Black Power/White Control

Studies in Religion and Society,
Center for the Scientific Study of Religion

FOR A LIST OF OTHER PUBLICATIONS IN THIS
SERIES, SEE THE BACK OF THE BOOK.

BLACK POWER/
WHITE CONTROL

*The Struggle of The Woodlawn
Organization in Chicago*

by John Hall Fish

PRINCETON UNIVERSITY PRESS

PRINCETON, NEW JERSEY

Copyright © 1973 by
Princeton University Press

ALL RIGHTS RESERVED
LCC: 72-5379
ISBN: 0-691-09358-X

This book has been composed in Linotype Caledonia

Library of Congress Cataloging
in Publication data will be
found on the last printed
page of this book.

Printed in the United States of America
by Princeton University Press,
Princeton, New Jersey

235199

To Sally

TABLE OF CONTENTS

LIST OF TABLES

PREFACE

THIS study is based upon six years of active participation in
The Woodlawn Organization (TWO). It was written over
a period of three years. A difficulty encountered in any study
based on extended participation is that the attitude and
perspective of the participant changes as well as the organization in which he is participating. While some effort has
been made to provide a consistent framework for the entire
study it may be apparent to the reader that the interpretation cast upon TWO varies at different points in this study.
It is recognized that this may be a result of changes both
in the author and in the organization. That I came very
early in my involvement in Woodlawn to care deeply about
TWO has undoubtedly influenced my research. This caring
I cherish. Whatever questions this poses for research purists
are welcomed but probably not, at least in this study, fully
satisfied.

I am deeply indebted to the many people in Woodlawn
with whom I have worked and from whom I have learned.
Whatever insights may be gleaned from this study have their
roots more in Woodlawn than in the University of Chicago.
I will mention specifically the three presidents of TWO,
Lynward Stevenson, Arthur Brazier, and Duke McNeil,
partly because their wisdom has been an influence upon my
own thought but more because they have been spokesmen
for the people of Woodlawn for whom the author has great
admiration and affection. In addition to the staff and participants of TWO I would single out John Fry, former pastor
of First Presbyterian Church, not simply because he has
been a friend and critic but because I think he is right.

To the north of the Midway there are four to whom I am particularly indebted: Alvin Pitcher, who nurtured my initial interest in community organization; Colin Williams, who saw my continued involvement in Woodlawn as part of my work with him in the Doctor of Ministry Program at the University of Chicago; Jack Meltzer and his Urban Affairs Seminar, who pressed me to clarify my ideas; and most of all my advisor, Gibson Winter, who guided, prodded, and reviewed my work all along the way.

I am grateful to Stephen Rose, John Fry, John Kretzman, and Harold Baron for reading portions of this manuscript and offering helpful suggestions. More than this editorial help they, along with the rest of the staff and students of the Urban Studies Program of the Associated Colleges of the Midwest, have sustained me, covered for me in teaching responsibilities, and borne with what must have appeared at times as an insufferable preoccupation with this study.

Most of all I am indebted to my wife, Sally, not so much for her essential and painstaking editorial work as for hanging in during the past five years and bearing, along with three growing children, the sacrifice of late evening meetings and preoccupied weekends.

JOHN HALL FISH
Chicago
July, 1973

Black Power/White Control

INTRODUCTION

BY THE early 1970s the large American cities were bogged down and nearly bankrupt, overwhelmed, on the one hand, by staggering social and environmental problems, and torn, on the other, by strife signifying an erosion of public authority. In addition, the nation seemed committed to an American-style apartheid with disadvantaged blacks segregated in urban and rural ghettos and upward mobile blacks offered marginal access to the mainstream in exchange for nonconfrontational postures on the racial front. The great issues of the 1960s of abolishing poverty, renewing urban America, ending the downward cycle of the ghetto through new policies of self-determination and community control, indeed, the very voluntarism and political optimism of the movements of the decade had given way to visions of escalating apartheid and repression on the one hand and politics-immune technocracy on the other. The decade of the Great Society with its promise of equal opportunity, participation, and access ended with a legacy of growing cynicism about the ability and willingness of urban governments to serve, or even to represent, the interests and needs of the citizenry and particularly the black and poor citizenry. Faced with mounting problems of survival in urban America, we were advised by Edward Banfield to choose "between getting things done by government and being democratic about the way we do them."[1] Bereft of effective channels of influence, the alienated urban underclass was faced increasingly with two choices: adjust to the offerings of white technocracy or flail out in anger. Such apocalyptic summations were perhaps premature, but they combined with the agony of Vietnam and a general weariness of activism to induce a national mood of considerable pessimism.

[1] Quoted in *Model Cities Target* (Chicago), March 1971, p. 1.

3

The aim of this study is to examine what might be called a third or middle way between the dualisms that were sharpened in the heat of the late 1960s: integration versus racial nationalism, repression versus revolution, politics versus culture, planning versus participation. More specifically, it is a middle way between increased institutional dependency in bureaucratized cities on the one hand, and chaotic and frustrating rebellion on the other, between technocratic urbanology and "power to the people" rhetoric. The middle way is not merely an idea but the specific incarnation of an idea at once simple and complex. The idea is that social injustice can be overcome and excessive concentrations of power can be checked without a fundamental restructuring of the total society. It is, further, that justice can be won only through power and conflict; that oppressed groups cannot wield power or generate effective conflict without organization; and that such organization generally requires the harmonization of conflicting interests—or bargaining—in order to gain the numbers and credibility to have substantial impact. The idea has become incarnate in a number of organizations in America; it is most clearly identified with a man, Saul Alinsky, and it attained its most forceful expression between 1960 and the present date in the Chicago community of Woodlawn. As a community organization the Alinsky-style Woodlawn Organization represents a middle way between, on the one hand, the "accommodative" agencies that seek to assimilate the alienated into the dominant society by strategies of socialization, rehabilitation, and therapy and, on the other, the "revolutionary" groups that form paracommunities rejecting the values and processes of the dominant society.[2]

This is a narrative study of The Woodlawn Organization. Although it abbreviates much of the history of TWO, it

[2] This argument draws upon a typology developed by Lawrence Witmer and Gibson Winter, "Strategies of Power in Community Organizations," in *Issues in Community Organization*, ed. by Lawrence Witmer (Chicago: Center for the Scientific Study of Religion, 1972).

makes an initial claim to be a more complete reference for future study of Woodlawn than any presently existing study.[3] Ever since Charles Silberman concluded his popular *Crisis in Black and White* with a tribute to the early TWO, commentators and scholars alike have made passing judgments about the organization based on several articles, brief visits to the community, or hearsay.

> TWO's greatest contribution is its most subtle: it gives Woodlawn residents the sense of dignity that makes it possible for them to accept help.[4]

> There is no evidence in Alinsky's TWO or any of his other projects that their gains are greater than those of comparable communities in Chicago or other cities.[5]

> To date, the principal result of The Woodlawn Organization in Chicago is the rise of a military cadre—the Blackstone Rangers.[6]

Unsubstantiated judgments, generated more from the ideological presuppositions of the commentator than from firsthand observations in Woodlawn, are recycled in the literature on community organization and have become part of a

[3] The only extensive document on TWO is Arthur M. Brazier, *Black Self-Determination: The Story of The Woodlawn Organization*, ed. by Roberta G. and Robert F. DeHaan (Grand Rapids: William B. Eerdmans Publishing Company, 1969). This book, devoted largely to an account of the TWO Youth Project, is a valuable contribution by TWO's president for six years. In addition to providing insights into Brazier's own perspective (esp. chaps. i, x and Afterword) and the Youth Project (chaps. vii, viii, and ix), the book includes descriptive information about TWO's formal structure (pp. 31-36) which will be omitted in this volume.

[4] Charles Silberman, *Crisis in Black and White* (New York: Random House, 1964), p. 348.

[5] Frank Riessman, *Strategies Against Poverty* (New York: Random House, 1969), p. 9.

[6] Milton Kotler, *Neighborhood Government: The Local Foundations of Political Life.* (Indianapolis and New York: Bobbs-Merrill Company, Inc., 1969), p. 30.

body of conventional wisdom about TWO. A more thorough study of TWO has been needed.

The narrative study that follows is a condensed reflection of six years of intense involvement with TWO both as a scholar-observer and as an active participant.[7] It is presented with the underlying sense that the social, political, and technical upheavals of the 1960s in the United States place a priority on the attempts to give, as far as possible, a true assessment of specific phenomena rather than the attempt to propound holistic theories with little reference to fast moving temporal realities. This study claims to be a contribution to knowledge not in the sense that it codifies existing theory or proposes alternative models or criticizes unproductive generalizations, but rather in the sense that it illumines an important phenomenon which has been distorted by conventional wisdom and by urbanologists.

More needs to be known about particular configurations in the urban scene. Foremost among present knowledge is, according to Robert Wood, that the urban political process is "chronically beset with such tensions, conflicts, and diversity of participants as to be always in danger of disintegration and collapse."[8] Indeed, as Wood sees it, our knowledge

[7] The primary resource for this study has been a personal involvement, in excess of 1,000 hours, in meetings, demonstrations, hearings, conventions, and other activities in Woodlawn or related to TWO. These have included seven Annual Conventions, over 150 steering committee meetings, and 50 delegate meetings. The writer was a member of the Woodlawn Community Board, The Mandel Legal Aid Advisory Board, the Greater Woodlawn Pastors' Alliance, the TWO Schools Committee, the TWO Model Cities Planning Council, and the Political Action Colloquium of First Presbyterian Church. Notes on these meetings, interviews and informal discussions with participants, and formal minutes have provided the basic source of data for Chapters II through V. Chapter I, dealing with the formative years of TWO is based primarily on interviews, newspaper accounts, and miscellaneous records.

[8] Robert C. Wood, "Contributions of Political Science to Urban Form," in Werner Z. Hirsch (ed.), *Urban Life and Form* (New York: Holt, Rinehart and Winston, Inc., 1963), p. 100.

of urban politics is embarrassingly scant, built on tenuous foundations and shaky generalizations. Scholars have suggested various reasons for the unproductiveness of the social sciences in dealing with urban problems.[9] Wood's observation is to the point:

In short, compared to criteria which suggests [sic] that government normally possesses qualities of purposefulness, rationality, regularized processes, and the power for the deliberate resolution of issues and conflicts, urban politics is devoid of most of the properties of a manageable enterprise.[10]

If this assessment is at all accurate, it is not necessary to apologize for a narrative study. Much can be gained from more detailed knowledge of particular urban processes, actors, and organizations. This is not to minimize the basic limitation of a case study approach, that it cannot yield firm generalizations. In the most obvious sense this is a truism. Woodlawn and, indeed, The Woodlawn Organization, are the result of particular forces and actions which are unique in time and space. These particularities—the presence of the University of Chicago, an independent alderman, the Chicago political Machine, to say nothing of numerous incalculable events—limit the degree to which it is possible to generalize from a close examination of this one organization.

In spite of this obvious limitation the narrative study has its own merits. On the one hand, it avoids the danger of excessive generalizing. Wood argued that the literature in urban politics "displays a strong preference to search for refinements in theory that make propositions self-evident or capable of easy generalizations."[11] A narrative study will

[9] Two examples, from differing perspectives, are Daniel Moynihan, *Maximum Feasible Misunderstanding* (New York: Free Press, 1969), especially chap. viii, "Social Science and Social Policy," and Philip Green and Sanford Levinson (eds.), *Power and Community: Dissenting Essays in Political Science* (New York: Vintage Books, 1970).

[10] Wood, *Urban Form*, p. 114.   [11] *Ibid.*, pp. 121-122.

certainly not yield easy generalizations. It can, however, shed light on the complexity and contingency of the urban political process and the struggles of neighborhoods within that process. The major strength of a narrative study is that it provides depth, insight, and "feel" for the issues which are at the core of the urban struggles. On the other hand, a narrative study can avoid the danger of barren hyperfactualism. By providing an in-depth and focused inquiry into one situation it can stimulate insights and yield suggestive or tentative—as opposed to "scientific"—generalizations. This argument is based on the contentions that Woodlawn, in spite of its unique history, is not essentially unlike other urban neighborhoods that have become part of what is referred to as the black ghetto; that Chicago, in spite of its particular political arrangement, is not essentially unlike comparable metropolitan areas; and that the aspirations as well as the powerlessness of Woodlawn residents are not unlike those of many other urban residents. The general configuration of the Woodlawn scene—physical decay, official neglect, latent hostilities—is found throughout urban America. A narrative study of one situation may provide insight into the character of the problems faced by an urbanizing nation.

The very theme around which the study is organized has been a major issue for numerous urban neighborhoods. Like other inner city communities Woodlawn has been a pawn in a larger game. Its conditions, institutions, and its future have been shaped and set by influences beyond its control. In essence TWO's story is the story of a struggle for survival and control. The way that TWO defined the urban situation, selected, pursued, and negotiated issues, and developed an organization, all make clear this central theme—the struggle of the people of Woodlawn for a voice, for participation, for power, for new relationships with established centers of control. This spokesman struggle has provided focus for this narrative and criteria for selecting relevant material from the multitude of data gathered.

The extensive attention to narration, however, does not obscure certain fundamental questions whose answers constitute the thesis of this study. The questions, in brief: What factors have contributed to the survival and growth of The Woodlawn Organization during a time when groups with similar objectives have met with little success? Does the strength of The Woodlawn Organization depend on a contradiction between rhetoric and practice? Or to put it another way, does the survival of The Woodlawn Organization bode well for the realization of the fundamental stated objectives of the organization?

Because this is a narrative, the propositions of the thesis emerge in the story of the development of The Woodlawn Organization, first as a fledgling body seeking birth (Chapter I); then as an established organization seeking a particular identity as a spokesman to and for a given neighborhood (Chapter II); later as the antagonist or protagonist in a series of confrontations which would test in differing ways the possibility of community control as the principal route to the advancement of people living in Woodlawn (Chapters III, IV, and V); and finally, after being stymied in these confrontations, as an experienced, battle-scarred, and increasingly competent initiator and manager of sophisticated community development programs (Chapter VI).

TWO emerged in 1961. Through the skillful use of conflict tactics it developed clout. By the mid-sixties it was hailed as a principal example of black power. It expanded. It did not spurn the materialistic values of the middle class; instead it combined them with a pragmatic militancy which erupted now and then on behalf of the poor. It rode out the storms of the late sixties. In 1970 TWO was still there. And one could say with confidence that it will be in place in 1980, or that the odds of this are better than for any organization of comparable goals in Chicago.

It could be argued that the price of survival was too high, that TWO compromised too much, lost its credibility as a spokesman for Woodlawn, and, unable to halt the enduring

9

cycle of neighborhood decline, exchanged its posture of militant defense of community self-determination for organizational survival as a privileged part of the Establishment. The suggestion of the narrative, indeed the thesis of this study is, on the contrary, that institutional survival, far from being a betrayal of TWO's vision, has been the guiding motif of the organization from the beginning and that through precisely this process of survival TWO stands to become the possible beneficiary of what might be termed community control by default. This analysis maintains that, as outside agencies of government prove ever more incapable either of imposing programs upon the ghetto or importing development schemes into the ghetto, it is the existence of a politically self-interested and, above all, organized and experienced mass organization within the ghetto that will determine the possibility of significant neighborhood self-determination. For if it comes at all, community control will come not by intent but by default. Liberal programs featuring "maximum feasible participation," shared decision making, and notions of "partnership" have been marked by duplicity and have, at best, resulted merely in decentralized service centers. Direct assaults on municipal sovereignty have elicited overwhelming resistance. Intentional efforts to move toward increased community control of public programs, either by central design or by neighborhood demand, have met with little success. However, the governmental and service bureaucracies, while protecting their claim to what Ivan Illich calls "a professional, political, and financial monopoly over the social imagination,"[12] have shown little evidence of being able to solve the major social problems that plague urban America. In fact, the failure of these efforts has been used to justify their increase. With continued failure, however, they may, out of their own self-interest, transfer levels of authority to those neighborhood

[12] Ivan Illich, "Why We Must Abolish School," *New York Review of Books*, July 2, 1970, p. 9.

institutions that have demonstrated paragovernmental competence.

In proposing the prospect of community control by default this study offers an implicit challenge to several urban and political theorists. It suggests that the current efforts to wish away such established phenomena as rising expectations, while they may simplify matters for Edward Banfield, will fail.[13] It suggests further that idealistic blueprints which fail to deal with existing power realities, such as Milton Kotler's neighborhood corporation and Theodore Lowi's "juridical democracy," are unproductive.[14] While this thesis offers no concrete proposal, it suggests perhaps a valid context for those who wish to ply a course between the simplicities of Banfield and the impossibilities of Kotler and Lowi.

One would be wrong to present what follows as a thesis in the sense that it resolves contradictions which may, themselves, be the very basis for change in the future. The future for TWO is open. The long-run significance of the organization remains to be documented. This is a study of preliminary success; and a probe both of the possible failure inherent in any success that depends upon the present system of power and the possible success inherent in surviving in the existing system of power.

[13] See Edward Banfield, *The Unheavenly City* (Boston and Toronto: Little, Brown and Company, 1968).

[14] See Theodore J. Lowi, *The End of Liberalism* (New York: W. W. Norton and Company, Inc., 1969), and Kotler, *Neighborhood Government*.

CHAPTER I

The Struggle Is Conflict:
The Origins of TWO

WOODLAWN in the 1950s was an old and deteriorating white neighborhood which had become part of an expanding black ghetto. Built up with luxury hotels for the World's Colombian Exposition in 1893, the neighborhood was later filled out with walk-up apartments. The post-World War II building boom, the dire housing needs of the black community, and the general real estate policy of racial control led to rapid change in designated older neighborhoods. During the fifties, one-fourth of Chicago's white population moved to the suburbs.[1] The black population, which tripled between 1940 and 1960, from 278,000 to 838,000, was steered into what the whites left behind—old housing and deteriorating neighborhoods.

Woodlawn became a natural focus of black in-migration. The 63rd Street train station provided a convenient port of entry for a continuing influx from the South. In addition, thousands of black families were pushed out of areas north of Woodlawn by slum clearance projects. Between 1950 and 1960, Woodlawn changed from 86 percent white to 86 percent black.[2] Nearly half (48.7 percent) of all housing units

[1] Pierre de Vise, *Chicago's Widening Color Gap* (Chicago: Interuniversity Social Research Committee, 1967), p. 17.

[2] The demographic data summarized here is more fully treated in the following: Evelyn M. Kitagawa and Karl E. Tauber (eds.), *Local Community Fact Book, Chicago Metropolitan Area, 1960* (Chicago: Chicago Community Inventory, University of Chicago, 1963); Welfare Council of Metropolitan Chicago, *Chicago Community Area Profile* (Chicago: The Council, 1964); Irving A. Spergel and Richard E. Mundy, "A Community Study, East Woodlawn: Problems, Programs, Proposals" (unpublished paper, Social Service Administration, Univer-

in East Woodlawn were substandard according to the 1960 census. For this housing the new residents paid more than the median rent city-wide out of a median family income of $4,400 as compared with the $7,200 median for white families in Chicago.

In East Woodlawn 12.2 percent of the male labor force was without work in 1959 as compared with 3.8 percent of male whites in Chicago. Nearly one-quarter (24.6 percent) of the residents were receiving some form of public assistance, primarily Aid to Dependent Children. The percentage of population under twenty years old had risen from 19 to 36 during the decade, forcing double shifts in the elementary schools. Transient hotels on 63rd Street became centers for dope and prostitution. By 1960 Woodlawn ranked among the least desirable ten out of the 75 Chicago community areas in seven major indices: family income under $3,000, male unemployment, substandard housing units, juvenile delinquency, public assistance, illegitimate births, and infant mortality. Statistically, Woodlawn had become just another slum.

In the spring of 1958, four Woodlawn clergymen began meeting regularly to discuss the social and physical problems facing the Woodlawn community. Martin Farrell of Holy Cross parish, Ulysses Blakeley and Charles Leber of First Presbyterian Church, and C. K. Proefrock of Immanuel Lutheran Church consulted with public officials, met with community groups, and considered possible forms of action. What bothered the clergymen most was not the magnitude

sity of Chicago, 1963); Department of City Planning, *Proposal for a Program to Meet the Long-Term Needs of Woodlawn* (Chicago: The Department, 1962); The Woodlawn Organization, *Woodlawn's Model Cities Plan: A Demonstration of Citizen Responsibility* (Northbrook, Ill.: Whitehall Company, 1970); Central Student Task Force, Model Cities Plan Project, "Preliminary Profile of the Woodlawn Community" (Chicago: Center for Urban Studies, University of Chicago, 1968) (mimeographed); Chicago Urban League, "Housing and Race in Chicago: A Preliminary Analysis of 1960 Census Data" (Chicago: The League, 1963) (mimeographed).

of the problems but the inadequacy of existing efforts to respond to them. Leber and Blakeley later wrote:

> The last ten years of Woodlawn have been largely a failure, innumerable civic groups (on paper chiefly) have come and gone, but the situation has remained the same. Everybody has tried to prevent a slide into slum. Businessmen have agitated; social workers have held conferences; city planners have shrugged and remarked, "You have your problems all right, but compared to a lot of places in Chicago, you're in good shape." We clergymen have worn out the seats of several good pairs of trousers while attending an uncountable number of meetings held to "do something about Woodlawn."[3]

The clergymen had had experience with three channels of action: governmental agencies, the University of Chicago, and local community groups.

The city government and the public agencies had not in the past demonstrated their ability to halt the cycle of decay. State and federal housing acts gave rise to renewal projects in the fifties. Major institutions such as Michael Reese Hospital, Illinois Institute of Technology, and the University of Chicago seized the opportunity to upgrade their surrounding neighborhoods. In the process tens of thousands of black families were forced to find housing elsewhere. Woodlawn was populated by thousands for whom city action meant "bulldozer." A growing number of Woodlawn residents felt that the city agencies, rather than helping to combat deterioration, would merely muddle along until Woodlawn too could be cleared and they again would be pushed out.

The University of Chicago, Woodlawn's neighbor to the north, had its own concern about the condition of neighborhoods surrounding it. In 1952, the University established an organization called the South East Chicago Commission. University Chancellor Lawrence Kimpton indicated that

---

[3] Ulysses B. Blakeley and Charles T. Leber, Jr., "The Great Debate in Chicago," *Presbyterian Life*, June 15, 1961, p. 36.

It is extremely important that we maintain a community in which our faculty desire to live and in which our students will be secure. In order to combat the forces of uncertainty, and deterioration at work in the neighborhood, the University had taken the initiative in the organization of the South East Chicago Commission.[4]

SECC was an instrument of the University and the prime architect of the Hyde Park-Kenwood renewal program. The University, in danger of being engulfed by a blighted and black neighborhood, spearheaded a major renewal and rehabilitation effort as the only alternative to moving from the area. The goal of the renewal program was to stop the cycle of deterioration and to develop a stable, integrated, middle- and upper-income neighborhood which would be compatible with the style and goals of an academic institution.[5]

Even though SECC did claim to include Woodlawn in its boundaries and did include people from Woodlawn on its Board of Directors and did open up a Woodlawn office, there was no doubt that the primary goal of the Commission was to protect, serve, and enhance the well-being of the University of Chicago.

There were enough civic-minded groups in Woodlawn. But none of them had either the support or the "clout" to deal effectively with the problems Woodlawn faced. The United Woodlawn Conference was the result of a merger in 1953 of two groups, United Woodlawn, Inc. and the Neighborhood Conference. Julian Levi of SECC helped engineer the merger in the hope that a strong improvement associa-

---

[4] Quoted in Julian Levi, "The Neighborhood Program of the University of Chicago" (distributed by the Office of Public Information, University of Chicago, August 1961), p. 7.

[5] Detailed accounts of the Hyde Park-Kenwood renewal program can be found in the following: Peter Rossi and Robert Dentler, *The Politics of Urban Renewal* (Glencoe, Ill.: Free Press, 1961); Julia Abrahamson, *A Neighborhood Finds Itself* (New York: Harper and Row, 1959); Muriel Beadle, *The Hyde Park-Kenwood Urban Renewal Years, A History to Date* (Chicago: n.p., 1964); Levi, "The Neighborhood Program."

15

tion could be developed. The UWC tried to do for Woodlawn some of the things SECC did for Hyde Park: secure adequate law enforcement, code inspection, and other city services. Even with SECC support it never developed strength. The Associated Clubs of Woodlawn, the oldest civic group in the area, had become more of a status organization and luncheon club than a community spokesman. The South Side Community Committee was a colloquium of service agency representatives. Its primary task was to serve as a clearinghouse to coordinate welfare planning and services. In addition, there was a Woodlawn Block Club Council, which was organized primarily in opposition to the UWC, a Ministerial Association, which had become inactive in the late fifties, and the Woodlawn Businessmen's Association.

The frustration arising from these efforts to deal with the problems Woodlawn faced was as disturbing to the concerned local clergy as the problems themselves. Powerlessness to act was seen as the major problem. Despairing of past efforts, they turned to Saul Alinsky. Leber and Farrell had been acquainted with Alinsky and his Industrial Areas Foundation. He was controversial. It would take major financial resources to secure his services. But in the fall of 1958 they went after him. Alinsky said later, "I was reticent about moving into Woodlawn but they kept pushing me."[6] After numerous visits from Leber, Farrell, and Blakeley, Alinsky finally agreed to consider their request seriously. The pastors went after financial support and denominational sanction. At a January 20, 1959, meeting of representatives of the Archdiocese of Chicago, the Illinois Synod of the United Lutheran Church, and the Presbytery of Chicago, Farrell indicated that the Catholic Church would put up $50,000. A second meeting involved a wider circle of leaders from the three church bodies. This time Alinsky was present. With his formal entrance into the discussions the three-church coalition began to break up. Walter Kloetzli, Secre-

[6] Saul Alinsky, interview, November 13, 1967.

tary of Urban Church Planning for the National Lutheran
Council, was the most vocal about his dissatisfaction with
Alinsky's approach. Proefrock and the other Lutheran representatives became increasingly cool toward any cooperative project involving Alinsky. There were no more meetings
of the denominational leaders. Progress on the Woodlawn
project was postponed. In the meantime, the Industrial
Areas Foundation became involved in another organizing
effort which eventuated in the Organization of the Southwest Community.[7] Presbyterian and Roman Catholic cooperation in the planning of that organization during the
spring and summer of 1959 provided experience in working
together with the IAF and an opportunity for continued
discussion of the Woodlawn proposal. From the summer of
1959 until the summer of 1960 these informal discussions
continued.

The entire project might never have gone beyond the discussion stage had it not been for the University of Chicago.
On July 18, 1960, the University presented its plans for expansion before the Chicago Land Clearance Commission.
Having solved its most immediate crisis through the Hyde
Park-Kenwood renewal project, the University, now pressed
for space, proposed to expand its campus to the south, clearing out a one-block-deep by one-mile-wide section of Woodlawn. Top University officials went to the Clearance Commission not merely with a request for a preliminary land
survey but with maps, models, public relations men, and
the press. They pointed out that the University already
owned 60 percent of the land and that most of the remaining could be termed "slum and blighted." The major point
in their argument was that the University's outlay of money
would generate $21 million of federal urban renewal credits
under Section 112 of the Housing Act amendments of 1959,
which would be available to the city for use in renewal proj-

[7] A brief account of the origin and early development of the Organization for the Southwest Community is found in John Fish et al., *The
Edge of the Ghetto* (New York: Seabury Press, 1968), pp. 1-36.

ects anywhere in Chicago. The amendments, extending to university expansion the same financial inducements previously reserved for housing programs, were the direct result of a lobbying effort organized by Julian Levi, administrator of the Hyde Park-Kenwood renewal program and University of Chicago trouble shooter. The Section 112 credits gave the needed leverage.

Phil Doyle, CLCC director, was, however, no supporter of the University. He opposed Section 112 on the grounds that it forced the city to do things for universities it might not otherwise do. Levi and Doyle had tangled earlier over the Hyde Park-Kenwood project. Sandburg Village, a housing project which Doyle helped develop, was delayed for several years because of the priorities Levi secured for the Hyde Park program.

Levi, sensing that Doyle would not be receptive to the South Campus plan, staged an onslaught more than a meeting. "We wired the room up on Doyle. He was on TV and couldn't make a move. This meeting had to be forced because Doyle didn't want it. He worked against everything I wanted."[8] The University strategy was initially successful. CLCC, on August 2, 1960, decided to make the requested survey. However, according to IAF organizer Nicholas von Hoffman, Doyle, having expected an informal meeting to discuss the University of Chicago proposal and discovering that the University was using his office for a press conference, was so furious that he "found" ways of delaying the survey for more than half a year.[9] This delay turned out to be very important for Woodlawn. Equally significant was the fact that in Doyle the Woodlawn groups found a sympathetic public official.

With the announcement of the South Campus plan, discussion in Woodlawn about clearance and renewal problems was intensified. The Ministerial Association became

[8] Julian Levi, interview, September 11, 1967.

[9] Nicholas von Hoffman, interview, April 11, 1966.

reactivated with the Rev. Blakeley as president. One intermediary, suspected of being an envoy from Levi, proposed a new community organization for Woodlawn to be spearheaded by the clergy and funded jointly by the Ford Foundation and the University at a level of $50,000 annually.[10] The Ministerial Association interpreted this as an attempt by the University to develop a front group to facilitate acceptance of the South Campus plan. A second "feeler," supported by the Lutherans, was made by D. E. Mackelman, Commissioner of the Community Conservation Board of Chicago. In this proposal the clergy would generate local support for a coordinated program of existing renewal and service agencies in Woodlawn.[11]

The increased concern about community rehabilitation, provoked by the South Campus plan and stimulated by the proposals being presented to community groups, provided the occasion for Leber, Blakeley, and Farrell to make their move with Alinsky. Financially, the way was clear. IAF had received a $69,000 grant from the Schwartzhaupt Foundation. Cardinal Meyer had contributed $50,000 from the Archdiocese. Presbyterian support was forthcoming. As a first move the Ministerial Association in October invited Father Farrell and other Roman Catholic priests to join the ministers' group which was changed to the Woodlawn Pastors' Alliance, a name more congenial to the priests. Blakeley, Leber, and Farrell assumed leadership in the Alliance and took the initiative in inviting IAF "to make a study" of the area. In November, Nicholas von Hoffman of IAF became a consultant for the Alliance. Von Hoffman's task was to survey the area and advise on next steps toward the development of an organization. The Alliance was by no means united on this move. But at least for the moment the oppo-

[10] Charles T. Leber, Jr., "Rev. Leber Tells History of 'Anti-South Campus' Group," *Chicago Maroon*, March 3, 1961, p. 4.

[11] Fr. Martin Farrell, in interview September 14, 1967, recalled several meetings in which Mr. Mackelman advanced this proposal.

sition was silent. Some of them were apparently not really aware of what was being planned.[12] The advantage lay with those who took the initiative. The Catholic-Presbyterian proposal had been brewing for two years. Now money was available, an issue was emerging, and a small number of people were prepared to devote themselves to it. This was sufficient. A basic Alinsky axiom is that the only way to start a community organization is to stop talking about it and start organizing.

The approach which Alinsky and von Hoffman brought to Woodlawn included three related dimensions: an interpretation of the Woodlawn situation, a strategy for changing that situation, and a method of organizing.[13]

1. What is deemed necessary or possible or desirable in any situation is dependent largely upon how that situation is defined and interpreted. Interpretation gives meaning to events and conditions. The plight of Woodlawn—deterioration, inadequate services, apathy, and internal discord—was

[12] Otto A. Sotnak, "An Experience with Community Organization in Woodlawn: Description with Observations" (paper presented at Lutheran Consultation on Community Organization, Chicago, January 4, 1966), p. 2.

[13] This summary of the Alinsky approach is based largely on the following writings: Saul Alinsky, *Reveille for Radicals* (Vintage Books Ed., New York: Random House, 1969); Saul Alinsky, "From Citizen Apathy to Participation," Paper presented at Sixth Annual Conference, Association of Community Councils of Chicago, October 19, 1957 (Chicago: Industrial Areas Foundation, n.d.); Saul Alinsky, "Citizen Participation and Community Organization in Planning and Urban Renewal," Paper presented before the Chicago Chapter of the National Association of Housing and Redevelopment Officials, Chicago, January 29, 1962 (Chicago: Industrial Areas Foundation, n.d.); Saul Alinsky, "Action to Equality of Opportunity" (Chicago: Industrial Areas Foundation, n.d.); Saul Alinsky, "Questions and Answers Regarding the Industrial Areas Foundation," March, 1959 (mimeographed); Nicholas von Hoffman, "Finding and Making Leaders" (distributed by Students for a Democratic Society, n.d.); Nicholas von Hoffman, "Reorganization in the Casbah" (*Social Progress*, April 1962, pp. 33-44). See bibliography for a more complete list of references by and about Alinsky.

placed in an interpretative framework which provided meaningful connection between apparently fortuitous events and conditions. In its simplest form the interpretation was that the Woodlawn community was controlled and programmed by outside forces and that the plight of the community could be attributed largely to this outside control. It was explicit in this interpretation that the hope for the community lay in breaking this control and developing means by which the citizens could influence decisions which affected their lives and their community.

Alinsky sought to identify and make clear the manner in which the ghetto was defined and thereby controlled by the dominant society. He argued that there is no such thing as a disorganized community. What existed in Woodlawn was not a disorganized community but a community that was organized against the people who live there. "Call it organized apathy or organized non-participation, but that is their community pattern."[14] Alinsky asserted, therefore, that "the first function of community organization is community disorganization."[15] The task of disorganization is addressed not only to the prevailing structures of organized power and influence but, relatedly, to the prevailing interpretation which legitimates those structures. Dan Dodson, a social scientist sympathetic to Alinsky, said that "if the little man ever succeeded in making upreach and outreach to full selfhood his first job would be to beat down the mythologies the scholars build about him."[16] For Alinsky, the first task is to beat down the mythologies which have maintained ghetto dependency; specifically, to beat down the "medical" interpretation of ghetto problems, an interpretation which legitimates outside control.

[14] Alinsky, "Citizen Apathy," p. 3.
[15] *Ibid.*
[16] Dan Dodson, "Looking Ahead to Health and Welfare" (paper presented before the Fifty-fifth Annual Conference of Health, Welfare and Recreation of the California Association for Health and Welfare, March 9, 1966), p. 8.

21

In this "medical" interpretation Woodlawn is defined as sick, the people are treated as patients, cures are sought, specialists consulted, and remedies prescribed. A situation of dependency is thus perpetuated as it becomes institutionalized in the ghetto and internalized in the life patterns of the residents. Those who shape life in the ghetto would like it to be believed that the social problems are "medical" because this interpretation legitimates their positions of influence and, if accepted by the citizens, makes outside control easier to maintain. As long as the dominant interpretation is unchallenged, Woodlawn, more like a colony than a garrisoned compound, can be controlled with a minimum of force and through relatively few functionaries. The first task in breaking outside control is not to cast out the agents but to cast off the interpretation which legitimates them.

The basic problems of Woodlawn, Alinsky argued, are not "medical" but "political"; that is, they stem from the arrangements by which power is acquired and exercised. Woodlawn residents are excluded. They have neither access to nor influence over the political processes. Woodlawn's condition is not one of sickness but of powerlessness. Dependency and apathy, regarded by outsiders as justification for expanded "branch office" activity, are, from Alinsky's perspective, the result of "branch office" domination.

Alinsky and von Hoffman claimed that they were not imposing this interpretation upon Woodlawn or even introducing it. It was there. They were merely articulating the pervasive, indigenous interpretation which had been systematically suppressed. Central to the IAF approach is that the ghetto residents have never fully accepted the definitions that have been made of them and their condition by the dominant culture. Von Hoffman regarded "the undiscovered leader" as an essential element in organizing the community. In a community which is dominated by the outside the undiscovered leaders remain undiscovered precisely because they think politically. The following observation by von Hoffman is quoted at length because it reveals the major dimension of the interpretation around which Wood-lawn was organized.

These undiscovered leaders are inconveniently realistic in their judgments. When you find them, which is very easy, they point to a system which they say is the cause of most of the community's and the people's woe. . . . The true leadership is remorseless in crying that the great money and power interests maintain and profit by the system.

We have come to the heart of the matter. The leadership is calling into question the conduct and arrangement of society. The leaders are demanding great and deep changes.

To me their demands place the whole discussion in the domain of politics. The arrangements of society and the conduct of the state are, more than anything else, the proper business of politics. . . .

The unrecognized leader in a lower class Negro community is absolutely right when he insists on keeping political consideration paramount. He knows that programs to curtail high school "drop outs" are worthless when high school students are barred by discriminatory hiring practices from employment. He knows that conservation and rehabilitation programs cannot improve housing because the people do not have the income to afford the improvements. He knows P.T.A.'s are laughable objects since they are creatures of school systems that deliberately fail to educate his children.

Because he knows these things he shrugs his shoulders at what the standard brands offer. The Church with its business-as-usual routine offers him little, not even a sympathetic voice. The recreational social agency gives second-rate athletic and social distractions that are not appreciated when present nor missed when absent. The

23

relief worker is an adjunct of an unfriendly government. To the unrecognized actual leaders, these services are barbituates. They anesthetize against the pain inflicted by a system of society and government that leaders and followers loathe and execrate. It may bother some people to learn that innocent health and education and general welfare programs are looked at this way. That is because they are not thinking politically. The unrecognized leader is thinking politically. The political mind looks broadly, sees interlocking factors as they operate on the totality and asks where is all this going? Do you want to go there? Political understanding quickly arrives at some very uncomplimentary judgments about the standardized programs. To many unrecognized leaders the major objection is not in the programs' inadequacy but a belief that their purpose is to keep the leaders and their people in subjection.[17]

For Alinsky, the ghetto is first of all a political reality. It has been created and is maintained by the prevailing power arrangements.

2. This interpretation of Woodlawn's situation provided not only a way of understanding what was happening but also a strategy for change. Commenting on the way Chicago was organized, Alinsky observed, "It is a wonderful system for everyone but its victims. Only if its victims organize for power will it be changed."[18] Viewed in terms of colonizer and colonized the Woodlawn situation would be changed only when the colonized resisted domination. "The first objective in the ghetto," Alinsky and von Hoffman repeated frequently, "is building an organization that wields power."[19] If outside control and citizen apathy are interrelated dimensions of the basic problem, the first step toward a solution is the development of a people's organization which would,

[17] Von Hoffman, "Reorganizing," pp. 37-38.
[18] Alinsky, "Action to Equality," p. 10.
[19] Von Hoffman, "Making Leaders," p. 1.

on the one hand, resist external domination by mobilizing indigenous power resources and, on the other hand, overcome apathy by offering opportunities for worth-giving participation. Alinsky's strategy is based on the premise that "prevailing arrangements of power can only be altered by power."[20] He does not discount good will or reason or persuasion, but he argues that in themselves they are ineffective instruments of social change. "Remember," says Alinsky, "to make even good will effective it must be mobilized into a power unit."[21] Organization is a means of coordinating and concentrating existing power resources. Alinsky frequently simplified the sources of power into two categories, money and people.

What happens when we come in? We say "Look, you don't have to take this; there is something you can do about it. But you have to have power to do it, and you'll only get it through organization. Because power just goes to two poles—those who've got money, and those who've got people. You haven't got money, so your own fellowmen are your only source of strength."[22]

Alinsky, a student and critic of labor organizing, applied to community organizing many of the principles of the labor movement. In a lower income community the first and preoccupying task is to organize the most available source of power—people.

In addition to generating power to challenge the practices of the colonizers, a people's organization also changes the attitudes and consciousness of the colonized. In fact, in the Alinsky model, it is only through an association in which the victim participates that victimization can be overcome.

They must have that vital self-respect which arises out of their having played an active role in resolving their

[20] Alinsky, "Citizen Apathy," p. 5.
[21] *Ibid.*
[22] Quoted in Marion K. Sanders, "The Professional Radical," *Harper's Magazine*, June, 1965, p. 46.

own crises rather than being in the degraded position of being helpless, passive, puppet-like recipients of special private or public services.[23]

Because the purpose of a people's organization is twofold, to generate power and to enable citizen participation, Alinsky stresses two essentials in the development of a community group: "1) the organization must be democratic, 2) it must represent most of the interests, no matter how small, of the community."[24]

In the IAF model, the development of power and the enabling of citizen participation are interdependent. And both are based upon the creation of a strong citizens' organization. A strong people's organization is a means of changing both the victim and the victimizer. Just as powerlessness and apathy reinforce each other in a ghetto cycle of dependency, so power and participation are mutually reinforcing in a process of decolonization.

In the Alinsky strategy, priority is placed on the development and maintenance of organization strength. All else follows. Organization generates power. Organization overcomes apathy. Organization enables citizen participation. Organization creates leaders. Organization is a means of education. Organization clarifies goals. Organization builds organization.

In the IAF model, a community is defined by the way it is organized. The underlying notion implicit in the IAF approach is that a successful community association provides an alternative interpretation of the situation: it exposes outside control, it identifies issues, it locates "undiscovered" leaders. The organization is the message.

3. Alinsky and von Hoffman brought to Woodlawn a specific method and skills in organizing. Central in this method is the role of the professional organizer. The organizer is not a community leader. He is not an advocate for any par-

---

[23] Alinsky, "Citizen Apathy," pp. 8-9.
[24] Alinsky, "Questions and Answers," p. 16.

ticular interest. "The best organizers," says von Hoffman, "have single track minds. They care only for building the organization." He adds

The organizer's first job is to organize, not right wrongs, not avenge injustice, not to win the battle for freedom. That is the task of the people who will accomplish it through the organization if it ever gets built.[25]

The ghetto community has a wide variety of small organizations and informal associations, each of which has particular interests and a particular stake in the neighborhood. Each group is seen as a force which could be channeled in concert with other forces. The organizer's task is to facilitate concerted action. In the beginning the common interest around which a variety of groups unite may not be a commonality of interest but rather a common desire for the benefits resulting from mutual support of particular interests.

The right balance of network, continuity and money is engendered by an organizational program containing a balance or mix of goals or would-be pay-offs (which organizationally is all that a goal is) for various groupings you need to recruit. For home-owners the program may be defense against venal building inspectors, for welfare mothers it may be defense against snooping welfare inspectors, for the unemployed it may be pressure on some well-known local firm that discriminates, for the church group or local civil rights sentiment it may be some sort of assault on the local educational system. Hence it has been said that organizing of this nature is, at least in part, building up a community-wide set of interlocking logrolling agreements; "You scratch my back and I'll scratch yours, but if we don't combine, nobody's back'll get scratched."[26]

[25] Von Hoffman, "Making Leaders," pp. 6-7.
[26] *Ibid.*, p. 10.

27

Three axioms underlie the IAF strategy for building organization: (1) People build organization, (2) success builds organization, (3) conflict builds organization.

(1) In response to the February 1959 meeting with the church leaders Alinsky wrote:

> Actually, we cannot organize a community. The community does it itself. The statement may be surprising but simple arithmetic bears it out. How can four or five men walk into a place where fifty thousand people are living and organize them? They cannot. Essentially what they do is get the people to organize themselves.[27]

(2) An organization is built around success. Failure and powerlessness have been the pattern of the past. People in the community are attracted to the organization when they discover that through it they can achieve particular goals. They may be limited, immediate "bread and butter" goals. The important point for the organizer is that the residents discover that their participation in the organization helped achieve the victory. The organizer as strategist will plan fights that can be won and avoid hopeless battles.

(3) An IAF organizer appreciates the role of conflict in building organization. The organizer begins with the presupposition that conflict already exists. However, for many people in the ghetto, avoidance of overt hostility has become a means of survival. This enforced role adoption is revealed in passivity, resignation, and hopelessness. The organizer presupposes the existence of dormant hostilities and hidden resentments which when released and channeled into effective action can be the dynamic which builds the organization.

> That organizer dedicated to changing the character of life of a particular community has an initial function of serving as an abrasive agent to rub raw the resentments of the people of the community; to fan the latent hostili-

[27] Alinsky, "Questions and Answers," p. 8.

28

ties of many of the people to a point of overt expression; to search out controversial issues, rather than to avoid them, for unless an issue is controversial it means that people are not sufficiently concerned about it to feel deeply and to act; to stir up dissatisfactions and discontent; to provide a channel into which they can angrily pour their frustrations of the past; to create a mechanism which can drain off underlying guilts for having accepted the previous situation for so long a time.[28]

When this latent energy is released and channeled into effective action it not only drains off the hostility but also deals, hopefully, with the objective conditions which were the occasion for the resentment. Conflict is regarded, by Alinsky, not simply as inevitable but also as desirable. His approach is based on the presupposition that "the powerless will not participate on a sustained basis unless there is considerable attention given to dramatic conflict-type activity."[29] Conflict is the telling attribute of a people's organization.

For Alinsky the heart of democracy is in the active, informed, and sustained participation of the citizens. What he decries most is the eclipse of citizenship.

It is a grave situation when a people have reached a point of resignation of citizenship. Even when a resident of any great metropolis may have a desire to take a hand, he lacks the instrument by means of which he can translate his desire into active participation. And so the local citizen sinks further into apathy, anonymity and depersonalization. The end is his complete dependence on public authority and a state of civic-sclerosis.[30]

[28] Alinsky, "Citizen Apathy," p. 3.
[29] Dan Dodson, "Does Community Organization Process Preserve and Enhance the Dignity and Worth of the Individual," in *The Church and Community Organization*, ed. John R. Fry (New York: Department of Publication Services of the National Council of Churches, 1965), p. 108.
[30] Alinsky, "Citizen Participation," p. 17.

Alinsky's approach to community organization—his interpretation of the situation, the strategy for change, and the specific conflict methods of organizing—are directed toward the end of overcoming "civic-sclerosis," of restoring to citizenry the active role of participating in those decisions that affect the quality of their lives and the direction of their future.

There were many problems in Woodlawn which could have been the occasion for an organizing effort—poor schools, slum landlords, exploitative merchants. To tackle some of these problems without a base of power sufficient to effect a favorable outcome would have been demoralizing. Implicit in the IAF approach were several criteria which guided the selection of the organizing issue. It must allow for the possibility of some kind of victory with limited resources. It should be symbolically significant, representing some form of outside control or exploitation. It should be an issue around which the greatest community unity can be generated, that is, an issue which could be convincingly interpreted as leading to dire consequences for the neighborhood if the people did not stand up and fight back. The organizer's task was to discern the occasion around which an organization-building issue could be generated. He had to capitalize on the events at hand.

Alinsky and von Hoffman claim that they had originally wanted to avoid tangling with the University of Chicago. Alinsky had talked with University officials about his invitation to work in Woodlawn and, according to von Hoffman, "Saul suggested that they get the expansion plans out of the way before we organize."[31] This never worked out. Although Alinsky claimed that "it accelerated our timetable and nearly threw us off,"[32] the University's expansion program was too good to be ignored.

On December 14, 1960, Fifth Ward Alderman Leon Despres alerted von Hoffman of an ordinance which Julian

[31] Von Hoffman, interview, April 11, 1966.
[32] Alinsky, interview, November 13, 1967.

Levi was going to present to the Chicago Plan Commission on the following day. According to Levi the ordinance was merely a "bookkeeping device" to enable the city to qualify for $960,000 in federal urban renewal funds in connection with a building the University was planning to construct on a plot of land it already owned. This would hardly have been an issue except for the fact that the site was in the South Campus area of Woodlawn which was the subject of the prolonged eligibility survey by the Land Clearance Commission.

Von Hoffman had a delegation of forty Woodlawn people, representing five community groups at the December 15 Plan Commission meeting to protest against the ordinance.[33] Blakeley, Farrell, and Alderman Despres argued that Levi and the University of Chicago were using the Plan Commission to bypass the Chicago Land Clearance Commission. Approval of the ordinance, they contended, would by implication place the city in support of the total South Campus concept even before CLCC had completed its survey. Farrell told the commission:

> You are being used by Levi and the University of Chicago. Levi is forcing his way into our community, wanted or unwanted, invited or uninvited. He is now attempting to sneak in and get your approval before you know the desires of the people.[34]

After heated debate the Plan Commission chairman, Claire Roddewig, announced that a decision on the ordinance would be delayed until the January meeting before which proper hearings and study would take place.

[33] When asked how many Woodlawn residents attended the December 15 meeting the Plan Commissioner responded, "Hundreds, you might as well say a thousand." Quoted in Jane Jacobs, "Chicago's Woodlawn–Renewal by Whom?" *Architectural Forum*, May 1962, p. 124.

[34] Ruth Moore, "Uproar Stalls U of C Plan OK," *Chicago Sun Times*, December 16, 1960, p. 5.

The participants left the meeting feeling they had won a victory and that the community groups could, if united, deal with the University. Von Hoffman had an organizing lever. One of the pastors recalled that "Nic sounded the alarm. He said, 'The University of Chicago will gobble up the whole area to 67th Street.' "[35] Visions of bulldozers and relocation were raised. Von Hoffman saw this occasion as the appropriate time to develop the nucleus of an organization.

Representatives from the five groups that had participated in the December 15 protest, the Pastors' Alliance, The United Woodlawn Conference, the Knights of St. John, the Woodlawn Businessmen's Association, and the Woodlawn Block Club Council, met on January 5 at the 63rd Street office of the United Woodlawn Conference. The meeting and agenda were, according to one participant, thoroughly planned by von Hoffman.[36] Leber presided, Blakeley took notes, and the necessary organizing action was taken. The temporary status of the initial structure and leadership was emphasized by the name of the new group, The Temporary Woodlawn Organization. The five initial officers represented the five convening groups. The Rev. Robert McGee, assistant pastor of the Apostolic Church of God, was president and the Rev. Arthur Brazier of the same church was designated "official spokesman" for the organization. Two committees were appointed: the city-wide Contacts Committee was to pursue negotiations on the ordinance; the Recruitment Committee was to seek additional community support and participation. In another action IAF was officially designated as technical consultant for the organization. Opposition to the University of Chicago action and, as the initial statement of purpose put it, "the need to assure common action and a single voice for the community of Woodlawn"[37] provided the common bond for most

[35] Rev. William Baird, interview, September 14, 1967.
[36] *Ibid.*
[37] *The Woodlawn Booster* (Chicago), January 18, 1961, p. 1.

of the participating groups. After the first meeting TWO secretary, James Mitchell, was quoted by the local paper as saying:

This organization will spike once and for all the charge that we are disunited. We have never been more united in our determination to see that our community is not cut up piecemeal and to make sure that we have a program for Woodlawn which will be of benefit to all of the community's citizens.[38]

In the controversy with the University two closely related issues became intertwined: the University's plan for the South Campus and recognition of TWO as the bargaining agent for Woodlawn. It is important to see how these two issues meshed because it is precisely this interplay that provided the dynamic for the growth of the organization.

The ordinance was the apparent issue. The city-wide Contacts Committee, chaired by the Rev. Leber, met with Mayor Daley, the Land Clearance Commission, and the Plan Commission in preparation for the January meeting on the ordinance. To reinforce this committee's effort, over three hundred Woodlawn people went to the Plan Commission meeting on January 26. This pattern of careful preliminary negotiations coupled with a show of citizen support became characteristic of TWO's emerging style of action. TWO won three important commitments from the Commission at this meeting. (1) It was clarified that the ordinance in no way implied approval of the South Campus proposal. (2) The Commission would recommend to CLCC that the eligibility survey be expanded to include more than the South Campus area. (3) The Plan Commission and the City Planning Department would begin to develop an overall plan for the entire Woodlawn area. "This," said TWO spokesman Brazier, "will help us in our fight to see that Woodlawn is not gobbled up piecemeal."[39]

[38] *Ibid.*, January 11, 1961, p. 1.
[39] *Ibid.*, February 1, 1961, p. 1.

When the ordinance came before the City Council's Housing and Planning Committee on March 14, Alderman Despres introduced amendments which specifically stipulated the commitments TWO had secured from the Plan Commission. Julian Levi again argued before this committee that the amendments might cause the city to lose the $960,000 of Section 112 credits. The ordinance was referred back to the Plan Commission so that Despres' amendments could be studied. By April, the ordinance issue was settled. TWO claimed victory in securing the amendments, particularly the extension of the land survey to 63rd Street, which would permit TWO to pursue the development of low-income housing to replace the loss of the South Campus area. The University claimed that the amended ordinance was essentially the same as the intent of the original. The two building sites were approved and the city qualified for the federal credits.

So why all the controversy? Levi, reflecting on this struggle, claims that the ordinance issue was "synthetic."

> I never could understand Leon Despres' fight. He knew all we were trying to do was to get the 112 credits for the city. I could see that the reference to the South Campus provided a hang-up for TWO. I suggested that we remove this reference and was pleased with the amended ordinance.[40]

For TWO the conflict was more important than the settlement. It is apparent that a settlement could have been secured fairly easily. Furthermore, a "synthetic" conflict, if that indeed is what it was, is often as useful as a real one. Sometimes it is more useful because the synthetic nature tends to infuriate the party that wants a quick settlement. It was the conflict and not the specifics of the ordinance that led to the public prominence of TWO by March 1961. Prior to March, TWO was virtually unnoticed by the metropoli-

[40] Julian Levi, interview, September 11, 1967.

34

tan press. The hearings, delays, and debates on the ordinance received extended coverage in the Chicago press under such headlines as *U of C, Woodlawn Push Showdown in Blight Area; U.C. Expansion Plan Furor Heats Up;* and *Seek Truce in U.C.-Woodlawn Renewal Feud.* If the University was satisfied with the outcome of the ordinance issue, TWO was more than satisfied with the process.

The issue behind the issue was running parallel in the controversy between the South East Chicago Commission and the Temporary Woodlawn Organization. The question, simply put, was who represents Woodlawn? SECC claimed that since its inception in 1952 it had served Woodlawn, received support from Woodlawn groups, and included in its membership representatives from Woodlawn. SECC would only recognize TWO as one among a number of groups in Woodlawn. TWO, however, viewed SECC as an arm of the University which neither represented Woodlawn nor expressed in any way the real interests of Woodlawn. TWO refused to recognize SECC's claim either to speak for Woodlawn or to determine who speaks for Woodlawn.

This controversy over recognition was carried on within SECC itself and through an extended correspondence between SECC and various TWO leaders.

Four days after the organizing meeting of TWO, Farrell, Leber, and Attorney Theodore Crawley, TWO activists who were also members of SECC, presented a resolution at the monthly Commission meeting. The four-part resolution read:

1. That the principle of community self-determination applies to Woodlawn as it does to all other communities.
2. That any project executed in Woodlawn must be an inseparable part of an overall Woodlawn plan drawn in accordance with sound professional planning procedures.
3. That any and all considerations surrounding the South Campus proposals should, after the most careful

consultation with the community of Woodlawn and the University of Chicago be settled by the appropriate municipal authorities under whose jurisdiction these questions fall.

4. The South East Chicago Commission stands ready to give every reasonable proof and security of a purely private organization to the people of Woodlawn that their fears and anxieties are groundless.[41]

SECC accepted the resolution only after the word "self-determination" was deleted and replaced by the word "participation." TWO, after considering the amended resolution, flatly rejected the "participation" position of SECC. In Brazier's announcement of TWO's position he said:

King George was willing to give the American colonies "participation" but George Washington wanted "self-determination." . . . We may have our little differences of opinion between ourselves but we are all firmly united against any attempt at foreign domination.[42]

TWO prepared a much stronger resolution for the February 13 meeting of SECC, which was prefaced in a characteristic Alinsky style.

Last month we came to the South East Chicago Commission Board meeting as fellow board members to propose a statement of policy in regard to the community of Woodlawn. We urged the South East Commission to recognize and accept the people of Woodlawn's right to self-determination. Instead the Board took the word self-determination from our resolution and replaced it with the word "participation." In Woodlawn the news that you would permit us to participate was greeted with a derisive snort. . . .

Tonight you must act on our resolution. There are only

[41] Julian Levi, "Levi Refutes Leber's Charges," *Chicago Maroon*, March 10, 1961, p. 4.

[42] *Hyde Park Herald* (Chicago), February 8, 1961, p. 3.

two choices: either you agree to respect our rights or you do not. If you agree you will be taking the first step toward an amicable, democratic, and permanent resolution of the differences between us. If you refuse, you must remember that Woodlawn will do unto you what you do unto Woodlawn.

Therefore, we offer the following resolutions:

1. The South East Chicago Commission recognizes and respects the right of self-determination in Woodlawn.

2. The South East Chicago Commission defines self-determination as meaning that the civic groups, churches, institutions, businesses and organizations of Woodlawn have the same rights and powers in Woodlawn as the South East Chicago Commission enjoys in Hyde Park and Kenwood.

3. The South East Chicago Commission pledges itself to find a means of open, public and equal negotiation to settle the difference outstanding between it and the people of Woodlawn.[43]

SECC rejected TWO's overtures and referred the whole matter to the Woodlawn Liaison Committee, which had been appointed by SECC to facilitate its relationship with Woodlawn groups.

More significant than the SECC resolutions was the extended effort to arrange a meeting between SECC and TWO. The hassle over the seemingly small point of who meets with whom, when, and where, continued for several months. The significance of this detail was grasped by the organizers. Letter after letter was written, but there was no meeting. On its part SECC wanted an informal meeting with TWO and several other Woodlawn groups to discuss and straighten out any misunderstandings over the ordinance. TWO had different interests. First, they were not interested in a private settlement of the ordinance issue. Second, and more important, TWO wanted a formal nego-

[43] Leber, *Chicago Maroon*, March 3, 1961, p. 4.

tiating session with SECC to symbolize TWO's role as the bargaining agent for the community. For years the pastors and other community leaders had met informally at the YMCA with University and SECC leaders. Now they were determined to meet only on their own terms. The terms were the issue at stake. TWO wanted a two-party negotiating session at the office of the Land Clearance Commission, the city agency most directly involved and, not incidentally, most receptive to TWO. After two months of sparring through an extended exchange of correspondence, George Watkins, chairman of the Woodlawn Liaison Committee of SECC, requested a meeting with TWO. TWO was quick to seize the opportunity. Brazier and Leber responded:

> Since your committee has been willing to recognize TWO and now desires to enter into direct conversation and discussion with us, we are glad to accept your invitation.
>
> Among the alternative dates you suggested was April 20, which is the date we hereby agree to meet with your group.
>
> Since you did not specify the place or time for our meeting, we have made arrangements with Mr. Phil Doyle of the Chicago Land Clearance Commission for the use of the commission conference rooms. He has agreed to be present with us at that time. . . .
>
> With the hope that this first meeting of your committee with the representatives of the Temporary Woodlawn Organization will provide a good beginning for constructive and productive relationship between our two organizations.
>
> Sincerely yours,[44]

As the date approached, there was a flurry of letters in which each group agreed to meet the other at different places.

On the evening of the 20th, SECC was meeting with rep-

[44] Letter, Rev. Arthur M. Brazier and Rev. Charles T. Leber, Jr., to George Watkins, March 13, 1961, on file at First Presbyterian Church, Chicago.

resentatives of the Associated Clubs of Woodlawn, the United Woodlawn Conference, and several block clubs in the Chinese Room of the Hyde Park YMCA. TWO's committee and Mr. Doyle waited two hours at the CLCC office for a meeting which they well knew would never take place. Brazier then released the following prepared statement:

> We are disappointed that the SECC failed to show up. They set the time and date. We want to talk about self-determination on an equal basis with them. The SECC has repeatedly said that they did too, but their actions show that they are not sincere.
>
> It is not clear to us why the University and the SECC seem to hold in contempt the idea of equality and respect for Woodlawn. The TWO represents the great majority of the organized groups and people in Woodlawn. The desire of our people to develop, plan, and rehabilitate their own community, deserves the greatest respect in all such planning and negotiations.
>
> Self-determination is not disregard for government. It is the participation by the people in the decisions of government. This includes the same rights, privileges, and responsibilities as all other communities enjoy. However, as representatives of the Woodlawn community, we are not discouraged by this unfortunate incident.
>
> It is becoming increasingly clear to us, how difficult it is for some institutions and individuals to understand the meaning of equality and self-determination. This is especially true when these ideas are taken out of text-books and are applied to real people in real communities, and those people who do not have vast financial resources to back them.[45]

SECC and TWO never did meet.

The ordinance issue set in motion an inner dynamic of controversy which carried the conflict far beyond the initial point of contention. Both TWO and the University moved from specific to general issues and from disagreement to

[45] *The New Crusader* (Chicago), April 29, 1961, p. 1.

39

antagonism very quickly. TWO was apparently regarded by some University and SECC people as illegitimate, power hungry, obstructionist, and dangerous. This portion of a published statement by Levi is an example:

> The fact that a community may be stirred and organized by "sharpening the dormant hostilities" or "rubbing raw sores of discontent" as suggested by the organizers of the Temporary Woodlawn Organization is not new. . . . The technique has been proven in practice in the assembly of lynch mobs throughout history.[46]

The University made direct attempts to discredit TWO through the press. The University public relations office gathered material which was supposed to discredit Alinsky, IAF, and TWO. When the major metropolitan papers did not use the material, it was released to the University student paper, the *Maroon*, which published a front page copyrighted article under the headline, "Church Supports Hate Group."[47] This article branded TWO as a segregationist hate group, sponsored by the Roman Catholic Church. The issues raised were not so much the pros and cons of the South Campus plan as the character, aims, and tactics of IAF and TWO.

To TWO, the University as an institution became the enemy. It was charged with paternalism, colonialism, manipulation, and blackmail. Julian Levi became a henchman symbol of evil and exploitation. A flyer circulated throughout the neighborhood included the following warning:

> Remember: Levi is against an over-all plan and an over-all eligibility survey and program for Woodlawn. He does not want Woodlawn to have a program. He wants to make Woodlawn a slum.

[46] Levi, *Chicago Maroon*, March 10, 1961, p. 5.
[47] Ken Pierce, "Church Supports Hate Group," *Chicago Maroon*, March 3, 1961, p. 1.

Be Careful: Anybody who is against an over-all plan and program is for Levi.

The controversy generated its own spiral of escalation. Each partner in this controversy developed an image of the other and then reacted to the other in terms of that image. As the controversy progressed, the image each had of the other tended to be confirmed. The University saw TWO as trying to monopolize the role of spokesman for the community and as threatening to undermine the University's expansion plans. TWO saw the University as an alien force that was expanding in its own interest without concern for the community and residents affected. Interacting in terms of these images, the University overreacted and over-anticipated so that what they did and said confirmed for TWO the image they had received from their initial contacts. As TWO responded in terms of their now confirmed perceptions, the University became more convinced that TWO was indeed as they had first believed, a major threat to their plans. This spiral led to a polarization which made discussion of the original point of contention impossible.

Seeing the conflict as an instrument in building the organization, TWO was more deliberate than the University in escalating and managing the conflict. Alinsky and von Hoffman were the principal strategists. Von Hoffman wrote most of the letters, testimony, speeches, and press releases. Together they planned moves which were designed to elicit predictable countermoves by the University. For example, both Alinsky and von Hoffman claim, and early documents bear them out, that TWO never intended to stop the South Campus plan. In fact, far from being opposed to it, they felt that it was not only inevitable but could be beneficial.[48] It was the University's perception, not TWO's, that TWO wanted to stop the South Campus plan. TWO did not wish to alter this perception. Rather they capitalized on it to strengthen their own position, to build the organization, to

[48] Von Hoffman, interview, April 11, 1966.

secure city commitment to a Woodlawn planning effort, and to bargain for new housing in other parts of Woodlawn. From TWO's point of view there was ample reason for maintaining the controversy. The University charged that TWO was an illegitimate spokesman for Woodlawn. But the charge, when continued, tended to create the legitimacy which TWO needed, a legitimacy based upon united Woodlawn support and sympathy from city agencies. The dynamic of the controversy made the University's charges against TWO less and less credible. On the other hand, the TWO charge that SECC was unrepresentative and therefore an illegitimate spokesman became, in the process of controversy, more and more credible. In other words, the controversy tended to equalize the strength and bargaining position of the contesting groups, enhancing the legitimacy of TWO and weakening the legitimacy previously held by SECC.

In the heat of the controversy with the University, attendance at the TWO meetings grew. On January 16, over 170 people met at St. Clara's Parish Hall. Over 300 people were reported to have attended each of two February meetings. The day-to-day strategy was carried on by an executive committee, an informal steering committee, and the organizers. Four organizations provided the initial strength and leadership for the temporary organization. The Pastors' Alliance, instrumental in initiating the organizing project, was perhaps the most influential. The Knights of St. John, Hijos de Boringuen, and the Club Social Familiar, three Spanish-speaking groups which formed the Woodlawn Spanish Speaking Council, were early supporters whose presence at some of the first TWO meetings was evidenced by signs reading "Woodlawn, Si, Universidad, No!" The Woodlawn Businessmen's Association was active in the organizing process. George Kyros, local restaurant owner and president of the WBMA, explained it this way in a newspaper interview:

When the University announced plans for the South Campus, Levi came to talk to our Woodlawn business men. He said we could accept the plan, help it or sit back and watch it go through. Then Phil Doyle of the Land Clearance Commission came out. He said that the biggest investment he would advise us to make in our businesses was one coat of paint. I've never seen people feel so bad. After that we had a unanimous vote to ask Alinsky in to organize.[49]

The Woodlawn Block Club Council brought into TWO numerous preexisting block organizations providing a pool of leadership as well as a widespread grassroots base. These four groups were drawn together by a common perception of the University as a menace proposing massive clearance of the community.

Much of the traditional leadership which had been recognized by the established agencies was indifferent or antagonistic to TWO. The United Woodlawn Conference, one of the five groups at the December 15 meeting protesting the ordinance and the host of the TWO organizing meeting on January 5, never really participated in TWO and was soon in opposition to it. A Conference board member, Mrs. Eugene Cooper, explained their attitude toward TWO this way:

The other group seems to be spreading the propaganda which would make outsiders feel the United Woodlawn Conference is part of it. That isn't so. We do not endorse their program. We do not want to be associated with them. They conduct that organization in an undemocratic fashion with just three or four people running the whole thing. The United Woodlawn Conference is run by a board of directors elected from the membership. We

[49] Georgie Anne Geyer, "War Over Renewal: The UC Campus Siege," *Chicago Daily News*, April 12, 1962, p. 31.

just want everyone to know our organization has not been replaced by the TWO. We speak for the Woodlawn community. We have for the past nine years.[50]

The Associated Clubs of Woodlawn, never inclined to active protest, unanimously passed a resolution stating that it would not work with the Industrial Areas Foundation or TWO. ACW president Eugene Harrison stated:

The temporary organization backed by the IAF lacks grass roots support. Spokesmen do not live in Woodlawn, have not been in close touch with Woodlawn or its organizations, do not represent Woodlawn.[51]

The most intense internal controversy centered on the churches. The question of the role of the church in community organization became a source of tension at several levels. In April 1961, five clergy withdrew from the Woodlawn Pastors' Alliance and formed an alternative Ministerial Association. Their charges against TWO and the Alliance, that they were undemocratic and were scapegoating the University, received front page press coverage.[52] Similar tensions, though with less visibility, arose in local congregations, particularly those whose pastors supported Alinsky.[53] Beyond Woodlawn, the controversy over church involvement with Alinsky was carried through the editorial statements of the *Christian Century*. The major editorial, entitled "Open or Closed Cities?" resurrected the charges that Walter Kloetzli had first leveled—that IAF was building walls around the community, fomenting "class war," creat-

---

[50] *Hyde Park Herald*, February 8, 1961, p. 3.

[51] *Woodlawn Booster*, April 19, 1961, p. 1.

[52] Ruth Moore, "Five Pastors Leave Woodlawn Alliance," *Chicago Sun Times*, April 12, 1961, p. 1. The full statement released by the five pastors is in the *Woodlawn Booster*, April 19, 1961, p. 1.

[53] The controversy within First Presbyterian Church is recorded in the minutes of the Session Committee on Community Relations, on file at the church.

ing antagonism, seeking power for power's sake, and that Alinsky was using Protestants as a front for his Catholic instigated power play.[54] To those who were directly concerned, von Hoffman circulated a detailed rebuttal of the *Century* editorial, correcting the numerous factual errors, and refuting, with appropriate documentation, the substantive charges.[55] Since residents of Woodlawn do not read the *Century*, TWO did not care to make an issue out of editor Harold Fey's attack.

Within Woodlawn the theological, ethical, and ecclesiastical subtleties of the arguments over church involvement in TWO were lost. The overriding issue around which the cleavages, even in the religious groups, were drawn was the TWO-University controversy. There with little room for an equivocating middle-ground position. Those who questioned the growing organization were viewed as University sympathizers and, therefore, as anti-Woodlawn. Opposition to the University united diverse groups of people overshadowing the more traditional cleavages of race, class, religion, status, politics. Protestants and Catholics, religious liberals and fundamentalists, blacks and whites, homeowners and tenants, businessmen and welfare recipients, all found common cause in the TWO struggle against the University.

[54] See Editorial, "Open or Closed Cities?" *Christian Century*, May 10, 1961, pp. 579-580; Readers' Response, "Woodlawn—Open or Closed?" *Christian Century*, May 31, 1961, pp. 685-688; Harold E. Fey, "Open or Closed Cities—A Reply to Replies," *Christian Century*, June 7, 1961, p. 711; Editorial, "Revolution—What Kind?" *Christian Century*, July 18, 1962, p. 879; Editorial, "Justice and Beyond Justice," *Christian Century*, February 24, 1965, p. 227; Editorial, "Thank You No, Mr. Alinsky," *Christian Century*, June 2, 1965, p. 701; Editorial, "The Greatest Good for All," *Christian Century*, June 30, 1965, p. 827.

[55] Memorandum from Nicholas von Hoffman to Richard Harmon, May 9, 1961, a 26-page refutation of the original "Open or Closed Cities?" editorial, on file at First Presbyterian Church (mimeographed).

The groups opposing TWO soon faded in significance. The United Woodlawn Conference, the Associated Clubs of Woodlawn, the Woodlawn Ministerial Association were never able to elicit much support or develop a base of influence. These three organizations did cooperate with each other on various projects and continued to engage in traditional forms of service, but they became less and less significant as community organizations. Otto Sotnak, recounting the aftermath of the split with the Pastors' Alliance, wrote:

> As an organization our re-constituted group reverted to more conventional modes of community involvement. We collaborated with the Chicago Woodlawn Boys Club, the local YWCA, the Associated Clubs of Woodlawn (a PTA-related organization, the oldest in Woodlawn) and with the South Side Community Committee, a red-feather agency with offices in Woodlawn.[56]

TWO, on the other hand, continued to grow and expand. By June 1961, TWO claimed over twenty constituent groups. The "undiscovered leaders" began to emerge, the most notable of which was the Rev. Arthur Brazier. Unheard of before 1961, Brazier, as the official spokesman of the organization, became TWO's major leader, a position he has enhanced throughout the decade. The early controversy itself provided both the occasion and the attraction for new community leadership. It was soon apparent that TWO was becoming *the* dominant community coalition. It had enthusiasm, financial support, a growing grassroots base, and determined leadership.

To take advantage of the enthusiasm engendered by the South Campus controversy, the temporary organization tapped resentments which lay deep in the hearts of Woodlawn residents. A variety of positive actions were launched, each of which reached a segment of the community, each

---

[56] Sotnak, "Community Organization in Woodlawn," p. 5.

of which appealed to some particular interest, and all of which together helped build a constituency prior to the organizing convention of the permanent Woodlawn Organization in March 1962.

In his initial survey, von Hoffman found that the problems talked about most by the ordinary citizens were not the general issues of segregation or urban renewal or the University of Chicago, but short weights at the meat counter, credit-traps, poor merchandise, overcharging, misrepresentation of products, high carrying charges, garnishments, and other malpractices through which Woodlawn residents were losing approximately $1,000 a week to dishonest merchants.[57] This differed from the South Campus issue in three significant ways. (1) Whereas the antagonisms toward the University had to be generated, the resentment toward the merchants was already widespread. (2) While the South Campus issue appealed to a limited number of community activists, this issue appealed to the ordinary resident, particularly the poor who were most abused by the merchants. (3) Action against the University was essentially negative and did not result in any visible or immediate changes. An attack on malpractices of merchants provided an occasion for positive action with immediate and visible outcomes.

The campaign was dramatically inaugurated on Monday evening, April 6, by a parade of over six hundred sign-carrying citizens down the 63rd Street shopping strip. The Spanish-speaking groups led the parade and were joined by local churches, block clubs, businessmen, as well as some nonresident groups such as the Chicago Theological Seminary student body and several labor union locals. The impressive demonstration was directed as much at the University of Chicago as it was at the slum merchants. One month after the first small meeting, this mass demonstration was a public display of strength. The message was summed up by one TWO leader this way:

[57] Jacobs, "Chicago's Woodlawn," p. 124.

47

There has been an awful lot of talk on the other side of the Midway against the self-determination of the people in the community of Woodlawn. I think we now see what self-determination means in action. It means that we who have the problem also know and can devise the best ways of eliminating the problem. Self-determination is not license, it is responsibility and progress.[58]

This campaign generated enthusiasm in the organization and the community. Squads of shoppers were organized to detect fraudulent practices. One notorious offender was boycotted until he got his scales and totalizer adjusted. Several other merchants negotiated with the organized consumers. However, having tasted victory on a homemade issue, TWO did not vigorously pursue its attack on the merchants. There were dangers in this issue. In its attack on the unscrupulous merchants, the campaign, if pursued, might cast TWO as an organization of the poor against the businessmen. While the businessmen initially supported the Square Deal, their support would wane if the momentum of the campaign led TWO toward a more general anti-merchant stance. To the organizer such a split would be unwise and unnecessary. The participation of the businessmen was essential if TWO was to become the multi-interest, inclusive neighborhood organization that IAF was out to build. Von Hoffman, in an article "Finding and Making Leaders," apparently had this issue in mind when he wrote about the organizer's task of securing the support of all major segments of the community through "interlocking log-rolling agreements."

Purists may find such a procedure intolerable. For example, you don't put pressure on the white small store owner past a certain point—even if he can hire an extra Negro clerk. The reason is you need his money which you will get if he fears you, but not if he hates you. You will also

58 *Woodlawn Booster*, March 1, 1961, p. 1.

<hr>

get his money, I hasten to add, if the organization's program includes objectives that are worth something to him.[59]

Some did find this intolerable. Fr. Dittami, who was active in the Square Deal campaign, was disillusioned by what he considered to be the failure of TWO to continue this fight. The Future Outlook League, one of the initial supporters of the Square Deal, withdrew from TWO because "TWO seems to have forgotten the Square Deal program it promised the people of Woodlawn."[60] The Spanish-speaking groups lost their initial enthusiasm for TWO and never reassumed the prominent position they once held.

It is clear in retrospect that organizational considerations dictated the decline as well as the initiation of this Square Deal campaign. In the limited campaign, TWO gained strength and prestige. In a continued campaign, the organization might have alienated the businessmen whose support was needed, particularly in the initial stage of the temporary association.

When seven of the CORE Freedom Riders who were burned out and beaten in the much-publicized Annistan, Alabama, incident were touring northern cities, TWO decided to schedule them for a community meeting on June 1, 1961. There was dissension in the TWO executive committee; von Hoffman claimed that he tried to dissuade the leaders from inviting the CORE group because he felt that the community would not respond and that a poor attendance would not reflect well on TWO.[61] The evening of the meeting von Hoffman went to St. Cyril's Church early, folded up many of the chairs, and spread out the others so that the small attendance he expected would not appear so disappointing. Von Hoffman claims that he was dumbfounded when the hall was packed with an estimated seven hundred

[59] Von Hoffman, "Making Leaders," p. 10.
[60] *Woodlawn Booster*, October 11, 1961, p. 1.
[61] Von Hoffman, interview, April 11, 1966.

49

people, many, of course, standing throughout the meeting. The Woodlawn people learned and sang "We Shall Overcome." A contribution of $600 was collected for CORE. Von Hoffman said that it was at that moment that he began to realize that there was a "movement" beginning in Woodlawn.

For the organizers the enthusiasm of this meeting was educational. Previously they had concentrated on specific neighborhood problems such as the University expansion and the 63rd Street merchants. They now realized that they could tap the issues raised by the emerging Freedom Movement, particularly voting rights and segregated education. It was after this evening with the Freedom Riders that the organizers decided to relate the appealing concerns of the Movement emerging in the South to local organization programs.

Soon a "northern version of the Freedom Ride," a bus cavalcade to transport Woodlawn residents to City Hall in a mass voter registration effort, was organized by TWO. Using the "Freedom Ride" theme, TWO organizers, as well as leaders of constituent groups, began a two-week campaign that finally involved over fifty block clubs, churches, civic and business groups, many of whom were not then members of TWO. The participating groups contributed the $1,600 necessary to hire the forty CTA buses. As the August 26 day of the bus cavalcade approached, the neighborhood newspapers announced that 1,000 and then 1,500 people would participate. The agreement with the CTA on the buses broke down at the last minute and TWO had to turn to a private company. TWO charged that CTA tried to sabotage the Freedom Ride by raising the price of the bus rental, refusing to permit TWO banners and signs on the buses, and refusing to allow the entire fleet to travel as a caravan. A private company was secured. At 9:00 a.m., Saturday, over two thousand Woodlawn people boarded forty-six buses for what was called a "vote-in." Adorned with signs and filled with black people the forty-six buses proceeded in caravan eight miles to City Hall, which became totally encircled by this impressive ring of buses. Election Commissioner, Sydney Holtzman, added forty-five extra clerks to process the registrants, which, by the end of the morning, totaled over two thousand. As the biggest mass registration ever staged in City Hall this cavalcade received wide publicity in the metropolitan press. The message, summarized for the press by a TWO spokesman, was clear:

People are always accusing us of being apathetic and lacking leadership. We are proving them wrong. The TWO registration program will open a lot of important eyes in the City of Chicago. It will demonstrate that the little people are on the move and demanding recognition.[62]

Like the Square Deal parade, this voter-registration cavalcade was dramatic and impressive. The South Campus controversy and the Square Deal had convinced a number of University people and local residents of TWO's growing strength. This "Northern Freedom Ride," TWO's largest show of strength, was clearly for the benefit of Mayor Richard Daley. As mayor, he had reason to be impressed. As head of the Cook County Democratic organization which was in the business of delivering votes, Chairman Daley had reason to be alarmed. TWO was playing his game. With the skills of precinct captains, TWO leaders were "delivering" voters themselves.

For TWO, this campaign provided another opportunity to build the organization. In promoting this noncontroversial drive (who is against voter registration?), TWO organizers developed a favorable relationship with additional block clubs, churches, and civic groups, several of which joined TWO shortly after the cavalcade.

The biggest single action in TWO's first year centered on the public schools. After the Freedom Riders visited Wood-

[62] *The Bulletin* (Chicago), August 17, 1961, p. 1.

lawn in June, von Hoffman claimed "then we decided to take on the school issue."[63] Unlike the noncontroversial registration drive, or the locally oriented Square Deal campaign, the school issue catapulted TWO into leadership of a city-wide controversy. TWO, more than any other organization in Chicago, raised the issue of school segregation for the city. For the first time, TWO entered into battle in a controversy which was not limited to the boundaries of Woodlawn. In the course of this issue, TWO became as much a leader of a movement as a geographically based neighborhood organization. It was in pursuit of this issue that TWO developed some of the tactics which became characteristic of the organization.

A major public hearing, scheduled by the Chicago Board of Education for October 16, 1961, provided the occasion for TWO to draw the lines of controversy. Over three hundred members went downtown to the hearing. More than half of them jammed into the hearing room while the others marched outside the building. After an hour, when only two of the sixty-five scheduled speakers had testified, a TWO spokesman tried to get the floor. "We have been here for several hours and our people are working people and I feel that we should have a chance to testify before evening."[64] When Board President William Caples refused to recognize him, Brazier and the large TWO delegation walked out and joined the others picketing outside. This stormy meeting, the walkout, the picketing, and the charges presented in the testimony of the scheduled TWO speakers received extensive press coverage. The TWO attack raised numerous points: "double shifts in black communities," "double talk public relations," two hundred vacant classrooms in white schools, segregated boundaries, and Superintendent Benjamin Willis' "mendacious public relations,

[63] Von Hoffman, interview, April 11, 1966.

[64] Charles J. Williams, "A Christian Approach to Community Organization—the Greater Woodlawn Pastors' Alliance" (unpublished B.D. dissertation, Chicago Theological Seminary, 1963), p. 73.

his secrecy and his unfeeling interest in Negro children."[65] At its next meeting, October 23, TWO demanded the resignation of Willis, marking the beginning of a long "Willis Must Go" campaign that in later years became the rallying cry of a city-wide movement. One pastor, a TWO delegate, expressed TWO's response to the Board of Education: "Rarely in the history of a democratic government have the people been confronted with such arrogance, stupidity, and racial prejudice as the Board of Education has displayed in recent weeks."[66]

Charging the Board with "fettering of facts" and "ridiculous rules," TWO scheduled its own public hearing on November 6 at the Southmoor Hotel in Woodlawn. An overflow crowd of seven- to nine-hundred people listened for four hours to a variety of statements from parents, teachers, community leaders, and Saul Alinsky. The highlight of the meeting was the testimony of three public school teachers who were draped with sheets to preserve anonymity and avoid reprisals. Specific grievances were repeated and detailed: double shifts, overcrowded classrooms, use of hallways for classrooms, no books, empty rooms in white schools. Two major points were underscored. The Chicago schools system is intentionally segregated to the detriment of black children, and the superintendent has refused to release information or make surveys (racial head count, facility use count, achievement scores) which would make this obvious.

TWO's next move was the "death watch" at the Board of Education. Small delegations began to attend all regular School Board meetings through the winter and spring, wearing black capes to symbolize "the mourning of Negro parents for the plight of their children."[67]

In January, TWO decided to confront Superintendent

[65] *Woodlawn Booster*, October 11, 1961, p. 3.

[66] *Ibid.*, November 1, 1961, p. 1.

[67] Ernestine Cofield, " 'Death Watch' Against School Segregation," *Chicago Defender*, November 27, 1962, p. 9.

Willis and Board President Caples directly. A group of forty to fifty made an unannounced visit to Willis on January 19. When he refused to see them, they sat down and had lunch in his reception room. Finally he agreed to talk briefly with three of the group. In answer to their charges of segregation, he showed his charts and statistics. When Jeff Williams, one of the three TWO representatives, objected he was forcibly removed by attendants. Immediately after this fifteen-minute meeting Willis called a press conference in which he denied that any segregation existed in the public schools.

Three days later, eighteen pastors from Woodlawn called on Board President Caples at his executive suite office in the Inland Steel Company Building. While the pastors were seeking to talk with Caples, an Inland Steel vice-president, fifty TWO pickets marched in front of the main door of the building. Convinced that Caples was out of town and not just avoiding them, the pastors conferred with other company executives while Caples was contacted by phone and a meeting was set for January 24. TWO prepared six proposals to present to Caples. The first three proposals called for the Board to recognize and admit that the schools are segregated, to set integration as a goal, and to commission an impartial outside group to develop a plan to implement integration. Caples met with the pastors but rejected the proposals. A month later he resigned as president of the Board.

In order to dramatize the overcrowding in the black schools TWO organized "truth squads" to visit white schools in the southwest area of the city, count empty classrooms, and take pictures. On February 2, 1962, the "squads" visited several schools and found six empty classrooms before one group of four women was arrested and charged with trespassing and disorderly conduct at the Kellogg Branch of Foster Park School. The arrest of women peaceably visiting public schools, more than the photographs of empty classrooms, confirmed in the minds of TWO supporters the image of an insensitive school system. The more parents and community leaders tried to find out about classroom use, the more resistant the schools became to any inquiry. In an article on TWO's battle with the schools, Ernestine Cofield of the *Daily Defender* observed:

> The "Truth Squads" visits had a curious twist. The "welcome" signs that had appeared in schools were suddenly removed. Parents in Woodlawn were threatened with arrest if they visited schools in which their own children were enrolled.[68]

After several court delays the mothers were found guilty and received suspended sentences. Although TWO's failure to appeal the verdict because of lack of funds created some internal bitterness, the truth squad mothers and their treatment became a symbol of a repressive and irresponsive school system.

The Board of Education's response to the double shifts was the use of mobile classrooms placed in parks, school play-yards, and vacant lots. TWO protested the use of what were soon called "Willis Wagons," arguing that vacant classrooms in white schools should be used first. As a demonstration of their opposition to a plan to erect a mobile classroom school in Woodlawn, TWO organized a one-day boycott of the Carnegie Elementary School in which, on Friday, May 18, 1962, 1,200 of 1,350 pupils stayed home. This boycott tactic, effectively demonstrated by TWO, later became the major tactic of a city-wide movement against the Chicago school system.

The strategy and tactics of TWO's pursuit of the schools issue revealed a new militancy that appealed to the black community. The dramatic walkout at the Board of Education hearing, the mass hearing with hooded witnesses, the forced meetings with Willis and Caples, the death watch,

[68] Cofield, "Death Watch," p. 9.

the truth squads, the boycott, all these were tactics to which the white community was unaccustomed. Although these tactics were ineffective in changing the school system, they did enhance the Temporary Woodlawn Organization. One commentary in a South Side weekly newspaper observed that TWO along with CORE was fast replacing the NAACP as the leader of the civil rights movement.

> The Temporary Woodlawn Organization has grabbed off a pile of publicity through a vigorous press relations program and through the engineering of dramatic news situations. TWO's now famous "walkout" of the Board of Education meeting and the staging of its own schools hearing not only made news but have appealed to the grass roots as well. . . . This type of direct action adds feathers to the TWO cap.[69]

Although TWO directed much of its attention during the first year to a variety of activities, it never forgot the issue around which it was formed. The original expressed purpose of TWO was community rehabilitation. The patterns of racial change, neighborhood deterioration, and finally, massive land clearance had the appearance of inevitability as the black ghetto expanded in Chicago. The founders of TWO argued that this pattern was a deliberate process, planned and controlled by established monied interests which created and maintained the ghetto. Conservation and rehabilitation of black communities were virtually impossible because the pattern was firmly fixed in the minds of established authorities and urban planners. If there was one single notion behind TWO it was to break this pattern. Charles Leber wrote, in the early months of TWO:

> There is a desperate need today to demonstrate the rehabilitation of such a community by its own indigenous leadership. Only then can direct encouragement be given to other communities. Only then can a new security be

[69] *Chicago Courier*, December 2, 1961, p. 1.

attached to in-migration into hitherto segregated areas. Only then can the forces of exploitation be shown up for what they are today.[70]

In the South Campus controversy TWO formulated its position on urban renewal, favoring rehabilitation and conservation of the sound, existing structures with some spot clearance of vice centers and structures beyond hope of rehabilitation. TWO vigorously opposed massive clearance and relocation. In exchange for approval of the South Campus plan TWO sought two things: (1) low-income housing on a deteriorated nonresidential section of Cottage Grove Avenue and (2) overall planning for the community in which the interests of Woodlawn would be represented through TWO.

It is one thing to prevent massive clearance and to develop a working relationship with city planning and renewal agencies. Preventing decay and deterioration is another matter. The ordinance issue was settled. The overall Woodlawn plan was promised. But the housing conditions in Woodlawn were not one bit affected by these moves. To families paying $115.00 a month for a three-room apartment with broken windows, faulty plumbing, falling plaster and rats, the culprit was not the University of Chicago or the Chicago Plan Commission, but the landlord. If TWO was to alter the pattern of physical deterioration, it would have to tackle the absentee landlord.

Absentee landlords have been a central part of the ghetto pattern. When a community was "written off," many landlords with large holdings profited. Apartment buildings were cut up to house more people. Rents remained high because the dual housing market allowed blacks few options. The absentee landlord often merely gathered the rent and let the buildings decay. Some, no doubt, felt that it was useless to maintain their buildings because anticipated clearance projects would wipe out their improvements or

[70] Leber, *Chicago Maroon*, March 3, 1961, p. 4.

THE STRUGGLE IS CONFLICT

because tenants would ruin them. But the more important fact was that the absentee landlord knew he could get away without maintaining his buildings. Inspectors could be bribed, court processes were slow, fines were small, and tenants had few rights (or knowledge of rights) by which they could force changes.

Since the city was unable or unwilling to enforce codes which would maintain basically sound buildings, TWO developed its own enforcement techniques to deal with slum landlords. TWO's direct action approach was based on organization, public exposure, pressure, and if necessary, rent strikes, and picketing.[71]

TWO would not take a case unless at least half of the tenants in the building agreed to form their own group to work with the housing committee. This procedure assured tenant support and it also served to build the organization. Members of the committee, with some of the tenants, would investigate the building, list the violations, and take pictures. The committee would then call for a meeting with the landlord. At the first meeting with the landlord and his lawyer, all the tenants making the complaint were present with members of the committee. A list of violations was presented and demands were made. These included a time-table for completion of repairs and sometimes a reduction in rent in line with city-wide averages.

Not all cases followed this simple pattern. Sometimes it was difficult to find the owner because occasionally landlords hid anonymously behind trusts administered by banks. In some of these cases a delegation from TWO visited the trust-holding bank and threatened a sit-in if the bank refused to reveal the owner's name. On occasion the bank decided to resign the trust and reveal the name.

A greater difficulty was getting the owner to negotiate with the tenants and TWO. In these cases, and only after

[71] An account of TWO's early tactics against the landlords is given by former staff member Charles Williams, "A Christian Approach to Community Organization," pp. 68ff.

several attempts to negotiate were made, the tenants, with TWO's backing, would call a rent strike. Two examples illustrate TWO's tactics with landlords.

In early November 1961, Julius Mark agreed to make specified repairs on a building he owned. The complaints included rotting floors, no locks, inoperative bathroom plumbing, falling plaster, and broken windows. When Mark reneged on his agreement, the tenants called a strike and placed signs in their windows (one large word per window) reading "This is a Slum" and "No Rent Till Fixed." Later, Mark entered one of the apartments and tore down a window sign. The tenant swore out a warrant for his arrest. A committee member said:

> We are taking Mark to court because the day is gone when a slum landlord can ignore the dignity of his tenants. You wouldn't see anybody going into his home tearing anything out of his windows. I don't see the difference.[72]

The coal supply in the building ran out in mid-December and Mark was accused of trying to freeze out the tenants. Fr. Farrell and the Rev. Charles Jordan soon appeared in a coal truck decorated with TWO slogans and delivered the fuel. Following this, a group of thirty-five TWO members picketed Mark's home in nearby South Shore on a Saturday afternoon and distributed in his neighborhood flyers which read:

> Did You Know One of Your Neighbors Is a
> Slum Landlord?
> He is Julius Mark, 2409 East 73rd Street.
> He Leases and Won't Fix A Slum at 6434-
> 36 S. Kimbark Where the Tenants Are So
> Mad They've Called a Rent Strike.

[72] Ernestine Cofield, "A Community Mobilizes Versus Absentee Landlords," *Chicago Defender*, November 26, 1962, p. 9.

With pressure from his white neighbors and the threat of a court case against him, Mark asked to negotiate. In a "public ceremony" an agreement was signed which stipulated a specific timetable for repairs, deconversion of apartments, and the hiring of a new janitor.

The week the Mark case was settled, tenants of a building owned by Millard Brown called a rent strike. Brown had signed a contract with the TWO committee on December 18 in which he agreed to repair his building by January 10. Two weeks after the deadline no work had been started. This strike lasted for more than two months. Most of the children of the building had to move in with relatives because there was no heat. Again TWO picketed the owner's office and his home. Finally, Brown came to terms with the tenants and the housing committee.

The rent strike and picketing were not always needed. One of the early TWO organizers observed that "after about the third bitter slum building fight, TWO's housing committee met with little opposition."[73] The effectiveness of this style of direct action was not seen merely in the repairs and improvements that were made to Woodlawn buildings. In the long run, the building-by-building, landlord-by-landlord negotiations did not prove to be an adequate solution to Woodlawn's housing problems. Although millions of dollars of improvements were forced by direct action against individual slum operators, this one-by-one approach was eventually too limited to halt the deterioration of the hundreds of buildings in Woodlawn. As in the schools issue the effectiveness of this direct action lay more in what it did for the organization. For the organizers these tactics were primarily a means toward building and maintaining a strong organization. Von Hoffman made this clear:

> If it still appears that a strike is feasible, he (the organizer) must ask what it will do for the organization. I will

[73] Williams, "A Christian Approach to Community Organization," p. 70.

list a few possible things it might do, again by way of illustrating the organizational mentality.

1. If the political climate is right and you know local government is with you it may provide a quickie victory—something every organization needs on occasion.

2. It can be a device to show people via face-to-face confrontation that a big, important white man like a slum landlord can be humiliated and beaten.

3. It may be a way to force a municipal government to begin rigorous enforcement of minimal housing standards.

4. It may be useful in building up general organizational cohesion . . . humor, color, the relish of a small triumph and greater organizational solidarity. . . .

5. The strike may also be a useful method for organizing the people in the immediate locale around the building in question. Unless you have all of officialdom on your side, a rent strike is liable to be a protracted contest of nasty little surprises which each side springs on the other. The landlords' surprises are usually legal ones, bailiffs, court orders, etc. If the whole area is mobilized and organized into a big warning system, the landlord can't pull off much.

But if the fight is really you and a few tenants versus the landlord in the midst of an indifferent populace, you are likely to invest hundreds of hours of time keeping the tenants morale up, with little to show for it but some publicity.[74]

For TWO the rent strikes along with the other direct tactics had many benefits: the emergence of new leadership, the creation of TWO-oriented tenant organizations, organizational solidarity, favorable publicity, exposure of slum landlords, victories, and the experience on the part of an increasing number of residents that "we don't have to take it." This is the stuff that was used to build the Temporary

[74] Von Hoffman, "Making Leaders," p. 8.

Organization into a strong bargaining agent for the community.

All of these activities—the Square Deal Campaign, the voter registration cavalcade, the conflict with landlords and public schools—were directed toward the one primary goal of creating a strong community organization. Some of the scholarly critics of TWO missed this point. They lamented that TWO was more concerned with protest than program, publicity than follow-through, and sociotherapy than social change.[75] What these critics missed was the essential, though unstated, aim of all of the initial activities, the building of a viable and permanent organization through which the residents of the community could acquire and exercise influence, an accomplishment which many of the same critics deemed unlikely. Charles Silberman was closer to the point when he observed that "What makes The Woodlawn Organization significant is not so much what it is doing for its members as what it is doing to them."[76] Silberman drew attention to an emergence of enthusiasm and hope that was revealed in this first year. This more than the accomplishment of any specific neighborhood improvements provided the dynamic for developing a mass-based community organization. To those whose first question of TWO was "What has it done?" the most appropriate reply might have been,

[75] For criticism of TWO in its early years see Philip M. Hauser, "Conflict vs. Consensus," *Chicago Sun Times*, December 13, 1964, sec. 2, pp. 1-3; Thomas D. Sherrard and Richard C. Murray, "The Church and Neighborhood Community Organization," *Social Work*, x (July 1965), pp. 3-14; Frank Riessman, "Self-Help Among the Poor: New Styles of Social Action," *Trans-Action*, September-October, 1965, pp. 32-37; Riessman, *Strategies Against Poverty*, especially chap. i, "The Myth of Saul Alinsky" (New York: Random House, 1969); Arthur Hillman, "Notes and Comments on the Alinsky Approach" (n.d.—mimeographed); W. W. Schroeder, "Protestant Involvement in Community Organization with Special Reference to The Woodlawn Organization," *Cognitive Structures and Religious Research* (East Lansing, Mich.: Michigan State University Press, 1970).

[76] Silberman, *Crisis*, p. 346.

"Organized." The greatest achievement of the Temporary Woodlawn Organization was the permanent Woodlawn Organization.

On March 23, 1962, over 1,200 people representing 97 community groups (35 block clubs, 44 church-related organizations, 18 social, civic, and ethnic associations) gathered at the Southmoor Hotel for the organizing convention. A constitution was adopted, officers were elected, policy resolutions were discussed and approved. The Woodlawn Organization, continuing with the initials TWO, was for real. Perhaps the most significant sign that it was for real was not the large crowd, the enthusiasm, the official business of constituting itself, or even the determination to continue what Alinsky called an orderly revolution. It was rather the presence of Mayor Richard Daley. The mayor knows the meaning of organization. And it is presumed that he is made aware of those groups he can afford to ignore and those he cannot. His last minute acceptance to speak, supposedly after having received a visit by Mr. Alinsky, indicated that he regarded TWO as an organization with which he would have to deal.

In 1960, Woodlawn was a powerless neighborhood deteriorating in a familiar pattern. The leaders and agencies recognized by the white community were either helpless to counteract these forces or were themselves part of the problem. The University of Chicago had little reason to suspect that it could not claim a piece of this decaying real estate. Two years later Woodlawn was a different scene. The residents had fought back. An impressive organization was firmly established. New leaders emerged. The Woodlawn Organization had to be taken seriously—by the University, by the mayor, by anyone who had plans, interests, investments, or programs in the Woodlawn community.

Attention to the creation of TWO is based on more than the obvious fact that an organization provides a channel for action. A community association, in the very process of organizing influence and enabling action, becomes a bearer of an interpretation of that community, its values, its problems, and its possibilities. Organizations are, by the very way they function, bearers of messages. As a community organization TWO provided a definition of the situation: that is, an organized interpretation of what was wrong with the community, what needed to be done, who should do it, and how it should be done. The initial significance of TWO and the controversy surrounding it lay more in the message it conveyed than in the neighborhood improvements it sought to secure.

A new rhetoric appropriate to this organized message emerged. It was rhetoric of demand and of self-determination. More significant for the images it evoked and the frame of mind it engendered than for any programmatic clarity it provided, this call to self-determination expressed both a rejection of outside control and an affirmation of corporate community planning and action. The specific workingout of community self-determination was the task ahead.

CHAPTER II

The Uses of Conflict: TWO as a Spokesman Organization

THE EARLY activities of The Woodlawn Organization did more to unite the community than to alter the practices and policies of the city. While the organization could be built initially around symbolic victories, it could be maintained only if it could demonstrate a capacity to influence the decisions and forces that shaped life in Woodlawn.

Accordingly, the basic strategy of influence characteristic of The Woodlawn Organization throughout most of its history has been its effort to establish and legitimate its role as spokesman for the 120,000 people of the Greater Woodlawn area.[1] This spokesman strategy was apparent at the beginning of the temporary organization, and was an integral part of TWO's general definition of Woodlawn's situation. The primary task of this chapter is to examine the development of TWO's spokesman strategy between 1962 and 1967.

One perception of the political process in Chicago holds that bargaining is a basic principle of government. This perspective, clearly articulated in Edward Banfield's *Political Influence* and shared by Alinsky, identifies a dual political system in Chicago held together by the Democratic Party Machine. The Machine provides the mechanism for achieving sufficient informal centralization of power to overcome the formal decentralization of authority.[2] As party "boss," Richard Daley, chairman of the Cook County Cen-

---

[1] Greater Woodlawn refers to the area within TWO's self-designated boundaries, including neighborhoods south and west of the specific community area of Woodlawn.

[2] Edward C. Banfield, *Political Influence* (New York: Free Press, 1961), p. 237.

tral Committee of the Democratic Party, has developed the power to enable Mayor Richard Daley to govern as the formal leader of the city.

The two hats of Richard Daley reflect the two political systems in Chicago. One is the formal overt system of government which could be outlined by boxes on a chart. The mayor is at the top of the executive branch. Fifty aldermen represent the people in a legislative council. The courts, the special districts, and the multiplicity of agencies are tied into the diagram by solid and dotted lines. The other system is the process by which the diversity and decentralization of the formal system is overcome. The key to this system is the Cook County Central Committee of the Democratic Party which controls high appointments, a vast system of patronage, and the nomination of candidates for public office. The Democratic Machine has, therefore, varying degrees of influence over the city council, the city agencies, state and national representatives, neighborhood political organizations, and even the supposedly autonomous boxes on the formal chart, such as the courts and the Board of Education. The Machine, in this Banfield model, seeks to maximize areas of control and minimize those areas where power-costly bargaining is necessary. Control is translated into program which can in turn be parlayed into additional influence. The desired outcome is increased capacity to govern and, of course, continued tenure in political office.

Banfield argues that the major actors in this process are persons and organizations which are best able to "play the game"—that is, to organize the action of others, withhold and deliver support, pyramid political resources into blocks of influence that need to be reckoned with by the formal or informal authorities. The formal governmental chart is regarded as a myth because the factors that shape the actions of representatives come not from below but from the Machine, to whom representatives owe primary allegiance. Were there no strong political machine the mayor and other top officials might seek black support by heeding the advice of leaders whom the black community regarded as representing their own interests. However, in Chicago, most of the black aldermen and the black appointees on boards and agencies are oriented not to the group they represent but to that organization that effectively determines their political future.

TWO was challenging such a process of representation in the black community. The *Daily Defender* saw this very early and editorialized in April 1962:

> Chicago has been in need of a militant group for a long time. Since political leadership in our midst is only concerned with preserving its own identity and control, and since that leadership willingly abdicates its prerogatives to the City Hall, someone had to step into the void. If given appropriate support, The Woodlawn Organization may become the most effective spokesman for our people.[3]

The informal process of political influence is such that the decision makers pay more attention to what Banfield calls "autonomous actors" in the political process. As a power broker, the mayor will pay most attention to those who can alter or veto the desired program or purpose. With "kept" constituencies where support, particularly at elections, is delivered by hard-working precinct captains, material inducements, and, in the eyes of detractors, threat or fraud, the political leader will be less responsive. The best way, then, to "raise one's price" in the political market place is to develop a base of influence which can be used for bargaining.

Thus, TWO, as an alternative to the inadequate formal process of representation, assumed the role of "spokesman" or corporate representative of the community, standing between the unrepresented, underrepresented, and misrepresented residents of Woodlawn and those officials who were making decisions that affected the community.

[3] *Chicago Daily Defender*, April 18, 1962, p. 7.

This was no easy task. As a voluntary association, TWO drew on the only accessible power resource—citizens with interests, frustrations and hopes. Not having formal authority over these citizens, TWO had to win its role as spokesman. It has done this through a variety of means—the development of community consciousness, appeals to self-interest, charismatic leadership, forceful rhetoric, services performed, victories won, and organizational skill. This constituency support and allegiance was converted into political influence as TWO was able to obstruct, veto, or alter plans and programs deemed important by public officials and to initiate, pursue, and negotiate plans and programs that are valued by the neighborhood residents.

During the week of the first convention in March 1962, the city presented a plan for Woodlawn—the outcome of a planning effort stimulated in part by TWO's conflict with the University of Chicago. The twenty-page booklet, entitled "A Proposal for a Program to Meet the Long Term Needs of Woodlawn," received a mixed reaction. While the proposal was marked "For Discussion Purposes Only," and while it did offer some assurance that Woodlawn would not be subjected to massive clearance, it was not welcomed uncritically by TWO leaders. The proposal embodied a traditional approach to planning and renewal. Even more disturbing to TWO, the proposal made no mention and gave no recognition of the existence or role of TWO in the planning process. At its convention, TWO resolved to "fight with all its strength to win for the people of Woodlawn the deciding voice in the development of a plan for Woodlawn."[4] Filled with the enthusiasm of their first convention and with the intoxicating notion of "self-determination," TWO was unimpressed by this proposal which they had no part in formulating. The content was not immediately questioned. The process was. The coordinator of the city planning project was quoted as saying, "There is nobody to

[4] *Woodlawn Booster*, March 21, 1962, p. 16.

speak for the community. A community does not exist in Woodlawn."[5]

TWO responded not with a demonstration but with a counter plan. Jane Jacobs, a critic of the traditional planning approaches, became an informal consultant to TWO. Through her, William Nelson, head of a Milwaukee architectural firm, was hired jointly by TWO and the Woodlawn Businessmen's Association to help the community develop its response to the city's plan. Nelson's professional help served a double purpose. He was able to interpret the city's plan in ordinary language to the people of Woodlawn. He also helped the community in the process of developing and articulating their own goals and plans for rehabilitation. Like Jacobs, Nelson believed that most renewal programs tended to destroy rather than renew the older areas of the city.

After four months and numerous discussions with neighborhood groups and individuals, Nelson made his report, and the TWO proposals were published in a special 32-page edition of the *Woodlawn Booster* in July.[6] The report included both a critique of the city's plan and an outline of what it called "A People-Oriented Approach to Urban Renewal and Planning." This document analyzed, interpreted, and severely questioned the city's plan, particularly the professional planner's "we-know-what's-best" approach and the lack of provision for citizen participation. The TWO plan called for (1) direct and decisive citizen participation, (2) a major emphasis on "rehabilitation" and "conservation" rather than "clearance" and "renewal," (3) a basic conviction that Woodlawn should be preserved for those who presently lived there.

Although this venture in planning was impressive and stimulated community enthusiasm and, more important, brought to coherent articulation TWO's position on urban

[5] Jacobs, "Chicago's Woodlawn," p. 122.
[6] *Woodlawn Booster*, July 25, 1962.

renewal, the plan itself was not to be implemented. The city's proposal and TWO's proposal neutralized each other. Nothing happened, not even opposition. The TWO proposal simply received no response from the city planners. A standstill. And a standstill posed the greatest threat to TWO. Opposition it could thrive on. But the lack of any response was discouraging. TWO's inability to follow up on its renewal plan seemed to confirm some of the charges leveled by critics that the organization was high on rhetoric but low on positive action. At this point, however, action by TWO depended on action by the city and the University of Chicago.

If the Woodlawn community would not support the city's plan, the city was apparently willing to wait. Furthermore, a shake-up in city agencies leading to the merger of the Chicago Plan Commission and the Land Clearance Commission into the Department of Urban Renewal (DUR) made communication during this period difficult. The University, burned once, was willing to avoid any further discussion with TWO. The University's failure or inability to pursue the South Campus in public negotiations presented problems for TWO. TWO was counting on the Section 112 federal credits generated by University expansion to be used for community planned renewal in Woodlawn. The lack of the credits and the defeat of a 1962 bond issue left Mayor Daley with nothing to offer and TWO with nothing to receive.

TWO had to force the South Campus proposal back into the public agenda so that it could negotiate for the low-income housing and spot clearance that the community wanted and TWO needed. It is apparent in retrospect that TWO needed the South Campus project as much as the University did. In a strange twist of events, it was TWO, in 1963, that was pressing for the reopening of the South Campus proposal. As long as it remained closed, TWO had nothing to negotiate about and no one with whom to negotiate.

70

In the spring of 1963 TWO applied increasing pressure on the mayor to call a summit meeting between the University, city officials and TWO. Failing in these attempts, the organization planned a more drastic measure—a massive traffic-stopping sit-down on the Lake Shore Drive to dramatize Woodlawn's anger and determination. Only intervention by Alinsky thwarted the use of this tactic. Alinsky argued that there were better ways to gain the ends TWO sought. The mayor's image of TWO was that of forty buses of voters registering at City Hall and 1,200 adults at the Southmoor Hotel for the first convention. This image of potential power, Alinsky argued, should be preserved because it is more effective than a demonstration involving mass arrests and a possible riot. Somewhat grudgingly the leaders called off the Outer Drive sit-in. When the mayor did not respond to this cancellation, TWO went to see him. On July 11, approximately seven hundred Woodlawn residents "visited" City Hall. The response was quick. University officials, Mayor Daley and his planners, and TWO leaders met five days later. An agreement was quickly reached because the University was also anxious to have something moving again on the South Campus. Julian Levi claimed that TWO pressure saved the South Campus plan.

> Our major concern was how we could get the South Campus off dead center. TWO did an invaluable thing for them and for us. We needed movement on the South Campus. The Mayor was down on renewal. He lost the bond issue and was broke. With Doyle downtown I couldn't get this clearance thing to move at all. . . . Brazier then broke the log jam by his demonstration at a time when I couldn't have. We were pleased to be "forced" to meet with TWO.[7]

The seven-point agreement was a high point for TWO, providing leverage for them that no black community or-

[7] Levi, interview, September 11, 1967.

ganization had ever had in Chicago urban renewal planning. The landmark agreement included the following:

1. The majority of the people to be appointed to the groups or committees relating to planning and renewal in Woodlawn will be people from TWO.

2. South Campus should be designed to continue to give Woodlawn residents continued access to the Midway recreation area. In other words, no Great Wall of China.

3. The demolition for South Campus should be delayed until the Cottage Grove strip has been cleared and some new units of low cost (221(d)3) housing have been built so that the people can be relocated directly out of the old housing on South Campus into the new.

4. It should be understood by all parties that, besides the Cottage Grove clearance, a fair amount of other spot clearance, particularly of vice centers, must be part of the program.

5. Re-sale of cleared land to non-profit and limited profit corporations that will build at prices Woodlawn people can afford. This may necessitate larger than usual write-downs.

6. The City should be willing to use the idle four million dollars being held by the Chicago Dwellings Association to aid the program. The program will probably require a much more adventuresome policy on the part of the Chicago Housing Authority and the Department of Urban Renewal than has been the case in the past.

7. The administrator for the Woodlawn programs will be acceptable to TWO.[8]

On October 19 Mayor Daley appointed the Rev. Blakeley chairman of a 13-member Woodlawn Citizens Committee, seven of whom were designated by TWO. The initial item of business for WCC was the pending DUR ordinance

[8] "Agreement Reached Between Mayor Daley and TWO on July 16, 1963," on file at TWO office.

which designated an L-shaped area (the South Campus and the land bordering Cottage Grove Avenue) as "slum and blighted" and appropriate for an urban renewal project. Blakeley outlined TWO's approach:

> TWO's position has been that we do not oppose expansion of the University of Chicago so long as there is an overall plan benefiting the citizens of Woodlawn. Our position has been that most of our housing is sound and should be preserved. Some of our housing is dilapidated and should be rehabilitated. Here and there throughout the community there should be clearance of slum buildings that are not repairable. Vice centers and Baby Skid Row should be scheduled for demolition. In other words, TWO's approach is one of conservation and rehabilitation with some selective clearance. Any ordinance that is adopted must include and reflect this position. Once the limited ordinance is approved, we will no longer have a lever on the University. They will have South Campus, we will have a small strip of Cottage Grove and the other problems of Woodlawn will be unsolved.[9]

The committee worked through the fall on the DUR ordinance. At a November 16 meeting, the TWO members, voting as a block, prevailed seven to six on a motion to reject the ordinance as presented. WCC proposed that the ordinance be revised as follows: (1) that the boundaries of the area designated "slum and blighted" be changed slightly to preserve several blocks of good housing; (2) that the area around 63rd Street and Dorchester Avenue (Baby Skid Row) be included in the ordinance and designated for clearance; and (3) that there be a survey of vacant land suitable for low-income housing.

The Citizens Committee met with DUR on February 3, 1964, armed with copies of the July 16 agreement (see items

[9] Ulysses S. Blakeley, Chairman of Woodlawn Citizens Committee, "Memo on Planning, Renewal and Conservation in Woodlawn," n.d., on file at TWO, p. 3 (mimeographed).

73

3 and 5) and a survey of existing rents ($100 to $155 a month) being paid by families in the South Campus area. After this session DUR agreed to revise the ordinance in accordance with the Citizens Committee's demands.

Even before it secured from DUR a firm commitment to 221(d)3 (low-to-moderate rent, not-for-profit housing financed through FHA) housing on the Cottage Grove strip, TWO was working with the Kate Maremont Foundation on a proposal for that area. After several months of planning, TWO and KMF announced at a press conference on March 24, 1964, a $10 million proposal to be submitted to FHA and DUR along with a request to the City Council for passage of an appropriate ordinance. The organization had come up with a major improvement project which it had initiated, fought for, pursued, and seemed about to secure. But celebration was premature.

In July 1964, Brazier's successor as TWO president, Lynward Stevenson, presented the steering committee with a four-point action program against what he called "Mayor Daley's refusal to keep his word on urban renewal."[10] A year had passed since the agreement with the mayor and the University. Four months had passed since TWO-KMF announced their proposal. However no official action was forthcoming. Stevenson's action plan called for (1) an immediate meeting with the mayor, (2) a major press conference, (3) a delegation to Washington to talk with FHA officials about the slowdown in City Hall, and (4) implementation of a plan to block any moves on the South Campus project until 221(d)3 housing on Cottage Grove Avenue was in the works. The city responded. By November, an ordinance designating the Cottage Grove area specifically for 221(d)3 low-rise housing was passed.

The next step was a study of the TWO-KMF proposal by the federal government. However, it was not until a year later, the fall of 1965, that the proposal was forwarded to the Chicago-based federal officials and then to Washington

[10] *TWO Newsletter*, July 29, 1964, p. 1.

for final approval. By the spring of 1966 TWO was becoming increasingly impatient with what appeared to be excessive delays. As a prod, the Woodlawn Citizens Committee planned a community hearing. The purpose was twofold: to demonstrate massive community support for the TWO-KMF plan and to express the community's impatience with federal and City Hall delays. In what was one of the most impressive demonstrations of TWO's organization skill, 1,114 Woodlawn people attended a March 14 meeting and heard brief testimonies from 87 community groups, all of whom requested that the Cottage Grove strip be sold to TWO-KMF on a negotiated bid so that the cost would be low enough to permit housing within the financial reach of Woodlawn residents. In less than a month after the hearing, Mayor Daley announced his support of the TWO-KMF proposal and promised to convey his feelings to the Department of Urban Renewal. Through a process of early acquisition the land was purchased by the city and demolition of the area was begun prior to final city approval of the project or the designation of a developer. The conclusion of this drawn out segment of the process did not come until a year, and numerous meetings, later when, by official vote of the City Council, TWO-KMF was designated as developer-builder of the project. TWO had a controlling majority on the TWO-KMF Development Association Board which was chaired first by Brazier and later by longtime TWO leader, James Grammer.

In the final stages this project faced further delays which thwarted some of the original purposes of the Woodlawn Gardens project. Even though the initial demolition was begun in July 1966, and the designation of TWO-KMF as developers was made in July 1967, the final transfer of land to TWO was not made until November 1968. During this final delay while TWO was preoccupied with a controversial Youth Project (see Chapter III), the South Campus area was being cleared and residents relocated. Since the buildings in the South Campus, destined for demolition since 1961, had become increasingly deteriorated, many of the residents had already left. Nevertheless, TWO protested that the city had broken the 1963 agreement which guaranteed that new housing would be available before South Campus clearance. Although the protests may have speeded the final transfer of land to TWO-KMF, it was clear that Woodlawn Gardens would not fulfill its original purpose in providing housing for the displaced South Campus residents.

It was also becoming increasingly clear that this 221(d)3 housing was not the answer to the housing needs of low-income people. A variety of forces pushed up the rental cost of the new housing. After a controversy with DUR, TWO had to reduce the number of units to 502 in order to provide required off-street parking. This increased the per-unit cost. Inflation took another toll. The final rentals at the time of occupancy in the fall of 1969 ran from $100 for efficiency apartments to $160 for three bedrooms, substantially higher than the original estimates. TWO had hoped to overcome this cost problem by a rent subsidy program negotiated with the Chicago Housing Authority. CHA had agreed that one-half of the units would be rented by welfare recipients through a subsidy program. Had this worked out, Woodlawn Gardens would have achieved that mix of public aid and private rental units which has eluded housing officials in centrally planned projects. This hopeful sign was thwarted in part by FHA requirements and, ironically, in part by a 1969 court decision against the discriminatory practices of CHA which forced the latter to abandon its concentration on black communities and to limit housing subsidies in those areas.[11] Woodlawn Gardens would not provide substantial housing for the poor.

[11] In a suit filed by the American Civil Liberties Union against the Chicago Housing Authority, Federal District Court, Judge Richard Austin ruled that, in order to remedy past practices, CHA must follow a "three to one" policy in placing families and building new units,

If Woodlawn Gardens did not meet its original expectations it was, nevertheless, a major landmark for TWO. A black community actually planned, developed, and built a major housing complex. The building itself provided further opportunities for TWO. A $400,000 electrical contract was awarded to black contractors who formed a combine to qualify and bid for the work. As the developer TWO cooperated closely with Operation Breadbasket in driving a wedge in the white-dominated building trades which were notorious in discriminatory practices. A majority of the electricians, plumbers, bricklayers, and carpenters who actually built Woodlawn Gardens were black. Although this in itself did little to solve the problem of racism in the trade unions, it helped generate a concerted campaign in this direction.

More than any other activity undertaken by TWO this project reveals the endurance and tenacity of the organization. From July 1960, when the University of Chicago announced its South Campus plan until Woodlawn Gardens was a reality a full decade later, TWO stayed with it. The hundreds of meetings and demonstrations, the thousands of man-hours of planning and negotiating resulted in more than a brick and mortar physical improvement for the community. Woodlawn Gardens became, for TWO, a monument. Through TWO as its representative, Woodlawn, unlike any other black community, planned, developed, owned, and managed its own housing.

---

three in white areas for every one in black areas. White resistance to public housing stymied the ruling for several years. In the meantime, black neighborhoods had difficulty securing CHA units or rent subsidies. See Vic Pilolla, "How Housing Bias Rule Backfired," *Chicago Today*, September 14, 1969, p. 20. For a full account of CHA past practices see Harold Baron, "Building Babylon: A Case of Racial Controls in Public Housing," *Focus/Midwest*, Vol. 8 (1972), No. 56, pp. 4-27, and Martin Meyerson and Edward Banfield, *Politics, Planning and the Public Interest* (New York: Free Press, 1955).

Unemployment in Woodlawn was several times that of the city as a whole.[12] The general pattern of discrimination, the exclusion of blacks from the building trades and vocational schools, the inadequacy of ghetto schools, the failure of traditional employment services to reach the hard-core poor were a few of the many diverse factors contributing to joblessness. Unemployment would not be solved by the kind of protest and pressure which TWO had used with effectiveness in fighting land clearance.

The Woodlawn Organization developed a job-training proposal which, with the support of the University of Chicago, was submitted to the U.S. Department of Labor. TWO was awarded a Manpower Development Training Act grant of $76,000 in July 1966, for training 200 hard-core unemployed. The project was characterized by three innovations. First, the traditional tests by which the most disadvantaged and alienated had been screened out of employment programs were abandoned. TWO sought to direct its efforts to those who had been deemed unemployable. Second, the TWO program hired indigenous residents to staff the program. Third, and perhaps the most important, TWO argued that the job-training program could not be divorced from the multitude of TWO activities. For TWO job training was part of community organizing. The trainees organized clubs and became constituent members of TWO. If job training were merely a means by which a few were enabled to gain employment and perhaps leave Woodlawn, TWO probably would not have desired to continue the effort. One of the major goals in TWO's job-training program, as in all of its activities, was to strengthen the organization.

The first program had many problems. One of the more pleasant problems was overresponse. According to its final

[12] Unofficial estimates of unemployment in Woodlawn in the early 1960s ranged between 30 and 40 percent. See Steven M. Lovelady, "Private Poverty War Stresses Self-Help," *Wall Street Journal*, February 18, 1966, p. 6.

report, 3,718 persons made applications for a program designed for 200. Additional problems in staffing and administrating the program consumed an inordinate amount of TWO's time and energy in 1964.

For a substantial length of time TWO's program on housing, welfare, etc. suffered because of the energy poured into servicing, or attempting to service, the flood of persons seeking jobs or retraining. Consequently the Organization at times was subjected to severe criticism from its own membership for engaging in such a program.[13]

Many of these problems were solved with experience. With each new program the organization not only developed greater competence in administration but also designed more adequate programs. In 1965 TWO received $169,000 for an on-the-job training program for 350 adults. Unlike the previous program where job placement followed classroom training and frequently resulted in frustrating disappointment because of the unavailability of jobs, the second program placed trainees directly on jobs. The third, and largest, program was a two-year project funded in 1966. Referred to as the "Coupled Project," this $1.9 million program combined the features of on-job and institutional training. According to TWO records, 813 previously unemployed persons were placed on jobs.[14] By the time of the fourth grant in 1969 ($408,000), TWO had clearly demonstrated, at least to the federal agencies' satisfaction, the effectiveness of community administered job training. Job training had become a permanent part of the organization. It no longer detracted from, but rather enhanced, other activities of the organization. Perhaps the greatest testimony

[13] From the final report of TWO's job-training program under contract MDS 31-61 with the U.S. Department of Labor, "Retraining the Hard-Core Unemployed Through a Grass-Roots Community Organization," September 1, 1965, on file at TWO, p. 6 (mimeographed).

[14] *Observer*, February 26, 1969, p. 1.

of TWO's competence in this area is that it attracted job-training contracts from other agencies.[15]

Aside from the obvious benefit of job training for the community residents, these programs were important to TWO for several reasons. They enhanced the positive image of TWO as a self-help organization. These programs also enabled the organization to develop administrative competence and a technical staff. This expanded staff was, in turn, used to develop further programs. Perhaps most important, TWO was regarded, at least by some federal officials, as having that support and confidence of the community which was deemed essential for effective job recruitment and training.

The organization's energies were consumed by the job-training program in 1964 and 1965. The new TWO president, the Rev. Lynward Stevenson, was less able than his predecessor to control a rapidly expanding staff. The influence of the middle-class homeowners in West Woodlawn and Essex became stronger within the organization. Internal tensions were arising. Busy with the relatively amicable negotiations with the Department of Urban Renewal, with a noncontroversial job-training effort, and with mending fences with the University of Chicago, TWO was living more comfortably with the outside world and was facing more dissatisfaction within. TWO president Lynward Stevenson put it this way:

> The first MDTA program came in 1964 and it tied us up. The year was hectic. It was all MDTA. Personnel problems were great. We moved in a year's time from a budget of $30,000 to $1,000,000 and from a staff of 6 to 30—this included the newspaper and special programs. A lot of this activity shut out the poor. There were also problems of staff dissension, suspicion of mishandling of

[15] In 1969 TWO contracted with the Illinois State Employment Service to recruit welfare recipients for paramedical training and with the Zenith Corporation to recruit and counsel hard-core unemployed.

funds, and many picayune things. I just didn't know how to be president during my first year. I didn't come to life until the O.E.O. controversy. TWO was revived again also.[16]

When the Economic Opportunity Act of 1964 was passed, TWO responded. The Poverty Program, argued TWO leaders, would enable the organization "to back up our program of self-determination with deeds."[17] TWO developed and submitted two proposals designed to facilitate and make more effective the job-training program. The two major reasons for dropouts in the training program were the lack of day care facilities for the children of trainees and the lack of medical care sufficient to help the hard core attain that health necessary for continued employment. TWO said it would match federal funds on a 25 percent basis as a demonstration of their willingness to pursue these proposals for day care and medical facilities.

Chicago antipoverty chief Deton Brooks and his staff said they would study TWO's proposals. Nine months passed. Millions of dollars of projects in Chicago were approved. But there was no word on TWO's proposals. Stevenson and Brazier went to Washington to confer with Richard Boone, a top aide of OEO director Sargent Shriver. "Boone told us," said Stevenson, "that we could get the money if Brooks says O.K."[18] There appeared to be two reasons, not unrelated, for Brooks' reluctance to support TWO. One of his staff members offered the manifest professional reason:

You have to consider the competency of the Agency. Self-help is a fine principle, but frankly, this just isn't a technically sound proposal. Day Care centers need professional handling. And the Board of Health is planning

[16] Lynward Stevenson, interview, September 27, 1967.

[17] Lynward Stevenson, "Open Letter to Sargent Shriver," *TWO Newsletter*, October 21, 1964, p. 1.

[18] Lois Wille, "TWO Wants to Know: Will We Share in Poverty Funds?" *Chicago Daily News*, April 7, 1965, p. 68.

health clinics. So wouldn't it make sense to let the professionals do it?[19]

A more apparent reason was that Daley was not going to fund organizations that were politically independent or critical of City Hall. Facing reelection in two years, Daley appeared determined to maintain tight control and to use carefully his poverty funds. One Washington observer, apparently knowledgeable about the Daley style of politics observed, "It will be a cold day in hell before TWO gets a penny."[20] What burned Brooks most was that TWO tried to bypass him by going directly to Washington. "If Brazier and Stevenson had come here in the first place instead of going directly to Washington, maybe we would have straightened things out."[21]

Stevenson, with TWO support, began a head-on attack of Chicago's antipoverty set-up. He charged that Daley and Brooks were subverting the Poverty Program by using it to maintain control of the poor and to feed his patronage system. Stevenson's attack was picked up in a series of articles by *Daily News* reporter Lois Wille.[22] The charges were given substance. Daley's blue ribbon poverty committee, the fifty-four-member Chicago Committee on Urban Opportunity included no representatives of the poor. More than half of its members were on government payroll and only one person, Edwin Berry of the Urban League, was a recognized civil rights leader.[23] It was also revealed that

[19] *Ibid.*
[20] *Chicago Daily News*, May 13, 1965, p. 3.
[21] Wille, "TWO Wants to Know."
[22] *Chicago Daily News*, April 5, 6, 7, 8, 9, 1965.
[23] According to Lois Wille, "The War Within Poverty War," *Chicago Daily News*, April 5, 1965, the fifty-four-member Chicago Committee on Urban Opportunity included twenty-five chairmen or directors of governmental agencies, five aldermen, one judge, nine business leaders, four union executives, six private welfare agency leaders, three clergymen and Edwin Berry. None were residents of the ghetto, none were poor. In testifying before the House of Representatives' Labor and Education Committee, Deton Brooks was pressed by chairman

applications for jobs in the poverty bureaucracy were being funnelled through ward committeemen. Congressman Adam Clayton Powell, Chairman of House Committee on Labor and Education, which was investigating the Poverty Program picked up the Chicago controversy. Powell, his own interests in Harlem threatened by Mayor Wagner's control of the Poverty Program, saw the Chicago situation as a means of exposing the Program as a "fiesta of political patronage" and of securing changes favorable to his own interests. Powell called Stevenson and Brooks before his committee on April 13, 1965. "Apparently," said Powell, "TWO is the only group with enough guts to stand up to the politicians on this poverty business."[24] After describing TWO's efforts to participate in the Chicago Program and outlining the politicians' control of the Program, Stevenson, in a classic example of Alinsky rhetoric, concluded his testimony this way:

> This is maximum feasible participation of the rich. This is maximum feasible participation of precinct captains. This is maximum feasible participation of ward committeemen. Where is maximum feasible participation of the poor? There is not even minimum feasible participation of poor people. . . .
>
> In Chicago, there is no War on Poverty. There is only more of the ancient, galling war against the poor.
>
> It is a war against the poor when the great ideas of two presidents and Congress are twisted into cheap slogans to benefit local politicians. It is a war against the poor when our hopes are lifted—only to be drowned once again in this sewage of phony promises.

Adam Clayton Powell on this point. "Powell: 'Who on the central board represents the poor people?' Brooks: 'We haven't broken our committee down that way.' Powell: 'Have you got any—yes or no?' Brooks: 'I believe our whole committee represents the poor.'" From James McCartney, "Poverty Probers Rake Chicago Chief," *Chicago Daily News*, April 14, 1965, p. 1.

[24] *TWO Newsletter*, April 14, 1965, p. 1.

83

It is a war against the poor when only the rich benefit from public funds. It is a war against the poor when the white-shirted social workers, the bankers who run the powerful charities, the ward committeemen get fat off money appropriated to help the poor lift themselves off the bottom.

It is war against the poor when we are told by the President and Congress that we can plan for ourselves, but then find that we can only stand in the waiting rooms of Chicago's City Hall, while plans are made for us. It is war against the poor when the Chicago Committee deals out its money to people whose only knowledge of the poor comes from the television set.

Oh, it is not a war of guns and explosives. It is an undeclared war by the rich, and by the local politicians. What they want to do is to destroy our dignity. That is why they insist on planning for us.

And how do you think we feel when we know that men who drive Cadillacs, eat three-inch steaks and sip champagne at luncheon meetings discuss our future while we are pushed off the highways of self-help and told to keep our hats in hand? As one of Deton Brooks' boys said, "I don't know what's wrong with Lyn Stevenson. He must have given up hope for a Poverty grant or why would he be taking a chance talking like that." Well I'll tell you Gentlemen, The Woodlawn Organization will not sell its right of every American to free speech for a token from Deton Brooks and the Chicago Committee on Urban Opportunity. . . .

We may be poor. But we are proud. And, Gentlemen, we would rather starve as poor men than get fat as pets of City Hall.[25]

Receiving national news coverage, TWO drew attention to that aspect of the War on Poverty which became a point of controversy for the next five years—the community ac-

[25] *Ibid.*, pp. 9-10.

tion program. The growing conflict over "maximum feasible participation" and control of poverty money was not merely between mayors who feared that the poverty program might undermine their base of power and community organizations who regarded poverty more as lack of power than lack of services. It was also an internal conflict in the federal bureaucracy. The federal "reformers" apparently hoped to use the community action program to put pressure on recalcitrant urban bureaucracies. The reformers liked TWO. But the Democratic administration in Washington also liked the votes that Daley and other big city mayors could deliver.[26]

TWO, under Stevenson's leadership, became a spokesman for the poor. The national publicity and the continuing local conflict with City Hall revived TWO. The poor in Woodlawn began to play a more active role in the organization. Early in the summer of 1965, when the city was initiating neighborhood Urban Progress Centers, TWO leaders met with Daley and sought a majority on the Woodlawn Advisory Committee. According to Stevenson, the mayor agreed and said that he would appoint a twenty-five-member committee after receiving nominations from TWO. The organization sent a list of twenty-one names to the mayor from which he could pick at least thirteen. The mayor accepted all twenty-one and could truthfully claim

[26] See Tom Littlewood, "Powell Calls Off His Fight Against War on Poverty," *Chicago Sun Times*, May 13, 1965; Paul Gapp, "The Poverty War Toe Dance," *Chicago Daily News*, May 13, 1965; Charles Nicodemus, "Who Tripped?" *Chicago Daily News*, May 13, 1965. For fuller accounts of the controversy over citizen action programs see Peter Marris and Martin Rein, *The Dilemma of Social Reform* (New York: Atherton Press, 1967); Daniel P. Moynihan, *Maximum Feasible Misunderstanding* (New York: Free Press, 1969); John C. Donovan, *The Politics of Poverty* (New York: Pegasus, 1967); Chaim I. Waxman (ed.), *Poverty: Power and Politics* (New York: Grosset and Dunlap, 1968), esp. Charles E. Silberman, "The Mixed-Up War on Poverty," pp. 81-100; Saul Alinsky, "The War on Poverty—Political Pornography," pp. 171-179; and James Ridgeway, "The More Glorious War," pp. 202-206.

that he appointed everyone that TWO requested. But, to the organization's dismay, the mayor increased the size of the committee to seventy-five persons. TWO felt betrayed but they could not alter the outcome. In the fall and winter months the organization continued the pressure. Three hundred Woodlawn residents appeared, uninvited, at a major poverty conference held at the Sherman House downtown. Shriver was the main speaker for the 1,700 delegates. Refused permission to attend, the TWO group sat in the lobby. Embarrassed, Daley was reported to have remarked at the time, "They're kicking the hell out of us."[27]

Within the Woodlawn Urban Progress Center the twenty-one-member TWO contingent tried to exert influence on an advisory board controlled by Daley loyalists. One short-lived moment of success came at the local board meeting on December 27, 1965, at which time a variety of projects were to have been approved by the advisory board. While a number of proposals was accepted, nine projects worth $4 million were rejected by the board. With Alderman Despres and TWO members taking the lead, the advisory board actually vetoed the staff recommendations. Members of the TWO contingent, more diligent than the others in attending board meetings, caught the Daley loyalists short-handed and rejected the proposals by an eighteen to eleven vote.

The city's response was forceful and immediate. The all-out effort removed, in the minds of many Woodlawn residents, any lingering doubts about the political control of the Woodlawn Urban Progress Center. In a quick series of activities the advisory board decision was reversed. First James Clardy, a precinct captain on the advisory board, led a campaign sponsored by a group called the Associated Block Clubs of Woodlawn. Clardy, other precinct captains, and the WUPC staff gathered 15,000 signatures in support of the nine proposals. Second, the minutes of the December

[27] *TWO News*, December 22, 1965, p. 3. See introductory note in bibliography.

86

27 meeting were not sent out to the members. TWO members claimed that the minutes were rewritten by WUPC staff to indicate that the decision on the nine proposals was "unfinished business."[28] Third, written proxy support was secured from absentee members. Fourth, by the January 12 meeting, the advisory board was back in line and the previous decision was reversed by a thirty-seven to sixteen vote. After the meeting Stevenson said:

> If anyone in this city doubted that Daley is running the anti-poverty program, then tonight's railroading should clear up these doubts. TWO has been charging for months that the anti-poverty program was in the hands of the politicians. Now Daley has documented our charge.[29]

After that incident, the participation of the TWO delegation on the advisory board dwindled. TWO and the Urban Progress Center went their separate ways. With token community support the "war on poverty" was carried on through such programs as a charm school for teenage girls, clean-up campaigns, and choral groups. TWO, having for the first time elicited the direct and decisive countervailing power of the regular political Machine, turned to other matters.

This struggle had an impact on TWO. The organization became increasingly attuned to the problems of the poor. And the poor became a more significant part of the organization. The Fifth Annual Convention in the spring of 1966 gave Lynward Stevenson a mandate to lead a drive to organize welfare recipients. The convention's resolution was that

> TWO should engage in direct action tactics against abuses by the Cook County Department of Public Aid.
> TWO should assist in organizing welfare unions in

[28] *Woodlawn Observer*, January 19, 1966, p. 1.
[29] *Ibid.*, p. 2.

Greater Woodlawn so that persons on welfare can have unity and self-protection.[30]

Under Stevenson's leadership, recipients—primarily ADC mothers—were organized into locals and together formed a Social Welfare Union which has become an advocate and negotiator for recipients in Woodlawn. For TWO this new move provided at first five, and two years later, eighteen welfare locals as constituent groups in the organization. This provided not only an expanded support base for TWO but also a significant source of new leadership.

The Poverty Program issue did for TWO what the South Campus controversy had done in the first year. It provided an occasion for TWO to interpret and define the issue. And the issue was the same: outside control vs. self-determination. In a document entitled, "TWO Black Paper Number Two: Poverty, Power and Race in Chicago," the organization made this clear:

> The root issue underlying poverty, power and race in Chicago is self-determination.
>
> We, in Woodlawn have fought for self-determination on the issue of urban renewal, and have forced a settlement between the community, City Hall and the University of Chicago that is a major victory for citizen participation. The battle over citizen participation in the poverty program involves many of the same forces, and tactics, that Woodlawn faced over urban renewal. . . .
>
> Just like urban renewal, the poverty program is handed down from on high. The decisions are made by so-called "experts" who supposedly know what is "best" for people—especially if those people are poor and black. . . .
>
> Just like urban renewal, the poverty program is benefiting the rich and powerful, with a pittance thrown out as smokescreen to confuse the public. . . .
>
> Just like urban renewal, the poverty program is not geared to forcing basic changes in the ghetto. . . .

[30] From 1966 Statement of Policy and Resolutions, on file at TWO.

In Chicago, the Chicago Committee on Urban Opportunity is the colonial power, and we black people are its "natives." . . .

TWO has said before that the so-called War on Poverty is actually a war against the poor. We mean this: It is a war when tax money (including Negro tax money) is used for programs which strip a man of his dignity and manhood. It is a war against us when money is used to buy off our rage against being confined in the ghetto. It is a war against us when public money is used to distract black people from building enough power to break out of the ghetto. But above all, it is a war against the poor when we are told what is good for us by others. We know what we want, and what is best for us. It is a war when we do not make these basic decisions for our own lives, but are told by "experts" what we need—especially when these "experts" are hired by men who make money off the ghetto. The root issue is citizen participation—whether "maximum feasible participation of the poor" means what it says, or is just a huckster's slogan. . . .

If this city, and the country at large, is to be a genuine democracy, then we insist that we be in on the decision-making of the War on Poverty—from beginning to end. That is what citizen participation means to us. That is what we mean by self-determination.[31]

The controversy over the Poverty Program reminded TWO of its origins. At a time when the demands of administering a job-training program and negotiating on urban renewal were sapping its strength and creating internal tensions, this conflict with the Chicago poverty structure unified and strengthened the organization around a common external threat. In one sense TWO lost in this issue. The organization's claim as spokesman for Woodlawn was not recognized by the city. However, in the struggle TWO

[31] "TWO Black Paper Number Two: Poverty, Power and Race in Chicago," *TWO News*, December 9, 1965, pp. 14 and 16.

gained in national stature, rediscovered its earlier militant spirit, and broadened its base of local support. As in many of TWO's efforts, it was the process and not the outcome of the issue which gave meaning to the slogan "self-determination."

Amidst the frustration and hopelessness of the school system in Woodlawn, the one source of hope had been the Hyde Park High School. This school, located in Woodlawn, served the Hyde Park neighborhood as well as Woodlawn. Although it had become increasingly black (93 percent in 1965) and woefully overcrowded (4,256 students in a school designed for 2,600), it still retained some of the diversity and excellence for which it was once so highly esteemed. In 1966, the future of the high school became the subject of intense controversy. It was clear that something had to be done about this aged, crowded, and faltering school.

The Board of Education, with urging from Hyde Park residents, was considering building a new school, to be located in the Hyde Park neighborhood. Throughout the summer and fall, groups in Woodlawn and Hyde Park were polarized on this issue. Although a variety of suggestions was made, two basic proposals emerged. One, with the vigorous but divided backing of the Hyde Park-Kenwood Community Conference, called for a new high school for the Hyde Park and Kenwood students. The other, supported by the Unity Organization—a coalition of PTA's, SWAP (Student Woodlawn Area Project), TWO, some University of Chicago faculty, and a significant segment of the Hyde Park community—called for the expansion of the present Hyde Park High School into an innovative educational park with four 1,500-student high schools on a common campus. TWO and the Unity people argued that a second high school would wall off Woodlawn, make the present high school a ghetto school, and demonstrate deliberate segregation on the part of the School Board. The Hyde Park-Kenwood Community Conference argued that only with a new school in their area could the Hyde Park experiment in integration be maintained.

90

In the fall the controversy heated up. TWO scheduled a mass rally on October 10 to demonstrate community support for the Unity plan. But only a handful of Woodlawn residents appeared. Undaunted, President Stevenson continued the fight. Three busloads of Woodlawn parents accompanied Stevenson to the Board of Education hearing on October 27. In his testimony to the Board Stevenson said:

> The Woodlawn Organization's position on this issue is very simple indeed and very direct. Hyde Park must be expanded and improved. The right of every black child to a decent education demands it. Democracy demands it. Decency demands it. And TWO, the voice of the people in Woodlawn, demands it. It can be no other way.[32]

The following week the Board of Education, in a rare display of independence, supported the Unity-TWO plea and voted against the wishes of the General Superintendent.

As weeks passed, however, and the Hyde Park-Kenwood Community Conference increased the pressure, the Board of Education wavered. In a November press conference, Stevenson, using even more forceful language, said that Woodlawn residents would not tolerate a reversal of the Board's decision.

> The Woodlawn Organization will not see our youth castrated by junk-heap, dead-end education. We absolutely refuse to watch money spent for an island high school in Hyde Park-Kenwood and a wall-to-wall carpeted school in South Shore and not a dime for quality education in Woodlawn.[33]

By the end of January, the Board did reverse its decision. In a seven-to-two vote, a new 2,500 student Kenwood High School was approved.

Woodlawn was left with a deteriorating ghetto high

[32] *TWO News,* October 27, 1965, p. 1.
[33] *TWO News,* December 1, 1965, p. 3.

school bounded by a thriving Skid Row area. Stevenson urged the Organization to take drastic action against the Board of Education. But no action was taken. TWO staff director, Squire Lance, and several of the TWO leaders wanted to avoid an all-out fight over the high school for two major reasons. First, they did not think the Woodlawn people would respond. The fall meetings on this issue had not attracted crowds from Woodlawn. It would take too much organizational effort to make this an issue for which large numbers of people would fight. More important, it was very hard to see how TWO could win. The Hyde Park forces and School Superintendent Willis were simply too strong. The staff director did not want to commit the organization to a losing cause.

A number of people were disturbed that TWO never went all out for the Unity plan. Some PTA leaders, SWAP people, and Unity supporters living in Hyde Park argued that if TWO had taken the lead and had invested more effort the Unity campus plan would have won. Stevenson was also disappointed. He maintained later that he was deceived by his own staff[34] and left in the embarrassing position of promising more support than TWO would deliver. It is apparent that the TWO staff never really organized around this issue. As a result it turned out to be one of the few times when TWO was caught bluffing.

Although this was a set-back, it was one that TWO could accept. TWO simply pulled back. The organization was unwilling to expand its energies on a cause for which there were both insufficient indigenous support and little hope for a favorable outcome. If, like the poverty controversy, a continued struggle seemed likely to generate support, TWO might have pursued the high school issue regardless of estimates of a successful outcome. But TWO was unwilling to lead a coalition made up primarily of white Hyde Park liberals.

The defeat of the educational park marked the end of

[34] Stevenson, interview, September 27, 1967.

TWO's pursuit of integrated education, which had been its stated goal since the first annual convention. The schools issue slowly became redefined. While integration was still an ultimate goal, the organization began to direct its energies toward up-grading the black schools in Woodlawn. Brazier argued that TWO would not sacrifice this generation of students for a distant goal of integration. Quality education in black schools was the new task. This then became the issue around which community interest was to be more successfully mobilized. Indeed it was clear that to be a spokesman, one had to speak the wishes of the people to gain recognition from the power structure.

A high priority issue for TWO in the area of community renewal, second only to the Woodlawn Gardens project, was the spot clearance and redevelopment of what was known as Baby Skid Row, an area on 63rd Street lined with over twenty taverns and liquor stores. As a center of prostitution and narcotics it was a serious blight in the community. Many children attending the five surrounding schools had to pass the area daily. Clearance of this blight was on the TWO agenda from the beginning. In February 1964, the Woodlawn Citizens Committee received from DUR a commitment to deal with this area. However, progress on this smaller program proceeded even more slowly than on the Cottage Grove project. In the meantime conditions on 63rd Street became worse. By the fifth annual convention in the spring of 1966, the elimination of Baby Skid Row became a major issue for TWO. The planning, schools, civil rights, and community maintenance committees each presented resolutions that "Baby Skid Row Must Go."

In the spring and summer of that year the Greater Woodlawn Pastors' Alliance took the lead. The pastors' group concluded that the clearance and renewal plans that were in process would take too long to help the immediate crisis. Even with stepped-up pressure on Mayor Daley and DUR, the slow machinery of urban renewal would leave Skid Row untouched for several more years. Furthermore, there was reason to doubt whether the city had any intention of closing down this multimillion dollar operation. The pastors decided to explore the possibility of "instant clearance" by drying up the 23rd precinct, which included fifteen taverns, in a local option referendum. The odds are against a local option victory in Chicago. The laws are so written that it is extremely difficult even to get the referendum on the ballot. If it does get on the ballot the liquor industry can pour thousands of dollars into a campaign which may need only a few hundred votes. A traditional tie between the tavern owners and the regular Democratic Party workers has assured the tavern owners of victory in many past elections around the city. Newspaper pundit Mike Royko expressed the odds this way:

> Maybe the influence of the churchmen will prevail. Maybe the concerned parents will overcome. Maybe the liquor industry will be defeated. Maybe the Bears will beat Green Bay last Sunday.[35]

The one sign of hope was that the 23rd precinct lost a previous local option referendum by only five votes in 1960, before the emergence of TWO.

After Fr. Tracy O'Sullivan, assistant pastor at St. Cyril's parish, and a small group of volunteers laid the ground work, TWO picked up the issue in the fall. This was no ordinary wet-dry referendum issue. TWO "cut" the issue differently. It was the poor black community struggling to rid itself of a blight against all those powerful, monied, and political interests that benefited from Skid Row activities. Black neighborhoods have long been blamed for the vice centers that exploit them. Thus, all of Woodlawn, and not just the 650 registered voters of the 23rd precinct, became implicated in the campaign. Parents groups were aroused. Woodlawn seemed to be united on the theme "Skid Row Must Go."

[35] Mike Royko, "Priest Tackles Little Skid Row on South Side," *Chicago Daily News*, October 19, 1966, p. 3.

The strategy was to "cut" the issue and to publicize it in such a way that the opposition would find it difficult, particularly in an election year, to use traditional means of defeating it. Petitions, with twice the necessary signatures, were obtained to include the referendum on the November 8 ballot. Lawyers of the tavern owners predictably filed for a hearing to have the petitions invalidated. On strictly legal grounds the referendum was in danger. Despite extreme care in securing the signatures there were sufficient "irregularities," such as uncrossed "t's" and the failure to spell out the word "precinct" on the top of each page, so that half of the signatures might be ruled out. Under ordinary circumstances the referendum would probably not have made the ballot. But this was not an ordinary campaign. Block clubs, churches, and TWO participants wrote letters and sent telegrams to Mayor Daley informing him of their support for the referendum. A press conference was called so that this issue would receive city-wide attention. Journalist-ombudsman Royko picked up the cause in his *Daily News* column. It would have been politically costly for the regular Democratic organization to have the self-help aspirations of a community defeated on a technicality. The pastors suggested to Marshall Korshak, Fifth Ward Committeeman and candidate for County Treasurer in the November election, that he convey this to Judge Charles Dougherty who was to preside at the October 24 hearing which the tavern owners had requested. To leave no doubt about the community's determination, TWO brought over two hundred Woodlawn residents to the hearing.

The lawyers for the tavern owners had handwriting experts and presented numerous points which could invalidate the petitions. But the Judge, examining the petitions himself, found them to be, with the exception of two signatures, entirely in order. Having succeeded in the most difficult part, TWO was not prepared to lose at the polls. Ward Committeeman Korshak had assured the pastors that his precinct workers would not intervene on behalf of the liquor interests. With support from the University, TWO was able to finance a campaign which, while it could not match the flow of liquor money, was sufficient to win a 287 to 80 landslide victory that Royko called "the biggest upset of November 8."[36]

Unlike the Woodlawn Gardens, which was achieved by extended negotiations with city agencies, the elimination of Baby Skid Row was a straight-out show of political independence. Few believed that even an organized black citizenry would take on the liquor-political complex. The combination of organizing skill and sophisticated pressure on relevant political figures was impressive. In addition to pursuing to a successful conclusion a popular local cause, TWO was able to demonstrate publicly its strength.

Even though one or two top priority issues may have loomed large in the life of the organization at any particular time and may have consumed much of the energies of the staff and leadership, TWO has been built and maintained by the concurrent pursuit of a wide variety of little issues. Some of these are grievances which individuals bring to TWO meetings. Others are community-wide concerns. Some are resolved quickly. Some escalate into major confrontation with city agencies. Others are never resolved.

Almost without exception these little issues pursued through the standing committees—housing, schools, civil rights, social welfare, community maintenance, and consumer practices—share three common characteristics. First, the issues are pursued by committees only with the active participation of the residents or groups who present the grievance. TWO has refused to become a problem solver. Rather, for organizational as well as psychological reasons, it has sought to help people help themselves. "More important than what they do or accomplish," said Alinsky,

is that they are doing something for themselves. . . . If the tenants in a building don't want to do their own

36 Mike Royko, "E 63rd's Barmen Tell Their Side of Dry's Victory," *Chicago Daily News*, November 18, 1966, p. 3.

picketing . . . we are not interested in them. They don't get dignity except by taking it. It's up to them to solve their own problems. Our task is to convince them that they, by themselves, can.[37]

Secondly, the target of TWO action is almost always some agency or institution that is controlled by people who are viewed as unresponsive to the interests and desires of the Woodlawn residents: the Cook County Department of Public Aid, Jackson Park Hospital, the Police Department, the Chicago Housing Authority, a school principal, a supermarket, the Department of Streets and Sanitation. Thirdly, the desired outcome of all of these issues is some sort of negotiated settlement whereby the dignity of the Woodlawn residents is affirmed and their sense of political efficacy enhanced. The strategy of TWO was not only to help change the objective conditions in Woodlawn but also to provide the occasions whereby the residents could participate in, even bring about, their own liberation from external domination. Regular, organized, and successful encounters with slum landlords and city agencies would, it was hoped, help overcome the hopelessness sustained by years of entrapment and help provide the interior psychological conditioning for neighborhood self-determination. The desired outcome is a "we-did-it" attitude where the emphasis is as much on the corporateness of the "we" as on the accomplishment of the "did-it."

In practically all of the issues, big or small, that TWO pursued, the questions of representation and accountability were paramount. Who represents Woodlawn? In claiming the role of corporate representative of Woodlawn, TWO labeled inadequate the existing, formally legitimated processes of representation. DUR, OEO, Board of Education, for example, possess legally constituted authority to act in Woodlawn as representative of the people. These agencies based their legitimacy on the grounds that they were responsible to the elected officials that Woodlawn residents

[37] Lovelady, "Private Poverty War Stresses Self Help," p. 6.

helped place in office. The University of Chicago, the tavern owners, the landlords, and the director of Jackson Park Hospital claimed that they operated within a political and legal framework maintained and enforced by representatives who were responsible to representatives that Woodlawn residents helped place in office.

TWO was not trying to eliminate, replace, or even question the constitutional legality of these agencies. TWO based its challenge on the simple contention that the public agencies operating in Woodlawn were not responsive to the needs and interests of the community. Unconstrained by any effective spokesman for Woodlawn interests, city agencies can only accidentally represent the community. Without effective representation Woodlawn remains a colony controlled by outsiders. The central point in every issue which TWO pursued was that the community, or the particular residents involved, were controlled, planned for, dominated, pushed around, and manipulated by outside agencies which were not accountable to a representative of the people of Woodlawn. The one thing which the University, CHA, DUR, Building Department, Board of Education, tavern owners, landlords, and Jackson Park Hospital have in common is that, from TWO's perspective, they are outsiders whose unilateral action, made in their own particular interests, determines the well-being of many persons to whom they have not been responsible. The agents acting in Woodlawn are responsible to bureaucratic institutions usually centralized downtown.

It was TWO's conviction, born out of experience and observation, that the adequacy of *what* happens in a community is dependent largely upon *how* it happens. Years of outside control had led to deterioration, exploitation, and deplorable housing conditions. The further proposals by outsiders, no matter how well-intentioned, were no longer credible. TWO was not opposed to the South Campus idea but rather to the process by which it was being planned. TWO was not opposed to public housing but rather to the lack of consultation with the community. TWO is not opposed to landlords or inspectors of the building department but rather to the lack of accountability these men have to the people of the community. This perspective is illustrated by the major achievements to which TWO points. The 1963 agreement with the mayor was significant because TWO gained recognition and a virtual veto power in urban renewal planning. The Cottage Grove housing was a major achievement not simply because there is additional housing in the community, but because TWO planned and controls the project. The Baby Skid Row incident is significant not simply because the area is closed down but because the community did it. The job-training programs are valued because they have been secured and administered by the organization. TWO's position has been that only when residents gain a significant voice in determining what happens in and to their community will significant and lasting rehabilitation be possible.

Without formally legitimated authority the only way TWO could establish its claim as the representative of Woodlawn was on the basis of massive, demonstrable, and organized community support. TWO operated with the understanding that in the informal political process in Chicago organizations are recognized as spokesmen not because of their intrinsic merits, but because of the intensity and scope of the interests they are judged to represent. This recognition, which in the operative political process can be regarded as informal legitimation, would be secured not because of TWO's constitution but because of its constituency.

Since the organization needs a broadly based and inclusive constituency, it must stimulate and build its base of power. Although it does not have to demonstrate this support on every issue, TWO does have to reveal its strength frequently enough to maintain its reputation and credibility as Woodlawn's corporate representative.

In order to make good its spokesman claim, TWO has to be concerned about both the inclusiveness of its support and its size; that is, about both neighborhood unity and citizen participation. To represent a neighborhood an organization must, argued Alinsky, be "broad enough so that it attracts and involves most of the groups in the community."[38] With a wide diversity of ideological, economic, and religious groups in Woodlawn, TWO sought neighborhood unity around the most common denominator. It has not sought ideological unity because ideology divides. It has not sought unity around particular interests because interests differ. TWO, rather, has sought a unity that can attract people of diverse political beliefs and diverse particular interests, a unity centered around place and control. A unity of place binds residents—tenant and homeowner, young and old, welfare recipient and businessman, radical and conservative, separatist and integrationist, Protestant and Catholic—around a common concern for Woodlawn as a neighborhood. A unity of control seeks to bind these same diverse groupings around a common concern for a greater voice in the decisions that affect their place. In fact, it is because of its need to develop unity around place and control that TWO has been attentive and responsive to various kinds of diversity within Woodlawn.

In addition to the development of neighborhood unity, TWO needed to exhibit the active support and involvement of a portion of the constituency it claimed to represent. The relationship between the organization and its constituency is complicated by the fact that there are three general categories or levels of participation, each of which commands the attention of the staff and leaders of the organization.

First, there are the active participants. This group of two to three hundred people participates in delegates, steering, and standing committee meetings. Between 1965 and 1970 the monthly delegates attendance varied between seventy and 120 and the weekly steering committee between forty and eighty. With the exception of about forty long-time activists there is a regular turnover in this core group that

[38] Alinsky, "Citizen Participation," p. 4.

100

carries on the week-by-week deliberations and activities of the organization.

In addition there are several thousand occasional participants. It is from this group that TWO attracts a thousand delegates to its annual conventions, 200-400 for community meetings with DUR, and large attendances at special meetings and demonstrations. It is through massive support at times of crises that TWO has been able to maintain its spokesman reputation. These crises supporters, most of whom are members of TWO constituent groups and, it is assumed, are somewhat knowledgeable about and sympathetic with the general aims of the organization, will occasionally participate actively in the organization on an issue that is of immediate interest to them.

The third group, by far the largest, are the nonparticipants. At best, approximately three percent (4-5,000 people) of the Greater Woodlawn Area are in any way directly involved in TWO activities. Even accepting the organization's claim that through its 100-plus constituent groups it represents in excess of 40,000 people, this still leaves a majority of residents that are in no way identified with TWO. Since TWO regards itself as spokesman for all of Woodlawn, and not merely as a representative of the three percent, the organization cannot ignore this largest segment of its constituency. Continually seeking to broaden its base of active support, TWO can ill afford to alienate any major segment of the community whether it is active in the organization at a particular time or not. In fact, TWO has taken stands and engaged in activities which were justified in terms of the perceived needs and interests of this nonparticipant segment for whom TWO acts as virtual representative.

TWO had to pursue issues, develop programs, and carry on its internal affairs in such a way that it could maintain that level of active participation necessary to make its spokesman claim credible. What would lead someone to participate in TWO? What leads someone to participate in any kind of political activity? Robert Dahl, responding to the negative form of this question, identifies factors that lead people to avoid political participation: (1) if there is a low valuation of rewards to be gained from involvement relative to other kinds of activity; (2) if they feel that they cannot influence the outcome or change the balance of rewards by their participation; (3) if they feel that the outcome will be satisfactory without their involvement.[39] In common language these three reasons are: (1) "I've got more important things to do"; (2) "You can't fight City Hall"; (3) "They can get along all right without me." In order to alter what, according to some sociologists, has been a traditional pattern of low political participation in black, and particularly poor black, communities, TWO had to demonstrate that participation in the organization was worthwhile, efficacious, and necessary.

(1) The low participation by the poor in parapolitical voluntary associations can understandably be attributed largely to the fact that the pressing survival needs take priority in the expenditure of time and energy over the dubious rewards of political activity. TWO had to demonstrate that involvement in TWO was a way of dealing with immediate survival needs. Increased welfare payments, job training, building repairs, etc. were the material rewards.

(2) Past frustration in political action had led to hopelessness. TWO had to demonstrate that concerted community pressure could make a difference in the outcome. The victories of TWO provided these psychic rewards. It is understandable that with its desire to demonstrate its message TWO would select targets against which citizen action might be most efficacious.

(3) TWO had to convince its constituency that citizen participation was necessary, that only through citizen participation—and no way else—could desirable change be brought about. The formula of TWO's message, conveyed

<hr />

[39] See Robert A. Dahl, *Modern Political Analysis* (2d ed.; Englewood Cliffs, N.J.: Prentice-Hall, Inc., 1970), pp. 79-84.

both in rhetoric and through its strategy of selecting and pursuing issues, was clear. The Woodlawn Gardens development is desirable, it can be achieved, but only through grassroots pressure. The elimination of Baby Skid Row is worthwhile and it can be achieved, but this will happen only through the active participation of citizens. A slum landlord's building is intolerable, he can be made to fix it, but only if the tenants organize. When TWO is not successful in achieving a desired outcome, the failure, conversely, is interpreted to reveal the undesirable consequences when decision making is unconstrained by community action. Unable to shape the Poverty Program in Woodlawn, TWO pointed to the ineffectiveness and waste of that program as an illustration of what happens when programs are implemented without citizen participation.

To elicit participation TWO had to demonstrate convincingly that citizen participation makes a difference and that the difference is worth the effort. However, in order to demonstrate this, TWO not only had to be strong enough to make a difference but also responsive enough that the constituents could say that it was the difference they wanted. The participant in TWO had to be convinced not merely that TWO can influence DUR but also that he or his block club could influence TWO. The organization elicited participation as much by its responsiveness as by its ability to achieve desired outcomes.

In order to secure week-by-week active participation TWO has developed an open process whereby the participants have had a real voice in the ongoing operation of the organization. The participants elect the officers, serve on the committees, and introduce the countless little issues which TWO pursues. In the weekly open steering committee meetings, the active participants serve as a legislature to support and sometimes defeat policies and programs introduced by the leadership. The most impressive aspect of these weekly meetings is the degree to which the participants feel free to object to, argue with, and question the president, com-

103

mittee chairmen, and each other. These meetings stand in marked contrast with staff-dominated meetings of the Urban Progress center and, later, the Model Cities Council where the only semblance of citizen participation is in the passive presence of selected local residents. A significant difference between the two types of meetings is in the role and visibility of the staff. In the Progress center or Model Cities meetings, the professional staff and resource persons are selected and provided by the city agencies to which they are responsible. They initiate business, participate in discussion, and are highly visible at meetings. In TWO, the staff is hired by and accountable to the organization. They are in the background as nonparticipant resource persons at all TWO meetings. It is a firm policy, even though not always implemented, that the staff carry out the directives and assignments given by the steering committee. In order to secure participation TWO tries to conduct all of its meetings in such a way that the participants feel that their participation helped shape the organization, elect the leaders, develop policy, and direct the staff.

The residents of Woodlawn have had leverage within the organization simply because they provided the thing TWO needed most: support or, at least, tacit approval. TWO, of course, has not pleased everyone. In almost every major issue TWO has alienated some of its participants. But the gains and losses, in terms of support and organizational strength, have usually been calculated.

The other side of the coin needs to be examined also. Not all the influence within TWO has been from the bottom up. As in most representative relationships there is a process of mutual influence between the representative and the represented. In a variety of ways the staff and leaders of the organization have been able to shape and even create the constituency TWO needs. Some of these can be identified.

1. The skills and role of the paid staff give them a leverage in the organization which is greater than that formally attributed to them. Although the staff director, Leon Fin-

ney, was seldom a spokesman for the organization and was never, if he could help it, quoted in the press, he and his staff of three to eight organizers were behind the scenes of almost all TWO activities. The organizing staff assisted block clubs, organized new groups, served as resource persons for committees, turned out people for meetings, rallies, and demonstrations, and did countless administrative and organizational tasks. In addition, the staff, along with several top leaders, provided political skills by which the interests of the residents were translated into power terms and channelled into political expression. The good TWO organizer not only listens to the community; he also knows how to identify and "cut" issues so that, for example, tenant grievances become, if necessary, rent strikes. By knowing how to operate in power terms the organizer has some influence which, however much it may be veiled by formal subservience to the will of the steering committee, is clearly evident in the day-to-day operations of TWO.

2. Basic to the Alinsky approach has been the use of conflict to develop a supportive and united constituency. The situational dependency and apparent passivity characteristic of many ghetto communities has been maintained, according to TWO's general philosophy, by the activities of outside institutions and agencies which seek to prevent neighborhood solidarity. Just as there is a mutual relationship between neighborhood disunity and "peaceful" relations with outside forces, so there is a symbiotic relationship between neighborhood unity and conflict with outside forces. On the one hand, conflict with outside "enemies" stimulates neighborhood solidarity. On the other hand, internal unity leads to further conflict with outside influences. The staff and leaders of TWO have used the dynamics of conflict to help create the constituency TWO claims to represent.

3. The staff and leaders were also able to shape the makeup of the active constituency by selective organizing. In the initial year TWO was most interested in securing the sup-

port of preexisting groups in the community. Many of these constituent groups were block clubs. Through heavy block-club representation TWO was soon overrepresented by homeowners, persons of middle age and older, and people whose income and social status were above the norm in Woodlawn. Although there were exceptions, the block clubs, as small improvement associations, tended to attract a slightly more conservative, property-minded constituency. The poor, the youth, the tenants, and the aid recipients, many of whom had neither the time nor the interest for block-club activity, were underrepresented in TWO. To correct this imbalance TWO consciously began to organize these previously underrepresented groups. By 1967, the Social Welfare Union, parent councils, and tenant organizations were as active and influential in the organization, if not more so, than churches, block clubs, and the businessmen's association.

4. A supportive constituency has been developed through the pursuit of issues. Not all issues are pursued with equal enthusiasm and not all conflict is escalated. The selection of issues is a major factor in constituency development. An issue, in this context, is an interest that has been identified, appropriated, and shaped by a significant "influence group" and placed within a larger framework of meaning. In short, an issue is a politicized interest. Most people in Woodlawn have an "interest" in slum housing, poverty, unemployment, poor schools, inadequate medical facilities, in the sense that they are affected by these social problems and have an attitude toward them. But these problems are not issues until the interests are lifted up by a group which interprets them, places them in a more comprehensive framework, furnishes them with tactics in order that they might be pursued to a successful outcome, and, hence, presses them onto the public agenda. Community organization is, in this sense, an attempt to convert interests into politically relevant issues. The way issues are identified, selected, pursued, and resolved, tasks that fall largely upon the staff and top leaders,

shapes the character of the active constituency that is developed.

5. The success of the organization, the growth of the staff, the expansion of program and budget, and the complexity of multiple negotiations with outside agencies and influentials have led toward more centralized influence within TWO. Knowledge of the multitude of programs and issues was beyond the reach of the part-time participant. One pastor, who had been far more active than most residents, expressed the change this way:

> We have a problem. The organization is at such a point now that only one man can function at a high level. Arthur [Brazier] is the only one we have who can lead this organization. The complexity is such that only Arthur is able to handle it. In the early days many people knew everything that was happening in the organization. Now Arthur and perhaps Leon [Finney] are the only ones who know what's going on. I used to express my opinions more because I knew what was going on. Now I am not included so I keep quiet.[40]

This in no way meant that the staff and the inner core of leaders dominated the organization. All major decisions, programs, and negotiations continued to be presented, discussed, and approved or rejected by the steering committee and reviewed at delegates' meetings. However, the simple fact of complexity and growth meant that fewer people had the knowledge or the time to exercise the deliberative and intricate decision-making functions. Increasingly, the participating constituency relied more on trust of TWO leadership than on detailed knowledge of the total operation. President Brazier, in particular, was the bearer of this trust. It is a major tribute to his leadership ability that he exercised that trust well. On a week-to-week basis, in the president's report at the steering committee and delegates' meetings, he informed the membership of the issues, sought the

---

[40] Ellis, interview, September 19, 1967.

will of the group, clarified problems, and reported his activities and negotiations. Through the advice of the staff, a close contact with a variety of TWO participants, regular feedback at weekly meetings, and his own charisma Brazier increased this trust. Although this trust did not give the top TWO leadership complete discretion or freedom, it is true that more of the initiative for major action and program lay with those who had the knowledge and time to oversee the organization.

6. TWO increased the variety of incentives through which it attracted support and developed, to some minimal extent, control. These were the victories, the jobs, the services, the improvements which were gained through TWO's organized power. With the growth of the organization and particularly the development of well-funded programs, TWO had additional resources to develop a constituency.

7. One important way by which the top leadership of TWO has continued to influence and shape its constituency has been through the skillful use of rhetoric. In times of difficulty or internal tension Brazier and Stevenson frequently made impassioned appeals for unity and solidarity. The reciting of TWO's past achievements, the vivid portrayal of the "enemies" of the community and of the tactics by which these outsiders sought to maintain their control, and the constant reaffirmation of self-determination and self-rule have tended to counteract the pluralism that existed in Woodlawn. This appeal to TWO's "sacred history" and projected destiny helped provide the glue which held the organization together and minimized internal squabbles.

TWO's spokesman strategy of influence has been the determinative factor shaping the organization's growth and development, its relationship with its constituency, and its approach to the power structure beyond Woodlawn.

An internal dilemma in this spokesman style, however, became increasingly apparent. This dilemma, partially disguised by TWO's outward success, was that although TWO had developed a supportive constituency and had gained recognition and had demonstrated competence in several areas, the basic social problems in Woodlawn remained unchecked. Indices of the organizational growth of TWO between 1962 and 1967—increased budget, staff, program, and membership—were impressive. But it was difficult to discover indices revealing that the quality of life in Woodlawn had improved. Physical structures were deteriorating and, either by fire or demolition, the slow process of land clearance continued. Public schools appeared to be worse than ever. Welfare, unemployment, crime, and school dropout rates remained high. Woodlawn was not transformed.

Is the root of this dilemma revealed in the spokesman strategy of influence itself? The key to the strategy lay in the selection, pursuit, and negotiation of issues, a process calculated to establish TWO's claim as the corporate representative of Woodlawn. In order to win TWO tended to pursue only those issues which did not basically threaten or directly challenge the authority of the existing political process and did not elicit an overwhelming counter-response from established agencies. Also by organizing around self-interest it foreclosed a social analysis which conceived of false consciousness as a complement to colonial domination from without.

This dilemma of the spokesman strategy deserves close scrutiny. For TWO there were several criteria, not always explicitly stated, which guided the selection of issues. The first was consistency with TWO's basic interpretation of the situation, that the major problems in Woodlawn stem from external domination and community powerlessness. The development of Woodlawn Gardens, the elimination of Baby Skid Row, the job-training programs, the continuing fights against slumlords, and the struggle over control of the poverty program all fit TWO's general definition of the situation. It was largely through the pursuit of these issues that TWO conveyed and clarified this interpretation of the situation. Second, TWO selected, shaped, and pursued issues which enhanced its role as spokesman. This has already

109

been examined. Issues were developed which, either in the process of pursuing them or in the outcome, contributed to neighborhood solidarity (Woodlawn Gardens project), developed increased participation (pursuit of welfare rights), or secured additional organization resources (job-training programs). Issues which would divide the organization or deplete its resources were avoided. Third, TWO selected and pursued issues in which there was a reasonable likelihood of success. TWO's reluctance to expend major energy in the Chicago Freedom Movement led by Dr. Martin Luther King in 1965-66 was based upon its assessment of the Movement's tendency, bordering on compulsion, to lose. TWO leaders were of the opinion that the Movement's open-housing campaign had little chance of a successful outcome, that the Movement leaders had little understanding of operating in the framework of the Chicago political Machine, and that the entire strategy of the Movement weakened those organizations that were drawn into it.

On the one hand TWO defined issues in such a way as to identify or expose external forces that dominated Woodlawn. On the other hand, TWO actually pursued issues in which the opposition was not so aroused, powerful or entrenched as to make the desired outcome impossible. TWO needed to stimulate conflict, but not too much. The "enemy" had to be defined in such a way that the issue corresponded to TWO's definition of the situation, but the issue had to be such that the full resources of the opposition were not unleashed. By defining the issues, TWO was, in a way, able to define its own "success." By mobilizing around issues which were deemed important by the residents of Woodlawn but did not pose a basic threat to Mayor Daley, the Machine, or the major governmental bureaucracies operating in Woodlawn, TWO could build the organization, pyramid resources, and extend influence without eliciting formidable resistance. Through skillful and determined organizing around selected issues, TWO was able to utilize what Robert Dahl calls "slack" or unused power resources without seriously challenging the existing power arrangements.[41] However, by the same token, TWO, although successful in building an organization, was unable to address some of the systemic causes of the social problems Woodlawn faced.

On a week-by-week basis TWO was most successful in what might be termed little issues that affected a relatively small number of people and could be pursued to a successful outcome with relatively meager organizational resources. A boy was kicked out of school, a woman was cheated by a merchant, a slumlord turned off the heat. These were bread-and-butter issues that helped build the organization. Since TWO had already established a reputation of being able to deliver massive support when necessary, intervention by a small delegation from TWO to the appropriate group or person usually was sufficient to achieve the desired outcome. These little victories were highly publicized and certainly the accumulation of them was impressive and should not be minimized. In advocating this approach Alinsky has referred to de Tocqueville's comment:

> It must not be forgotten that it is especially dangerous to enslave men in the minor details of life. For my own part, I should be inclined to think freedom less necessary in great things than in little ones, if it were possible to be secure of the one without possessing the other.[42]

In these little issues the institutional processes which gave rise to the grievances were not seriously challenged. Grievances were satisfied one at a time. But the basic conditions remained.

[41] Robert Dahl, "The Analysis of Influence in Local Communities," in Charles R. Adrian (ed.), *Social Science and Community Action* (East Lansing: Michigan State University, 1960), pp. 25-42.

[42] Quoted in Alinsky, "Citizen Participation," p. 16. Reference is to Alexis de Tocqueville, *Democracy in America* (New York: Vintage Books, 1945), II, 338.

TWO points with most pride to the successful pursuit of major issues that affected a large number of people and involved sizeable resources such as the development of Woodlawn Gardens, the job-training programs, or the closing of Baby Skid Row. As important as they were for the organization these major achievements similarly did not threaten the established power of City Hall or the urban bureaucracies and did not draw massive opposition. The housing program demanded protracted and painstaking negotiations but there is no evidence that the mayor was strongly opposed to the project. The job-training programs met little or no opposition from city officials. In the Skid Row struggle TWO worked through the electoral process after neutralizing political opposition. The point is that the major issues for TWO were simply not major issues for the established power groups that had the potential of stopping TWO. Concerned with demonstrable victories, TWO, by the way it selected and defined issues, only rarely drew overpowering opposition. In the two major controversies which were deemed important by countervailing forces, TWO was either outmaneuvered or bypassed. The Poverty Program issue, in which TWO directly challenged Mayor Daley's strategy of centralized control and disbursement of Chicago's poverty money, aroused the forceful and determinative opposition of City Hall. In the Hyde Park School controversy TWO lost for a variety of reasons, not least of which was the countervailing influence of organized Hyde Park interests.

In issues of vital importance to the mayor, TWO carefully evaluated its position. An illustrative example was the June 1966, referendum on bond issues. The mayor went all out for passage of this referendum authorizing $50 million in bond issues which, supplemented by federal funds, would enable a $195 million improvement program in basic facilities such as street lighting, sewers, fire and police stations, mass transit. With the mayor running for a fourth term, the referendum was regarded as a vote of confidence in his administration. The bond issue was opposed by most groups that opposed the mayor. Civil rights groups opposed it on the grounds that the black community would not benefit from more of the same kind of services. Alderman Despres opposed it primarily because there was no overall plan for the disbursement of funds. TWO was the first major black organization publicly to support the bond issue. Brazier's position, which was supported in a split vote at the steering committee and triggered vigorous debate at the following delegates' meeting, was that if TWO wanted physical improvements in Woodlawn, the organization could not very well oppose the referendum. Brazier argued that TWO had the power to get its fair share. According to one member of the small TWO delegation that visited the mayor to discuss the referendum, the message of the meeting, though never explicitly stated, could be expressed this way: "Mr. Mayor, we aren't dumb. We know you want this badly. We know the referendum will win. And we aren't about to fight you on this." TWO had nothing to gain by opposing the referendum. Since the final decision on the Woodlawn Gardens housing had not yet been made by City Council, TWO had something to gain by revealing to the mayor that it was politically sophisticated. In less than a month after the referendum won by an overwhelming five to two margin, the mayor, along with Lew Hill of DUR, appeared in Woodlawn for a ceremony initiating clearance for the TWO-KMF housing program.

The basic dilemma of TWO's strategy of influence was becoming apparent. In order to achieve and maintain its spokesman claim, TWO had to work within the constraints of the existing political process and to develop a base of power in ways that did not basically threaten the system and elicit forceful counterpressure. However, the long-range solution to Woodlawn's most severe social problems, according to TWO's interpretation of the situation, demanded significant changes in the political process. But TWO was not able to bring about those structural changes

113

which were necessary to deal with the root causes of the deteriorating ghetto condition. TWO could win victories which resulted in more favorable treatment by outsiders but it could not alter the basic structure of outside control.

Even the major highly publicized accomplishments of TWO had limited impact on the total life of the community. In the areas of housing, welfare, and education there are a multiplicity of bureaucracies that are, at best, loosely co-ordinated and, more likely, working at cross purposes with different programs, different approaches, and on behalf of different constituencies. The application of pressure by TWO could, to be sure, result in a change in policy or a reallocation of resources in one or another of the agencies or in one or another problem area. However, the benefits of TWO's hard-won accomplishments in one area were often negated by the activities of some other agency or process over which TWO had little control.

TWO did indeed acquire influence. It was recognized as the spokesman for Woodlawn. TWO could veto or obstruct certain projects which were opposed by the community. It secured countless victories for residents against a wide variety of exploiters. In housing, education, employment, and mental health there was an increasing number of programs in Woodlawn that could be attributed, in part, to the organized impact of TWO. But the limits of influence without control, power without authority were becoming clear.

CHAPTER III

The Limits of Conflict:
TWO, the Blackstone Rangers,
and Mayor Daley

By 1967 TWO bore the outward marks of success. It was independent of the Industrial Areas Foundation. It had gained increased local support, city-wide recognition, and a national reputation. It had developed administrative competence in a variety of projects and had access to new financial resources. "Woodlawn is ready to make it," wrote *Chicago Sun Times* reporter Ruth Moore in a feature article headlined "NEW WOODLAWN: A HAPPY FUTURE."[1] She pointed to the plans for Woodlawn Gardens, the $1,900,000 job-training program (TWO's third), the closing up of Baby Skid Row, the improved relationship between TWO and the University of Chicago, and several other projects and improvements. But Ruth Moore did not live in Woodlawn. Woodlawn was not making it, at least not yet. No one was more aware of this than the leadership of TWO. Despite its impressive list of accomplishments TWO had been unable to deal with the underlying web of forces that sustained the ghetto cycle. The most destructive social problems, unemployment, poor schools, physical deterioration, and inadequate services continued to plague the community. What had been accomplished, the continued development of an effective spokesman organization, was no small achievement. But the social conditions in Woodlawn were not significantly altered.

Frustrated by the ineffectiveness of piecemeal action, lured by new possibilities of federal funding, and carried

[1] Ruth Moore, "New Woodlawn: A Happy Future," *Chicago Sun Times,* July 5, 1965, p. 4.

forward by the dynamic of its vision of self-determination as well as by the emerging Black Movement, TWO began to explore major ventures in the direction of community control.

TWO never explicitly articulated a philosophy of community control. The term simply was picked up. It was assumed that this was what self-determination meant all along. This central symbol of TWO, self-determination, has evolved with the development of the organization. During the first year of TWO, self-determination meant militant resistance to outside domination. With the emergence of an effective spokesman organization, self-determination was seen as the capacity to confront and influence existing agencies and institutions. In this phase of TWO, self-determination pointed toward the necessity of control.

The concept of community control, particularly as it was expressed in black urban communities, was as much a response to the staggering problems of centralized urban government as it was a response to the failure (and, to some degree, the success) of the Civil Rights Movement. The roots of the problems facing Woodlawn were untouched by the existing approaches and the existing agencies. It was not enough simply to get "a bigger piece of the pie," if you could not trust the baker. Through organized pressure TWO had succeeded in getting a fairer share of public services and resources. But if the services and approaches are inadequate, more of the same would not provide the answer to Woodlawn's condition.

From TWO's perspective, the existing agencies, institutions, and special programs were failing in Woodlawn. This included the public schools, the youth-serving agencies, the police, the Poverty Program, the welfare system, and urban renewal. Traditional methods, insensitive bureaucracies, vested interests, professional domination, and political control all served to defeat whatever good intentions lay behind the existing community-serving programs. TWO's capacity, through organized pressure, to block some programs or to

116

expand others had not basically changed the picture. Alternative approaches to Woodlawn's problems were needed. These, at least in TWO's experience, were not to be found in the existing agencies and not to be secured through usual political channels and could not be administered adequately by the existing bureaucracies. Militant resistance and organized pressure, although necessary for the development of TWO, had not led to new kinds of programs and structures of accountability.

The term community control, so laden with overtones, is of dubious descriptive value. It is used here in the same way that it has been used in TWO, to refer to a direction for political change rather than a specific goal, plan, or ideology. TWO was not advocating neighborhood autonomy, total control, or any specified administrative structure. The attractiveness of this term came more from the experienced inadequacy of pressure group politics than from a compelling vision of neighborhood government. TWO's efforts toward neighborhood self-determination through spokesman influence had been subverted by entrenched bureaucracies, professional domination, and the political Machine. The spokesman strategy was aimed at making agencies, institutions, and actors in Woodlawn more responsive to the citizenry. The move toward community control pointed to the need for neighborhood decision making and administrative processes in order to provide structures of local accountability for public programs, channels for participation and leadership development, avenues for local initiation of ideas and programs, and more adequate services.

What was soon to be seen as a nation-wide movement toward community control found expression in most large cities. Woodlawn was in a better position than many urban neighborhoods to move in this direction. It had in TWO an organization with experience, community support, and demonstrated competence. The movement within TWO, from a primary concern about distributional change to major

117

efforts toward structural change, from responding to out-side initiatives toward initiating programs itself, from a pressure group toward community control, was revealed in three major activities which consumed much of the organization's attention and energy between 1967 and 1969. These concerns, the Youth Project, the Woodlawn Experimental Schools Project, and the Model Cities program, will be examined in detail in this and the following chapters.

These three ambitious undertakings represented TWO's determined effort to get beneath the surface and reach some of the basic causes of Woodlawn's condition. In them TWO nurtured and made visible its hope of increased community control. The pursuit of these projects pressed TWO into direct confrontation with the city of Chicago and its agencies. The issue at stake was similar in each: municipal sovereignty versus neighborhood control. However, the three efforts represented different approaches, strategies, and dimensions of TWO's struggle for influence and control as well as for solutions to Woodlawn's lingering problems.

The emergence in 1966 of the Blackstone Rangers as a youth "supergang" was, among other things, testimony to a set of facts practically obscured by the relative success of TWO. These Rangers were not a part of TWO's world of negotiations and achievements. Neither were their parents. They belonged to no block clubs, churches, or social groups. They were the unrepresented, unrecognized underclass in a poor black community, a rung below even the hard-core poor of TWO's job-training program. What TWO had done and what TWO meant had not touched them. These youth were products of the school system, welfare system, unemployment situation, police strategies, and poverty in Woodlawn. The growth of the Rangers and the violence that surrounded them posed a threat to Woodlawn and to TWO.

In 1966, the Rangers, a small neighborhood gang since the late 1950s, were locked in combat with a rival gang, the Eastside Disciples, which shared the Woodlawn turf. Attack, retaliation, and escalation continued throughout the winter and spring of 1966. Partly for protection and survival and partly out of zeal, the Rangers entered into intense organizational activity recruiting youth not only in Woodlawn but in neighboring communities and even distant parts of the city. The core leadership began talking about the Ranger Nation, a confederation of Ranger units. The 1965-66 growth from a neighborhood gang of 200 to a new kind of youth organization estimated at 2,000 was impressive. One midsummer Ranger meeting at First Presbyterian Church was attended by 1,500 youth. A new style of organization began to emerge. A group of 21, referred to as the "main" or simply "the 21," operated as a "board of directors." The 21 met frequently to make decisions for the Nation, plan action, and exercise formal or informal sanctions over the group. Control of the subgroups was not always tight. However, one dominant factor mitigated internal dissension: survival in a violent surrounding meant joining together and staying together. For protection and support as well as for the nurturing of their own hopes, the Rangers were determined to stay together and to resist all attempts to break them up, take them over, or buy them off. This characteristic was highlighted in a proposal for Ranger leadership training.

> The successes of the organization have resulted in providing both the membership and the non-member related groups with protection, prestige, and hope—things that no agency, the community, family or program has been able to do. . . .
>
> When confronted with the choice between continuing with his organization or initial, even continued, involvement with an agency's program, the youth consistently chooses his organization. Pressures to destroy the organization have been frequent, but unsuccessful. The normal attrition that characterizes many other kinds of informal gangs does not apply to the Rangers. The youth's identity in the ghetto and outside of it is intimately tied to his

119

membership in the organization and even when he assumes family responsibilities, he maintains his membership.[2]

The emergence of this youth organization was not well received by the Woodlawn community. The spray-painting of buildings with Ranger names incurred the anger of many residents. But it was the violent shooting war with the Disciples that generated the greatest fears of the adult community. Woodlawn was a battleground. The fear of the adult community turned to hostility against the Rangers who were soon regarded as the creator and cause of the increased overt violence.

In the late spring of 1966, the police were becoming alarmed. It is ironic that they appeared to be alarmed less by the violence and shootings which had increased in April and May than by another series of events which signaled the independence and, indeed, the peacemaking hopes of the Ranger Nation. Having severed a relationship with the Woodlawn Boys' Club, the Rangers' connection with any of the established youth-serving agencies was virtually non-existent. Two new relationships elicited the increased hostility of the police: one with the Southern Christian Leadership Conference and the other with First Presbyterian Church.

The Rev. James Bevel, the advance man for Dr. Martin Luther King in what was to become known as the Chicago Freedom Movement, met with the Rangers. SCLC had plans to pacify the gangs and redirect their energies into the Rights Movement. At a May 9 meeting at First Presbyterian Church, Bevel showed a movie of the Watts riot revealing the futility of violence. Bevel's speech developed the same theme. Mayor Daley, Bevel argued, is "just out scheming and keeping people fighting each other. The thing that's kept him in power is he's kept Catholics fighting Protestants,

[2] Richard H. Davis, "A Proposal for a Leadership Training Program for the Blackstone Rangers," developed in consultation with the leadership of the Blackstone Rangers and their adult contact, January 1, 1967, on file at First Presbyterian Church, p. 4 (mimeographed).

Negroes fighting Polacks, and gangs fighting each other, while he gets away free."[3] Bevel's message was simple. Stop fighting and help get all black people together to change Chicago. The law enforcement officials in attendance were disturbed. It is hard to believe that they were disturbed by the prospect of peace in Woodlawn but that possibility cannot be ruled out. Rather than observe that the Rangers were not particularly turned on by Bevel's call for nonviolence, the police interpretation of the meeting was that the Rangers were very much turned on by an SCLC call for violence. Unable or unwilling to understand or respond to a new phenomenon of cool black youth organized, the law officers posited on the part of Rangers and SCLC attitudes, intentions, and strategies for which the police had a ready response. The Rangers' lack of enthusiasm was reinterpreted as vigorous support. The white commander of the police district for Woodlawn, Captain Martin O'Connell, argued that King had turned to the Rangers because without them "King would fall flat on his face in Chicago. He hasn't gotten anywhere with the adults. Chicago has been good to the Negroes. They have it nice here."[4] The editor of the *Woodlawn Booster*, Hurley Green, decried Bevel's approach to the Rangers. "Forsaking conventional dress and manner, the good Reverend has gone even further, with a real call for juvenile disorder."[5] The May 9 meeting soon came to be regarded by city officials as a riot-training session. Despite all contrary evidence, the cause for alarm seemed to be that the SCLC could actually enlist, mobilize, and use the Rangers and that Bevel's peacemaking rhetoric was a guise for a violent and criminal strategy. The contact with SCLC, although brief and one-sided, placed the Rangers in the spot-

[3] James Bevel, from transcript of speech delivered at First Presbyterian Church, Chicago, May 9, 1966, on file at First Presbyterian Church, p. 4 (mimeographed).

[4] Morton Kondracke and June Carey, "Youth Gangs Grow; Fear More Strife," *Chicago Sun Times*, June 5, 1966, p. 4.

[5] Hurley Green, "Rev. Bevel's Rangers No Help to Woodlawn," *Woodlawn Booster*, June 1, 1966, p. 1.

light where they were identified as a threat to society and deserving of special police and judicial treatment.

By the summer, the Rangers came to regard First Presbyterian Church as their home. "The castle," as they referred to it, was open to them for dances, meetings, and recreation at all times. Neither the pastor, John Fry, nor the youth workers, Charles LaPaglia and Bob Keeley, intervened in internal Ranger affairs. After a period of testing the Rangers found this to their liking: a place where they could assert their independence and maintain their identity. According to a report in the *Woodlawn Observer*:

> Rangers assert that every offer of help from city agencies has involved "strings." One agency offered them a place to meet, but insisted, according to a Ranger spokesman, on sitting in on meetings and "controlling things." Rangers said that the only institution which has not placed "strings" on them is the First Presbyterian Church.[6]

The position of the church was made clear in a document approved by its governing board:

> The Blackstone Ranger Nation has stumbled into the precincts of potential greatness by driving out of the parochial confines of a neighborhood gang. We desire that greatness to be expressed in ways directly beneficial to the youth themselves and to Woodlawn as a whole. . . .
>
> The power of this group will not be diminished by lessening the force and incidence of violence. The power of this group is its numbers and its point of view regarding self-determination. We are thus actively seeking to interpret to the Rangers the possibilities for securing benefits to them and their families without resorting to violent means.[7]

---

[6] *Woodlawn Observer*, August 4, 1966, p. 2.

[7] "A Statement Regarding the Relationship of the First Presbyterian Church and the Blackstone Rangers," October, 1966, on file at First Presbyterian Church (mimeographed).

The church's efforts to reduce violence were, like the efforts of SCLC, interpreted as the opposite by the police. "We didn't have a gang problem," one police officer was reported to have said, "before everyone discovered them [The Rangers]."[8]

The new situation, apparently perceived by the police as an ominous sign, was that the youth had rejected traditional youth-serving agencies and were relating to institutions over which the police had no direct control or influence. The peacemaking efforts of SCLC and First Presbyterian Church were distorted by officials who feared this growing independence. The response of the police was a strange and inconsistent mix of a tough and soft policy. Head cracking, harassment, arrests, and high bonds were interspersed with negotiations, the appointment of a black police commander for the district, and promises.

On May 24, the police, following a tip of a Ranger-Disciple rumble in a local school yard, arrested eighty-five youth over a three-day period. Upon the recommendation of State's Attorney Richard Elrod, a bond of $500.00 was set for each youth. When the session of First Presbyterian Church voted to provide bail money for thirty-seven Rangers, the church was, in fact, reprimanded by the judge for interfering with the court. The church was interfering with efforts to remove Rangers from the community by frequent arrests and high bonds. As summer approached, officials of the U.S. Treasury Department, interested principally in illegally altered weapons, made overtures for a disarmament. The Rangers in a meeting with local police officials, the Treasury Department, the First Presbyterian Church staff, and an investigating unit from City Hall agreed to a plan. The Rangers would turn in their weapons. The police, on their part, were to secure similar disarmament with the Disciples, and to intervene in several pending court cases against Ranger leaders. On July 4, the Rangers, after an

[8] Lois Wille, "Inside Ranger Gangs," *Chicago Daily News*, August 3, 1966, p. 1.

official inventory and signings, deposited over forty weapons in a vault at First Presbyterian Church. When harassment by police and armed attacks by Disciples continued, the Rangers felt betrayed.

In mid-July, the West Side of Chicago erupted. The Rangers organized a concerted effort to cool it in Woodlawn. Working in cooperation with the police, the Rangers manned an around-the-clock phone service, dispatched leaders to cool any trouble spots, held dances at the Church every night during the week of the riot, and enforced the curfew. The major role of the Rangers in preventing a conflagration in Woodlawn did not go unnoticed. But it led to no alteration in police harassment.

Hoping to capitalize on what he regarded as a good relationship between the police and the youth, the new district commander arranged a hasty truce between the Rangers and Disciples which was signed on July 21 before Superintendent O. W. Wilson. Neither the youth nor the police took it seriously. Hostilities grew as did the "crackdown." In late July, a controversy emerged between the Rangers and the Urban Progress Center, the local Poverty Program agency. Jeff Fort and Lamar Bell, two top Ranger leaders who were hired by the Progress Center for community work, were transferred to inside jobs. Progress Center director Frank Bacon said that the transfers were necessary because professionals were being hired to work with the Rangers. Bell put it this way:

> He said he didn't want me working with kids any more because I was too much for the group. So I was given a choice—working indoors, sweeping floors and stacking books, or changing tires at the police station. I couldn't take that, but Bacon said it was that or nothing.[9]

After 250 Rangers picketed the Progress Center demanding more significant programs, Bacon suggested that they draft

[9] Lois Wille, "City Gang Afflicted by Betrayals," *Chicago Daily News*, August 3, 1966, p. 1.

and present a proposal. A simple, imaginative, and direct proposal was developed. It called for a $6,500 grant to help the Rangers begin operation of a small restaurant, $4,400 to lease and equip a Ranger center, and a $129,000 proposal for a recreation program for the entire community. The Urban Progress Center officials never acknowledged the proposal.

To the Rangers the adult world appeared violent, capricious, and hypocritical, an upside-down world. Arrests were not related to particular crimes, bonds were not commensurate with charges, and punishment was meted out more by the policemen than by the judge. Promises by serving agencies were not kept. They felt betrayed by the Boys' Club, the police, and the Urban Progress Center. Those relationships with people who talked of peace, the SCLC and the Church, were viewed as dangerous. Their own acts of peacemaking, the July 4 disarmament, and the determined "cool" during the riot, were not honored. They saw Poverty Program money wasted and their own modest proposals unanswered. In this jungle of betrayal and denial the one place of significance, protection, dignity, and sanity was, for them, their own institution, created, as John Fry put it, "in the bowels of anti-democracy,"[10] the Mighty Blackstone Ranger Nation. Here trust, loyalty, dignity, and democracy took on meaning, however strange or distorted that meaning might appear to the non-Blackstone world. Traditional approaches to gang activity, exemplified in numerous ways by the police and the agencies during the summer of 1966, did not seem to work. The gangs would not be broken up, bought off, tricked, or truced into submission. These efforts merely served to confirm their strange vision that the only hope for the future was with themselves.

The leadership of The Woodlawn Organization faced a serious dilemma. In previous issues the organization had been able to identify "outside enemies" such as DUR, the

[10] John R. Fry, *Fire and Blackstone* (Philadelphia and New York: J. B. Lippincott Company, 1969), p. 42.

School Board, landlords, or the University of Chicago against which they could arouse solid community support. For most of the adult community the gang issue was already set. The enemy was within. The threat to the health and safety of the community was seen in the violent activity of the Rangers and Disciples. The sensitive leaders of TWO were caught in the middle. On the one hand, they could not fail to understand Ranger hostility toward the police and they could not fail to appreciate the aspirations, the power, and the future possibilities of the Rangers. TWO could not thwart these aspirations, discredit these hostilities, or ignore these future possibilities without denying its own past and foreclosing its own future. On the other hand, TWO was spokesman for an adult population which was increasingly frightened by and hostile to the youth.

Tension between the adult community and the gangs posed a threat to TWO's claim as spokesman for Woodlawn. The Rangers, in particular, were emerging as a significant organization that did not accept TWO as its spokesman. The adult population was being drawn into the orbit of those agencies and institutions that were seeking to crush the gangs. The police, press, and youth agencies offered a readily acceptable interpretation of violence in Woodlawn: the kids are tearing the place up and they have to be put away. The issue of youth gangs was being defined by events and activities over which TWO had little control. The issue was being interpreted along generational lines: adults vs. youth.

TWO's problem was apparent. How could it deal with the youth problem in a creative way consistent with its own history and aspirations and, at the same time, maintain the support of its constituency? The major task of the leadership of TWO was to redefine the issue so that it was consistent with TWO's general definition of the situation. The events from June 1966, to June 1967, reveal how this issue was redefined. In the summer of 1966, the major cleavage was between the youth and the adults. The issue was what

126

to do about these violent criminal kids. In the summer of 1967, the major cleavage was between Woodlawn—youth organizations and TWO working together on a common problem—and Chicago officialdom. The issue was community self-determination.

With the emergence of major gang activity in the spring and summer of 1966, TWO made several initial moves to address the situation. (1) The organization hired a special staff member to work with Fry and LaPaglia at First Presbyterian Church. This provided TWO with a contact with the Rangers. When asked, in the midst of the summer crisis, what TWO was doing, President Brazier responded, "We are working hand-in-glove with First Presbyterian Church."[11] (2) Brazier had contacted OEO officials in Washington about the possibility of a significant, innovative community youth project which might attack some of the roots of gang violence. Brazier received TWO support to pursue funding of what he called an "in-depth" program.

We don't want a namby-pamby program which has the kids picking up bottles in empty lots for $1.25 an hour and playing ping-pong in the evenings. They don't want it and won't accept it. We want an in-depth program to meet their needs.[12]

(3) TWO, in meetings and through its newspaper, began to praise the positive actions of the Rangers in order to counteract the adverse coverage in the daily press. The Rangers' role in keeping Woodlawn cool during the West Side riot and their peaceful picketing of the Woodlawn Urban Progress Center were highlighted. (4) The organization at the same time assured the adult community and the police that TWO was in full support of police efforts to curtail violent or illegal gang activity.

The position of TWO's staff and top leadership was presented in *The Woodlawn Observer*. A front page editorial,

[11] Brazier to steering committee, July 18, 1966.
[12] Brazier to steering committee, July 26, 1966.

127

"The Times They Are A'Changin'," questioned the prevalent community response to the Rangers. Then it went on:

> It seems to us that these reactions to the Rangers and their parents are based on fear. Many adults in today's world are petrified of youth—both black and white. Especially when the sins of the fathers, sloughed off onto the sons, come back to visit the home and the home community.
>
> For what we have bred in Woodlawn—and across the country, especially in ghetto communities—is a new breed of cat. Our youth simply will not accept the old, tired slogans, the fatuous, empty talk about workshops, summer camps recreation, brotherhood and decency.
>
> Our youth want jobs—but the $1.25 an hour jobs just won't work any more. And they demand, and will get the dignity.
>
> There are probably two reasons why the Rangers have upset so many people. First, the Ranger leadership is demanding honest answers from City agencies, and promises that are kept. . . . The second reason the Rangers upset people is that they are visible. . . . Our youth are visible because they have organization. They have realized that if they are to be honest with themselves, get what they want for the future, and force the institutions of this city to give them honest answers then they have got to organize.[13]

In a situation of continued gang warfare the force of this position was not compelling to most adults. TWO's appeal for calm assessment and for time to develop an in-depth program was challenged in the fall when the internal polarization of the community almost reached the breaking point.

The resumption of school in September posed the possibility of intensified gang conflict. During the summer, the

[13] Editorial, "The Times They Are A'Changin'," *Woodlawn Observer*, August 4, 1966, p. 1.

Rangers and Disciples occupied clearly demarked areas of Woodlawn. However, the high school, located in solid Ranger turf, served both groups. In September it became a Ranger-only high school. The most sympathetic account put it this way: "It was the decision of the Rangers to reduce the threat of daily Ranger-Disciple mass-confrontation at Hyde Park High School by reducing as far as possible the number of Disciples students at Hyde Park."[14] The school noticed a 25 percent drop in enrollment. Requests for transfers flooded the office. Refused transfers, the parents kept their children home or sent them to live with relatives. The community was incensed. A group called the Concerned Parents of Woodlawn was organized to demand more police protection of students and a crackdown on Rangers. The Concerned Parents charged TWO with failing to do anything about this situation. With the killing of a Boy Scout leader and increased publicity of violence and widespread gang extortion in Woodlawn, more and more groups in Woodlawn were demanding action. The consensus at a September 20, TWO schools committee meeting, attended by forty angry parents and several agency people, was that TWO's "work slowly" approach had failed. The suggestions from the audience were varied but the theme was the same: let the police take care of the Rangers any way they can. Although TWO held firm to an official calm, the police got the message. Commander Griffin and other law enforcement officials talked with the Hyde Park PTA and the Concerned Parents of Woodlawn and received what was interpreted, probably correctly, as a mandate to crack down. One hundred residents attended the monthly police-community workshop on September 26 at Holy Cross Church in Disciple turf. A report of the meeting included this observation: "Comments such as 'To heck with getting accused of police brutality, let's use some force on these punks,' 'Call

[14] John Fry, "Statement to TWO schools committee," September, 1966, on file at First Presbyterian Church (typescript).

in the canine corps,' and 'Stop trying to talk to them and get tough' were numerous."[15] A police crackdown, with apparent community support, was on.

The Rangers held a press conference at which time they offered to use their organization, which they claimed had been falsely accused of extortion, to help stop any violence or extortion around Hyde Park High. Commander Griffin immediately rejected the idea of Ranger assistance in helping to cool the situation. In what Griffin termed a move "to break the back of the Rangers this time,"[16] the police rounded up and arrested fifty Rangers on charges from disorderly conduct to inciting a riot following what eye witnesses have termed a police-instigated incident.[17] On the evening of November 10, a police task force raided First Presbyterian Church and confiscated the weapons that had been surrendered by the youth in the July 4 agreement in which the police themselves were involved. The interpretation picked up by the press and television was that a police agent, infiltrating the Rangers, "discovered" that the gang used the church as a storage depot for their weapons. The arsenal was captured. The church was exposed. The police were heroes. Only several days later did the police admit that they knew of the gun storage and had earlier agreed to this peacekeeping effort. The first story, however, was the one that was heard and remembered.

The police activities during the fall did not "break the back" of the Rangers. But they came close to breaking The Woodlawn Organization. TWO faced one of its most severe internal crises. In October it had severed all relationships with the Industrial Areas Foundation and became self-sufficient. It was entering into the hard stages of negotia-

[15] Noble de Salvi, "Angry Demand for Police Crackdown," *Daily Calumet* (Chicago), September 28, 1966, p. 1.

[16] J. E. Williams, "Crackdown on Blackstone Rangers Scheduled by Police in Woodlawn," *Woodlawn Booster*, October 18, 1966, p. 1.

[17] "History of Ranger Activity, Summer, 1966," on file at First Presbyterian Church, p. 8 (mimeographed).

tions with the Department of Urban Renewal on the Cottage Grove housing. It was trying to get the community together to do something about the ten elementary schools in Woodlawn. And TWO was, with the help of OEO officials and other consultants, developing a major proposal to address the basic problems raised by the gangs. This full agenda was being jeopardized by a divided constituency.

Agencies in Woodlawn were becoming increasingly critical of what they regarded as TWO's lack of action on the gang issue. Block clubs in west and central Woodlawn, Disciples' turf, were critical of TWO's continued relationship with First Presbyterian Church. The Pastors' Alliance was divided. Some of the top TWO leaders were urging Brazier to lead the organization toward a hard line on the Rangers and to forget any long-range proposal that would involve TWO in a working relationship with the gangs which, by now, were increasingly discredited in the eyes of Woodlawn residents.

Brazier and the staff remained committed to a long-range plan. The key to the plan was a major, federally funded youth program. This was to be TWO's response. Encouraged by Jerome Bernstein, the deputy director of the Manpower Division of citizen action programs in OEO, who more than anyone else shaped the basic concept, Brazier continued to develop the proposal with the help of First Presbyterian Church staff, consultants for Xerox Corporation, and OEO officials. For this proposal to be secured and to be effective, TWO needed time and constituency support. The organization also needed to avoid any precipitate action which would run counter to the general intent of the proposed program.

During these critical months in the fall, President Brazier made frequent appeals for unity and perseverance. The basic formula of these stirring appeals was repeated at various steering committee and delegates' meetings: a telling of the TWO story, its past and its achievements, a call for unity as the key to continued success, a chastising of de-

131

tractors who have no positive programs, an outline of the deeper problems behind youth gangs, and an indication of TWO's positive approach—the proposal that was being developed. The following summary of the president's report at the steering committee meeting on September 26, the very night of the police-community workshop at Holy Cross Church where residents were demanding a get-tough police policy, is an example:

> People are getting hysterical about the gangs. All we hear are accusations and counteraccusations. TWO is doing more than any other group. Others are just talking. We met with Jerome Bernstein from Washington on Thursday morning. The solution to this problem doesn't happen overnight. It took a long time coming and it will take a long time to deal with it. We are doing all we can. We are working responsibly and meaningfully. Of course we have our enemies. Some people don't like TWO because it is successful. These people who are asking, "What is TWO doing about the Blackstone Rangers?" are the same people who have spread gossip about TWO in the past. When they find an issue TWO can't handle immediately they scream and holler. Let us not allow any group to start a campaign to divide TWO. Our strength is in our unity. If you stick together you've got to win. I'm sticking with Woodlawn.[18]

Unity and support were essential. The development and promotion of a TWO youth program involved an extremely complex process demanding skillful leadership. TWO had to develop a proposal which the federal government would fund, the Rangers and Disciples would accept, the TWO constituency would support, the Pastors' Alliance would endorse, the agencies would not block, the political leaders would tolerate, and for which community support could be engendered. Given the temper of the community in September and October there appeared to be little chance that TWO would succeed.

[18] Brazier to steering committee, September 26, 1966.

Brazier was in the middle being pressured by two segments of the active constituency of the organization represented by Fry of First Presbyterian Church and Father Martin Farrell of Holy Cross. Fry was disturbed with TWO for their failure to criticize the illegal and inflammatory action of the police. Farrell was disgusted that TWO had not censured First Presbyterian Church, called for even stronger police coverage, and clearly repudiated gang activity. This split in the TWO constituency came to a head on the Monday after the November police raid on First Presbyterian Church. On that morning Brazier heard, and informed Fry, that Farrell was planning to introduce six resolutions for official vote at the steering committee that evening. The two of them decided that it would be wise to meet with Farrell before the meeting and, hopefully, dissuade him from this action. Brazier urged Farrell to reconsider because the TWO proposal would be presented shortly and the issues could be debated then. Farrell said he would not withdraw his resolutions and that he felt he had the support of the steering committee. He further suggested that Brazier's and Fry's action was a form of intimidation. Farrell brought enough support to swing the already divided steering committee. Four of his resolutions dealt directly with TWO's policy on the youth gangs: (1) that TWO make it known to the Third District Police Commander that TWO supported more vigorous enforcement within the limits of the law, (2) that TWO officially oppose illegal gang activity and express its disapproval of the "glamor" that gangs have received by their association with some Woodlawn groups, (3) that any federal grant be designated for the youth of Woodlawn and not for the gangs, and (4) that this new TWO position be made public at a press conference. In the preliminary debate it appeared likely that the resolutions would pass. The first and least controversial resolution received overwhelming support. Then ten Rangers entered the meeting and made their presence conspicuous. Farrell objected to the presence of the Rangers but it was to no avail. Fry had simply out-organized him. Brazier responded that the meetings were open and, furthermore, that the people of the community, Rangers included, should be free to participate in decisions that affected him. Farrell tried to argue the merits of the other resolutions as they came up but they were quickly defeated. Before the last two resolutions were even presented, Farrell and his supporters walked out.

This minor split within TWO may have been fortunate. When the TWO Youth Proposal was announced for the first time, the following week, on November 21, it received unanimous support from the steering committee. With the absence of the vocal dissidents and the announcement of a major TWO program with the prospect of federal funding, TWO was pulling itself together. At various steering and delegates' meetings in the winter Brazier explained the details of the proposal and kept the constituency abreast of the progress toward funding.

In brief, the original proposal was a multipurpose youth project directed toward the problems of the youth gangs. It included four major components: (1) basic education for school drop-outs; (2) recreation; (3) vocational training; and (4) job placement. The most significant aspect of the program was that it was to include the youth in the planning, development, and administration of the program. It was this aspect about which Bernstein and other OEO officials were most enthusiastic. At the December delegates' meeting Brazier explained it this way:

> Washington people say that there is not one successful program with gangs in the country and they don't want to throw anymore money down the rathole of traditional agency-run programs. We have the missing ingredient: self-determination. Our program will be administered by the community, by TWO. And it will utilize the unique aspects and advantages of the existing gang structure. Many fear this. They say it won't work. We think it will.[19]

[19] Brazier to delegates' meeting, December 5, 1966.

This major innovation, a community-planned and community-administered youth program, was highlighted on the first page of the final proposal:

> The Woodlawn Organization has a history of deeply successful programs in the areas of slum fighting, citizen participation in urban renewal, job training, early childhood development centers, and voter registration education. Its fundamental philosophy is that the only long-range solution to poverty and discrimination in this country is for the people of poverty communities to solve the problems themselves by exercising their own self-determination. Engagement in real issues restores human dignity. That same philosophy will succeed with youth because youth demands not just freedom and not just imposed authority, but a structure within which they can change their own destiny, yet know their elders support them.[20]

The central element in the entire proposal, the one that Bernstein was insistent upon and which made the proposal a significant demonstration project, was the inclusion of the youth themselves in the final development and administration of the program. The youth leadership was to be employed in running the program and to serve on the governing boards guiding the policy of the program.

Both Brazier and TWO steering committee as a body, were now committed, theoretically at least, to working with, and not on, the gangs. The negotiations with Washington continued through the winter. Bernstein had made it very clear that unless the youth organizations were deeply involved in the planning and development, TWO should not look to Washington for funding. However, TWO had to this point developed no close working relationship with the gangs. Although the proposal spoke of Ranger and Disciple

[20] "Total Manpower Demonstration Program for 700 Unemployed Young Adults," application to Office of Economic Opportunity, November 1966, on file at TWO, p. 1.

involvement, up to now there had been none. Bernstein was coming to Chicago on February 24 to talk with the gang leaders themselves. TWO had not even discussed the proposal with the two youth organizations. Realizing that the youths themselves could undermine the proposal by revealing to Bernstein the lack of relationship between them and TWO, Brazier had the staff at First Presbyterian Church arrange for a meeting between him and the Ranger leadership. What was supposed to be a brief meeting became a four-hour session. At that point Brazier's commitment to working with the Rangers became more than theoretical. After this meeting he was convinced of the practical feasibility of the proposal.

The final draft of the TWO proposal contained segments of a leadership training proposal which had been developed by First Presbyterian Church in close collaboration with Ranger leaders. This Ranger proposal identified clearly their understanding of why so many city and federal programs had failed to have any impact on the Rangers and other youth organizations:

First, the programs, either by accident or by design, tend to require that the member make a choice between continued involvement with his group or participation in the program. When confronted with that choice, the youth turns to his organization. . . . The youth will accept this decision because his membership represents one of the few successful experiences he has had during his life in the ghetto. . . .

The second reason for the failure of programs is that they often appear to be unrelated to the Ranger member's major concern. If, for example, an agency offers some sort of training program, the individual may not be interested in it, or he sees that it is unlikely to accomplish its stated objectives, or he perceives that if he did complete the program, he has no guarantee of employment, or if

136

employment is guaranteed, he perceives the job as a "dead end."

Third, the program is always "offered" to the youths by the agency. That is, the organization has played no part in the design of the program and individuals must participate in the proposed program on the terms set forth by the agency offering it. The program is never designed to take into account the existing relationships within the youth organization, nor has the agency sought the organization's approval. . . .

Fourth, the various programs fail to capitalize upon the nature of the organization and to take into account the unique functions it performs for its members. . . . Most programs fail to capitalize upon the positive leadership role and the existing strengths of the Rangers. Instead they tend to weaken the organization, or replace it with less satisfactory ones. The Ranger leadership perceives these consequences of member participation in various programs, even though the city or federal agency may not.[21]

Many of the innovative aspects of TWO's final proposal were based on some of the insights that had been contributed by the Ranger leaders.

The Disciples were more difficult to contact. TWO had no connections with them. It was not until mid-March that a meeting between Brazier and the Disciples was arranged. Although the Disciples were initially disturbed that they had not been contacted earlier, they voted to support the proposal provided they too would have a voice in altering and developing various aspects of it. This was assured. Leaders of both youth organizations met with Bernstein on several occasions to iron out the details. Perhaps the most significant meeting was on April 19, 1967, when the entire

[21] Davis, "Proposal for Leadership Training," pp. 5-7. Also see "Manpower Demonstration Program," pp. 7-9.

proposal was reviewed with both groups. At this meeting the leaders were informed that

> the probability of obtaining funds for the proposed program was virtually nil as long as the feud between the two gangs continued; that the shootings, killings, and other forms of violence would have to cease if the proposal was to be given a consideration by OEO.[22]

Three days later a truce between the two youth organizations was signed. Although, or perhaps because, this truce received no widespread publicity, it turned out to be the most effective truce up to that point. The spring and summer were cool.

TWO had endorsed the proposal and the youth organizations had agreed to participate. There were still, in the winter months, occasional flare-ups at TWO meetings. At the February 20, 1967, steering committee meeting one block club leader introduced several extreme resolutions. He proposed that all out-of-school youth without jobs be sent out of Woodlawn to detention camps. At the same meeting another member said, "We don't have time for a youth program now. We should demand that Commander Griffin put up or get out."[23] Brazier was able to handle these occasional outbursts calmly and diplomatically because the dissidents no longer had major support within the organization.

The April truce reduced violence in Woodlawn. TWO leaders were now speaking about "youth organizations" rather than "gangs." TWO was pulling itself together for its annual convention which, even with the absence of Holy Cross Church and a number of block clubs in that parish, was larger than ever. The major additions to the TWO constituency were the newly organized locals of the Social Welfare Union, primarily ADC recipients, many of whom were more sympathetic with the youth than other participants in TWO. A change, reflected both in discussions at meetings

[22] Brazier, *Black Self-Determination*, p. 80.

[23] Steering committee meeting, February 20, 1967.

138

and in the TWO newspaper, was taking place within the organization. The constituency of TWO was becoming less disturbed by the activities of youth organizations and more disturbed about agencies which might undermine the community's youth project. The gang issue, which had been interpreted as an internal Woodlawn problem of youth versus adults, or criminals versus law-abiding citizens, was being reinterpreted into the kind of issue TWO liked; that is, Woodlawn people with a program to deal with their own needs versus outside agencies, politicians, and professionals. Instead of becoming an issue which would split the community, the gang issue could help unite the community around TWO's basic definition of the situation. It was TWO's basic understanding that the black community has been dominated by white, alien institutions and that conflicts and cleavages within the community have their roots in this external control. The way to begin to solve the real problems is to organize people, develop a base of power, and pursue programs which unify and strengthen the community. In doing this, TWO has found that the opposition comes less from within the neighborhood than from the agencies and institutions who have previously benefited from having a divided and underrepresented community.

The youth controversy developed into TWO's kind of issue. TWO and the youth organizations were being drawn together by a common project. The differences between the styles of the two organizations and the constituencies were always clear. But the similarities were becoming more important than the differences. They were black organizations sharing the same "turf." They both shared the rhetoric of self-determination.

By spring, TWO, the youth leaders, and the Washington-based OEO officials were together on the proposed project. The biggest hurdle still remained—the city agencies and the local political leaders. The TWO proposal did not go unnoticed by Chicago officials, especially those in the youth-serving and youth-control agencies and those in the Poverty

Program. Agencies responded quickly. Hull House, the Chicago Boys' Club, and the YMCA cooperated in a program they called Youth Action. In mid-March, Youth Action approached TWO for support of a proposed $119,000 program for Woodlawn. The director of Youth Action began contacting Woodlawn pastors about use of church buildings for the new program. TWO, suspicious of the intent of the new proposal, appointed a committee to meet with Youth Action. The press accounts of the outcome of the meeting confirmed TWO's suspicion that Youth Action was an attempt to undermine TWO's long-range plans. The story, released by Youth Action without consulting TWO, implied that the Youth Action proposal was supported by Woodlawn and would be implemented. Brazier and TWO staff immediately broke off any further discussions with Youth Action. If Youth Action wanted to develop a program they would have to recognize and work through the corporate bodies of TWO and the Pastors' Alliance. The Alliance concurred with the decision to refuse to discuss any program with Youth Action until after the TWO proposal was funded by Washington. Then, if Youth Action wanted to support and add resources to a Woodlawn-controlled program, the discussions could be resumed. They never were.

A development, scarcely noticed at the time but of far greater significance than the agency counterproposal, was the creation by the Chicago Police Department of the Gang Intelligence Unit on March 22, 1967. Previously, dealing with gangs had been the special responsibility of the Youth Division. The establishment of a new unit, "for the purpose of eliminating the anti-social and criminal activities of groups of minors and young adults,"[24] at the very time when the major youth organization in the city, the Blackstone Rangers, was entering into a relationship with the strongest black community organization in the city, making peace with its rival gang, and anticipating an OEO program

[24] Chicago Police Department Order No. 67-6, March 21, 1967, on file at First Presbyterian Church.

140

in which they would participate fully, was significant. The Gang Intelligence Unit was given broad powers. It was clear from the police order given by Superintendent O. W. Wilson, that one of the major tasks was to identify, investigate, and infiltrate adult groups that were relating to the youth organizations.

The Gang Intelligence Unit will:

A. Identify the forces which encourage anti-social and criminal tendencies in groups of young people and identify the organizations and individuals which influence or lead such groups to engage in such behavior.

B. Investigate the organizations and individuals involved in the leadership or direction of such groups . . . for the purpose of determining what sanctions might be effective against such organizations and individuals. . . .

C. Infiltrate such groups for the purpose of determining what future anti-social and criminal activity is contemplated.

D. Develop cases of criminal conspiracy against those individuals, both minors and adults, whose leadership and influence has resulted in such criminal activity.[25]

When TWO's youth proposal was taken seriously and the prospect of federal funding became a real possibility, "every alarm system in the white establishment in Chicago," as Brazier puts it, "flashed red and clanged loudly."[26] The objections by city officials and agencies are not difficult to discern. They were stated frequently. Police Superintendent Wilson supported his GIU in opposition to the proposal. In utilizing the existing gang structure, in paying the leaders of these organizations to supervise parts of the program, in paying the youths who would participate in the program, the TWO proposal would run directly counter to the existing police strategy of breaking up youth gangs and scaring off resources that might help them. Wilson was opposed to

[25] *Ibid.*
[26] Brazier, *Black Self-Determination,* p. 92.

141

the program because he felt the TWO project would strengthen the gang structure and make his "busting-up" job more difficult.

The youth-serving agencies also had reasons for alarm. The approach suggested in the TWO proposal posed a threat to the professionalism of the agencies. If it were to be demonstrated that the youth themselves, with the aid of a community organization, could administer an effective program, this could set a pattern which might not be welcomed by those who made a living in the "helping" professions. In simplest terms, there was competition over the limited resources in the youth-serving business. The more that is channelled through nonprofessional community organizations the less that is available for agencies and their professionals.

The poverty bureaucracy in Chicago was deeply disturbed at the prospect of a major OEO project being funded directly from Washington to TWO. The Chicago Committee on Urban Opportunity (CCUO), directed by Deton Brooks, had been, since the inception of the Poverty Program in Chicago, the central policymaking and channelling organization for all OEO projects in Chicago. The centralized control of the poverty structure had enabled the mayor, through the CCUO and the councils of the neighborhood Urban Progress Centers both of which he appointed, to use poverty funds to build a loyal black bureaucracy which helped maintain political control of the black community. Brooks administered $22 million worth of OEO projects in Chicago. When he first heard of the TWO proposal he was receptive, presumably because he assumed that it would be under his financial control. His opposition was vigorous when he discovered that the project was to be funded directly, bypassing CCUO. If this program proved successful and became a pattern for future OEO funding, Brooks' operation might be in jeopardy.

The leaders of the police-agency-poverty complex made a concerted effort to block the funding. Brooks and John

Root of the Metropolitan YMCA went to Washington to persuade OEO chief Sargent Shriver not to approve the proposal. Caught between his own staff that was pressing for action and the opposition from the Chicago CCUO, Shriver held up signing until the proposal was completely cleared by the OEO midwest regional office and by Mayor Daley. During May, Brazier met with Wilson, Brooks, and Daley (individually and together) on several occasions. Brazier reported that Daley informed him that he would not approve any program that "had political implications which might hurt him."[27] Daley had to decide which would hurt him least. Bernstein and his Washington staff were pressing for it. Regional OEO had approved. TWO and the youth themselves were ready to begin implementation. Commander Griffin of the Third District, apparently impressed by the April truce, was more favorable. Ed Berry of the Urban League, Fifth Ward Committeeman Marshall Korshak, and Julian Levi of the University were supporting TWO. On the other hand, Daley's "cabinet on urban affairs," Brooks, Root, and Wilson, were opposed. To protect himself, Shriver had insisted on Daley's approval before he signed. Daley was on the spot. With summer approaching, it would be hard not to allow a federally funded program to operate in Woodlawn. He must have been aware that in anticipation of this program the Rangers and Disciples had been peaceful since April and that this determined "cool" could not be expected to continue if the program was not funded. He must have been aware that TWO would place on his shoulders the blame for summer violence were he to block a job-training program. On the other hand, if he supported the program he could establish a pattern which might weaken his own political base and also offset the programs of a variety of agencies represented by his advisors who were against the proposal. Furthermore, if he supported the program and it was a flop, he, and not Shriver, would be the scapegoat.

[27] Brazier to the Woodlawn Pastors' Alliance, May 25, 1967.

143

In the negotiations between Brazier and the top city officials the basic issue, always present but seldom discussed directly, was control. If funded this would be the first major OEO funded program not channelled through CCUO. TWO made it clear that this aspect of the proposal was absolutely nonnegotiable. TWO would withdraw the proposal if the basic control was not placed in TWO. Most of the discussions were to give assurance and develop safeguards to meet the objections of Wilson and Brooks. On May 18, in his third meeting with the mayor in less than a month, Brazier was accompanied by Berry, Levi, and Korshak. According to Brazier, Berry cleared the way with the mayor by proposing two stipulations that were fully acceptable to TWO: that nongang members would be accepted in the program and that no money would go directly to the youth organizations. Daley appeared satisfied with that assurance. It is interesting to note that on the same day Brazier appeared on a panel at a U.S. Senate Subcommittee hearing in which Senators Joseph Clark, Jacob Javits, and Robert Kennedy were probing the Chicago poverty operation; Brazier did not take that occasion to contest Daley's operation of the war on poverty.[28] It appeared that Daley would give the nod Shriver needed.

Just when the way seemed clear TWO was informed by Donald Hess, Bernstein's superior in Washington, that he, in conjunction with Regional OEO Director Alan Beals and Brooks, had, without consulting TWO, drawn up fifteen conditions to which TWO would have to agree before final approval was granted. Most of the special restrictions were technical in nature and involved bookkeeping, accounting, monitoring, and evaluation of the program. TWO had no quarrel with most of these restrictions. Only one restriction posed a major problem: "In view of the importance of this demonstration to the City of Chicago, the Office of the Mayor of the City of Chicago shall be invited to concur in

[28] See Frank Sullivan, "Daley Defends Poverty War Role," *Chicago Sun Times*, May 19, 1967, p. 3.

the grantee's selection of the Project Director."[29] At the time this restriction hardly seemed major enough for TWO to refuse the near-million dollar grant. All the basic aspects of the program were preserved. TWO would receive the funds and would have direct responsibility for administering the program. It was reasonable to suppose that the mayor, who had, after all, supposedly approved the concept of the program, would not block the appointment of a qualified director. What was not perceived at the time, at least by the TWO constituency, was that Brooks, whether acting on Daley's behalf or out of his own concern to undermine the project, had, through this restriction inserted at the last moment, provided the mayor with a way out. The mayor could approve the proposal and still not lose total control over its future.

On May 31, 1967, the $927,341 job-training program was funded. There was a new optimism in Woodlawn. TWO had succeeded in a complicated and politically sophisticated process of developing an innovative proposal and had negotiated its funding. The Rangers and Disciples were continuing the April truce. Woodlawn was calm. The Rangers were beginning to project a new image in the community and the city at large. They secured talent and staged a successful musical production under the direction of Oscar Brown. *Opportunity Please Knock* received good reviews in the metropolitan press and played before a packed house at First Presbyterian Church for six weekends. A great many citizens were forced to make some reevaluation of the Blackstone Rangers. *The Woodlawn Booster*, a long time critic of the Rangers, First Presbyterian Church, and TWO, headlined full praise for the Rangers in their May 23 issue. In addition First Presbyterian Church received a $50,000 grant from the Charles Kettering Foundation to expand its program with the Rangers. The basic aim of the Kettering Grant was, says John Fry, "to provide Blackstone Ranger leaders time and incentive to develop programs and

[29] Brazier, *Black Self-Determination*, pp. 93-94.

have them funded. It was an educational grant made on the presupposition that self-determination must be identified, treasured, supported, and its fruits honored."[30] Fr. Tracy O'Sullivan of St. Cyril's parish, who had worked closely with Fry and the Rangers, was guiding the implementation of a Neighborhood Youth Corps program in which fifty-five Rangers were employed to tutor children in the neighborhood. Tutoring, job training, musical reviews, economic development, political action, proposal writing—the Rangers were busy. And they had friends: TWO, the churches, Oscar Brown, a number of businessmen in the area, the Kettering Foundation, and increasingly, the general Woodlawn community. The Rangers had made peace with and had helped to bring peace to the community. Here was the alternative to violence—expanded relationships with the adult community and possibilities for real opportunity.

TWO had reason for confidence. The pieces were fitting together. The constituency was united behind the project. The youth organizations were ready to participate. The job development segment of the project was subcontracted to the Urban League which had contacts in business and industry. The setting was right for a significant demonstration of an innovative approach to job training for "severely disadvantaged youth." With the exception of the mayor's concurrence on the selection of the project director, the program would be controlled by the community through TWO and the program policy board appointed by TWO. It was projected that with the use of gang leaders as recruiters, center chiefs, instructors, and assistant teachers the project could reach those youth that professionally run agency programs had so consistently failed to touch. These two demonstration features, community control and youth involvement, were prominent in the "expected demonstration outcomes" listed in the proposal.

[30] Fry, *Fire and Blackstone*, p. 13.

That the natural structure of two street gangs provided an excellent vehicle to guide and develop skills and attitudes beneficial to the young adults of Woodlawn, the local community and the larger community of Chicago. That a community-centered manpower program, planned with the cooperation of the leadership of the street gangs, is a natural and logical vehicle to reduce community tension and to bring about a cooperative and coordinated community concern by youth, adults and local institutions in Woodlawn and Chicago.

That the ability of sub-professionals in counseling roles to communicate, understand and guide peer clients in a manpower program is more supportive and more acceptable to clients than the interactions between professional counseling staff and alienated young adults.

That a community organization can plan, develop and run programs in cooperation with street gang groups to the advantage of all members of the community.

That the principle of total involvement by gang members in all portions of the planning, developing, staffing and evaluating of a manpower program is central to the ultimate involvement and success of the said program. This expected outcome argues against unilateral planning for social service programs where the proposed clients do not have any inputs in the development phases.[31]

This manpower program to recruit and train 700 out-of-school youth was what is termed a high risk program. It did in fact turn out to be a high risk program, but in ways not immediately foreseen. The high risk aspect generally referred to the demonstration features, the acceptance of the gang structure, the use of gang leaders as subprofessionals, the employment of youth with criminal records, and the general attempt to alter the direction of street gangs. Since

[31] "Manpower Demonstration Program," application to OEO, pp. 15-16.

there was little or no precedent for success in this effort the probability of failure was real. TWO was aware of the risk and willing to take it. The leaders of the organization had confidence in the design of the project and confidence in the efficacy of the basic concept of self-determination as a means of solving the problems of the black community.

But the projects turned out to be high risk in another sense. The risk was not so much in dealing with severely alienated youth as it was in incurring the hostility of Chicago officialdom. The risk was not in working with those with whom past programs had failed, but in declaring independence from the control of those who had investments in past programs. Simply put, the risk of innovation was not in failure, for that is often expected, but in success. Success in the expected outcomes would have posed a threat to the welfare, education, and control institutions in the city of Chicago. Suppose it was demonstrated convincingly that the youth gang structure "provided the natural and logical mechanism" to recruit staff and participants for educational and manpower training programs? What would this mean for the youth-serving professionals and their agencies? What would it mean for the Gang Intelligence Unit whose stated purpose was to break up youth organizations? Suppose it was demonstrated that a community group could "plan, develop and run programs" independently of the control of the Chicago Committee on Urban Opportunity? What would this mean for the centralized poverty bureaucracy in Chicago? What would it mean for the mayor whose power has been buttressed by the vote-getting patronage made possible through control of federal money? For TWO the risk of failure was slight compared with the risk of success.

The manpower program did not last long enough to demonstrate in any thorough systematic way the expected outcomes. But it did demonstrate that those outcomes were sufficiently threatening to various official interests to warrant a concerted attack on the program from its inception.

148

It is the contention of this analysis that the program was murdered. It was made to fail. The way in which the project was killed is the most telling evidence in support of the expected outcomes. The concentrated attack on the program throughout its brief history is the strongest evidence that even those who wanted the TWO program to fail were convinced that, if left alone, it might succeed. If the police-agency-local government complex was convinced that the innovative concepts in the TWO program were demonstrably inadequate, they could have allowed the project to fail. They did not do so. They killed it. The project was undermined and attacked with such vigor that it is difficult to imagine that its demise was not the result of a calculated and coordinated effort by those who stood most to lose from a successful outcome.

1. The very first meeting after the funding proved to be a sign of what was to come. The youth leaders were meeting with TWO staff and Bernstein at the TWO office on June 6 to discuss the special conditions imposed by OEO. Before the purpose of the meeting was accomplished, a combined force of twelve police officers and six GIU members arrived, entered the office, prevented anyone from leaving, and threatened to arrest all present, including the OEO deputy director. It was only after a lengthy hassle and several phone calls to higher authorities that the police withdrew. By then the meeting was "busted." The gang leaders decided that it was best not to continue the discussion. As it turned out, this initial raid helped the project get started. On that same Tuesday, the *Chicago Daily News* printed an account of the funding. The story began: "The Woodlawn Organization, once one of Chicago's most independent neighborhood groups, has received an anti-poverty grant that ties it in with Mayor Richard J. Daley's office."[32] On reading this the youth leaders were disturbed and suspi-

[32] Peter Deuel, "Woodlawn Group Gets $927,000 to Train Poor," *Chicago Daily News*, June 6, 1967, p. 14.

cious. What were the ties? Was TWO really "slicking" them like all the other agencies? What were the special conditions of the grant? The gangs were ready to call off the entire project. Then, in charged the GIU ready to arrest Bernstein, Brazier, Leon Finney, along with the youth. TWO's role and independence were cleared in the minds of the gang leaders. If the youth had been more cynical, they might have suspected that TWO arranged the raid. As Brazier observed later, "the very program that the GIU despised and City Hall did not want would have died aborning had it not been for the bungling of the Gang Intelligence Unit."[33] Brazier complained to OEO regional headquarters that this sort of incident could have resulted in a riot and that continued harassment would disrupt the federal program. He was assured that the incident would not be repeated. And TWO accepted this assurance.

2. Anxious to get the program underway, TWO had begun a search for a project director. Following a lead from Washington officials, Brazier contacted Edward Elwin of New York City, a man with outstanding credentials and experience in youth programs. TWO had every reason to believe that the mayor would concur with the choice. He did not. Then TWO opened up the selection process and appointed a blue-ribbon committee to make a recommendation. After considering several candidates this committee also recommended Elwin as the best qualified. The mayor still did not concur. He claimed that he wanted a Chicago man. Finally, TWO secured a staff person from the Urban League who, although less qualified professionally than Elwin, at least fit the mayor's major requirement. But again the mayor did not concur. September came, the project was underway, but there was no director. The project was suffering and it had now become clear that the mayor would not concur with any TWO recommendation. Members of the TWO steering committee were becoming furious be-

[33] Brazier, *Black Self-Determination*, p. 100.

cause the mayor and Deton Brooks were apparently using the one small lever of control they had, a negative control of vetoing the top appointment, to undermine the agreed-upon intent of the project. The mayor's strategy was becoming clear. TWO would not be permitted to select a director. TWO would either have to allow the mayor to select the director or continue without one. TWO faced a dilemma. If the director was appointed by the mayor and under the virtual control of CCUO, then many of the demonstration aspects of the program would be subverted. If TWO refused to "select" the mayor's director, the program would have no permanent director and would suffer because of it.

In September, the steering committee of TWO was beginning to urge direct and forceful action. Several prominent members called for a massive demonstration. A direct confrontation with the mayor on this issue would make it clear where the community stood and who was subverting the project. The steering committee agreed to wait until there was one more meeting between the project advisory committee (the blue-ribbon special committee on the search for a director) and the mayor. After an October 4 meeting, Brazier reported to the steering committee that the mayor had assumed that he, the mayor, was to appoint the director and that he wanted TWO to approve of James Griggs as project director. Brazier suggested to the steering committee, "perhaps we ought seriously to consider it." The committee was incensed. Griggs had been the staff director of the Woodlawn Urban Progress Center during the controversy between TWO and the Poverty Program. Mrs. Phyllis Hubbard, a longtime TWO stalwart, said, "If we accept Griggs, we can kiss TWO's power good-bye."[34] Without a dissenting vote the forty-five people at the steering committee meeting rejected the recommendation of Griggs.

Again the question of massive action against the mayor was entertained. Brazier was on the spot. He did not want TWO to jeopardize the project by staging an all-out con-

[34] Steering committee, October 9, 1967.

151

frontation with the mayor. Many young people had salaried jobs with the program and as of September 8, 108 were in training. Brazier did not want the organization to do anything that would give the mayor grounds for demanding the cancelling of the program. Brazier never stated these reservations at the steering committee meeting. When asked by a member what his position was he responded, as he frequently did, "My position is the position of the steering committee. I will carry out the will of this committee."[35] After extended and heated debate, the committee, by a two-vote margin, decided that the organization should not be provoked into "open war" with City Hall. A direct confrontation was not made, but the war was on. The intentions of the city officials were becoming clear. Brazier put it this way:

I have lost all faith in the political establishment of this city. They do not want to stop riots. They will not let people help themselves. They want control and will stop at nothing to deny independent groups from gaining power. We will not transfer our power downtown. This is the first time a community organization has had the authority to spend a million dollars. Brooks and Daley can't stand that.[36]

TWO side-stepped the mayor's attempt to control the project by appointing an acting director, a position not needing the mayor's concurrence. Anthony Gibbs of the TWO staff assumed the position and the project continued.

3. The police raid at the opening of the project did not turn out to be an isolated incident or a case of misunderstanding. It was the beginning of a continued assault on the program. In July the potential for renewed gang warfare was evident all over Chicago. In hopes of averting this, Jerome Bernstein, who had become the Washington mana-

---

[35] *Ibid.*
[36] Brazier to Woodlawn Pastors' Alliance, November 2, 1967.

ger of the TWO project, contacted a group of Watts youth leaders and flew them to Chicago to meet with the top gang leaders. The meeting, at a downtown hotel, proved successful. The Rangers and Disciples came to the TWO office the next day and reaffirmed the truce. However, the Watts meeting was "busted" by the police and the participants arrested, allegedly for possession of marijuana and weapons (later the charges were dropped). The peace efforts were interpreted as a war council and Bernstein lost his job. However, Woodlawn remained "cool."

It was not until fall, when classes in the program began, that a clear and regular pattern of police harassment became evident. GIU officers regularly entered the four training centers and questioned the participants. This police interference and intimidation continued through the duration of the project. More devastating than the week-by-week harassment was the implementation of the GIU strategy of arresting the youth leaders.

In September and October, Gene Hairston and Jeff Fort, the two top Rangers, were arrested on separate charges of murder and held without bond. Later Nic De Renzo, a Disciples' leader, was arrested for murder. Three of the original four youths on the Project Policy Board were thus removed. Others in the project were arrested for rape, murder, or lesser charges. According to the account given by First Presbyterian Church, which had assumed the task of legal defense for the Rangers, twenty-three out of the twenty-four arrested in the fall were either acquitted or, in the majority of cases, never came to trial. Fort's case, the most flagrant example, hurt the project most. Fort was arrested on October 20 and held in jail for five months without bond or trial. On March 25, the State's Attorney dropped charges for lack of evidence. The impact of this campaign was so clear that it is difficult to imagine that the strategy was not employed precisely for the impact. The top leaders like Fort and Hairston provided much of the organizational skill which held the Rangers together. With-

153

out the top layer of leadership, the discipline and cohesion loosened. The second-level leaders were not as able to exercise control over the organization. The Third District police statistics for the period between June 22 and October 11, 1967, had shown a significant reduction in crime and violence in comparison to the same period in 1966: a decline of 23 percent in robberies, 20 percent in serious assaults, and 44 percent in shooting assaults.[37] This decline in crime, which coincided with the first four months of the Youth Project, came to an end when the program was denied the services of Hairston and Fort. A research report by the social action committee of a Hyde Park church emphasized this point:

> Most top Ranger leaders are in their early 20's and are primarily interested in political or economic ways of gaining power. When they are imprisoned, younger members step into the leadership roles. They are personally more violence-oriented, and have less authority over the early adolescents, who are the most violent of gang members. When Buckney's "arrest the leaders" strategy has been successful, organization has lagged and small-scale violence has markedly increased. In fact, the period of Fort's imprisonment (which was on a charge initiated by police and finally dismissed for lack of evidence) was the only break since Autumn 1966, in a consistent decline of crime in Ranger territory.[38]

[37] Reported by Brazier to delegates' meeting, November 6, 1967 and by Don Blakiston of the South East Chicago Commission at a conference on the TWO Youth Project at the Center for Continuing Education, November 2, 1967. More complete statistical data is included in Irving Spergel, Project Director, *Evaluation of the Youth Manpower Demonstration of the Woodlawn Organization.* Submitted to the Office of Economic Opportunity, February 1969 (Chicago: University of Chicago, School of Social Service Administration, 1969); see especially the appendix, "Gang Violence and the Woodlawn Youth Project," by Richard Appelbaum, September 8, 1968.

[38] Brian W. Grant, "A report by the Social Action Committee of University Church of Disciples of Christ," 1969, on file at the Church, p. 2 (mimeographed).

154

The police directed their efforts not only at the youth but also at the project staff. On December 11, acting director Gibbs was arrested for resisting arrest in the youth project office. The final evaluation of the project described the general situation with the police this way:

> The organization which led the attack in the winter of 1967 was the Chicago Police Department, particularly the Gang Intelligence Unit. The community force, probably more responsible than any other for directly hindering and destroying the project, was the Chicago Police Department. Its lack of commitment to the objectives of the program, its gross failure to understand the complexity of the problem of gang delinquency in the Black Ghetto, its reluctance to cooperate with The Woodlawn Organization in the implementation of the program, and its punitive law enforcement attitudes and activities were elements in the systematic attack.[39]

4. The TWO Youth Project received no cooperation from the public or private youth-serving agencies. TWO was regarded as a competitor by most and as a destructive threat by some. The schools, Boys' Club, YWCA, Urban Progress Center, and youth welfare agencies had never had a cordial relationship with TWO.[40]

In order to facilitate communication with all agencies and related programs in Woodlawn, TWO held a conference on November 2 to explain the program, invite cooperation, and answer questions. Representatives from the Joint Youth Development Commission, the Chicago Commission on Youth Welfare, Youth Action, the Board of Education, the

[39] Spergel, *Evaluation*, p. 215.

[40] An unpublished study by Neal G. Lund, "East Woodlawn Pilot Study," October 10, 1966, on file at University of Chicago, Divinity School, indicated the antipathy of agency leaders toward TWO. Lund interviewed leaders of eleven agencies in Woodlawn. Some of the responses toward TWO: "It does not seek improvement for people and conditions, but is mainly political"; "It manipulates people"; "TWO doesn't teach responsibility"; "It doesn't represent the community," pp. 106-108.

Woodlawn Mental Health Center, the Woodlawn Urban Progress Center, the Third District Police, the Cook County Department of Public Aid, the Chicago Human Relations Commission, the South East Chicago Commission, the University of Chicago, and numerous other agencies and institutions met with the project staff and youth leaders. Edwin Berry of the Urban League, Alderman Leon Despres, Dr. Sheppard Kellam of the Mental Health Center, and Fifth Ward Committeeman Marshal Korshak voiced their support. The rest either expressed doubts or remained silent. The major reservations centered on the use of unqualified gang leaders as teachers and supervisors. The basic intent of the meeting was to preclude the charge that TWO did not let anyone know what it was doing and that it would not allow anyone to cooperate with it. It is doubtful if any minds were changed. The agencies kept their distance and continued to attack the concept and the operation of the program. The evaluators of the project maintained that

> The agencies in Woodlawn, whether public or voluntary, serving gang youths were hostile to The Woodlawn Organization and strongly opposed to its Youth Manpower Project. The agencies varied only in the depth and bitterness of their hostility and in the emphasis given to various reasons for why the project was "no good" and could be of little or no positive value to youths and the community. While the public agencies stressed the political arrogance of Reverend Brazier and the extreme self-interest of The Woodlawn Organization, the voluntary agencies emphasized the faulty rationale and operational concepts of the program.[41]

Whether the agencies refused to cooperate because of instructions from their downtown offices, or because of their general antipathy toward TWO's approach, or because the success of TWO's program would signify their own failures

[41] Spergel, *Evaluation*, p. 251.

is perhaps immaterial. In any case, if the TWO Manpower Project was to succeed it would be in spite of the lack of cooperation of the existing youth-serving agencies.

5. The controversy over the project and the attacks upon it were soon expanded beyond the confines of Woodlawn. Through the efforts of Representative Roman Pucinski, a leader of the Chicago contingent of congressmen loyal to Mayor Daley, the TWO project became an issue on the floor of the U.S. House of Representatives. The TWO project became the most illustrious example of what the big city mayors and representatives fear most—direct OEO funding of citizen action programs. Teaming up with Southern congressmen who were interested in limiting OEO, the big city Democrats secured a number of amendments which so locked the poverty funds into the hands of existing local officials that the Poverty Program was again palatable to many of its former critics. What is commonly referred to as the Green amendment, and might more appropriately be termed the Pucinski amendment, was passed by the House on November 15, 1967. This amendment required that in the future all funds for local community action programs be funnelled through existing governmental agencies. In other words, no more demonstration programs funded directly from the Washington OEO office to community groups without first securing the full approval of local governments and local OEO officials.

6. The major and most damaging flurry of publicity came in late December. Beginning on December 22, the *Chicago Tribune* began a crusade which received national coverage. TWO was informed that Mayor Daley's public relations man, Earl Bush, fed the *Tribune* with front page material. Without checking its story the *Tribune* ran sensational articles daily for a week. The charges against the project of hiring murderers and rapists, of forcing youth to quit school and join the project, of flagrant misuse of federal funds were circulated to a public apparently willing to believe them.

157

The stories were so twisted that it is hard to contest the conclusion that they were politically motivated and were instigated by GIU-CCUO-City Hall direction. The charge that TWO had "murderers" on the staff was based on the correct fact that Fort and Hairston had been on the staff until they were arrested two and three months before the *Tribune* "report" and charged with murder. While held in jail they were, of course, neither on the staff nor paid. The so-called rapists were never jailed or tried because of lack of evidence. They remained on the staff. TWO's position had been made clear. The youth in the program had arrest records and would probably continue to have arrests. If arrest and accusation, and not conviction, became the criteria for participation in the project, then the GIU would be able to destroy the program simply by arresting the leaders. The charges published against the program were a mixture of truth and fantasy. In some cases, the program was accused of doing exactly what the federal government had intended it to do. In other cases, the charges bore no resemblance to fact. The clarification and refutation of this *Tribune* crusade never received press coverage.

The press attack on the program escalated the conflict. The impact of the widespread publication of charges against TWO and the project was felt in several ways. The job placement phase, handled by the Urban League, became much more difficult. Employers backed off from commitments which they had previously made to the League. Brazier argued that this was one of the major factors that crippled the program.

> I cannot overemphasize the damage the *Tribune* articles did to our ability and the Urban League's ability to get jobs. Employers are at best reluctant to hire this population. The constant, day after day series of articles by the *Chicago Tribune* on each and every youth that was picked up and arrested—not convicted—who was associ-

ated with the project caused the employers to feel that we had nothing but killers, murderers, or rapists on this project.[42]

The press charges also provided Representative Pucinski and other critics of the program with grounds for demanding a series of investigations. OEO investigators and then a team from the General Accounting Office (GAO) made a thorough study of the operation. Three GAO men were with the project from January until March examining in detail its management. Neither investigation found signs of mismanagement of government funds. The program was cleared. However, the very process of investigation hampered the effectiveness of the project. Much of Brazier's time was spent in exploring and investigating the charges. The need to accommodate the federal investigators also consumed valuable staff time.

While the attack by the press hampered the effectiveness of the project, it also served to elicit a greater unity within TWO in support of the youth and of the project. A press campaign against the Rangers in 1966 or 1967 would not have stirred up the community, at least not in support of the youth. But the experience of the training project led to new relationships within Woodlawn. In the winter of 1968 this attack on the youth and their program was seen as an attack on TWO and it became regarded by many as an attack on Woodlawn. Two of the regular TWO steering committee meetings in January were converted to mass meetings. On January 3, over 400 residents assembled at the Woodlawn Methodist Church to demonstrate support for the project. At this meeting Brazier outlined the history of the project, the failure of the mayor to concur with TWO's appointment of a director, the record of police harassment, and the lack of cooperation from established agencies. He answered in detail the specific charges of the press and

42 *Ibid.*, p. 262.

159

made very clear his interpretation which, it appeared obvious by the reception it received from the meeting, was shared by those attending. Support within Woodlawn for TWO and the Youth Manpower Project was greater than it had ever been.

The press attack socialized the controversy, brought in new partisans on either side, hampered the continued effectiveness of the Manpower Program itself, and signaled the fact that refunding was doubtful. This extensive press coverage also gave credence to Brazier's interpretation of the entire struggle which was that the city administration did not want TWO to succeed in this project and that it was using all available resources to make the project fail. The issue was not the gangs. The issue was black independence.

Even though the project had been under constant attack from these opposing forces from the beginning, there was still the possibility that it would be refunded. TWO was willing to continue the project. OEO officials were satisfied with the administration and progress of the project during its first eight months. Many of the anticipated outcomes were being realized: gang members were being placed on jobs, violence in Woodlawn was reduced, and, most dramatically, after the Martin Luther King assassination, when the West Side was in flames, Woodlawn was "cool." Furthermore, refunding of a demonstration program would normally be expected. It would take at least two or three years to demonstrate the feasibility of the innovative approaches being tested. Therefore, despite the heavy opposition it was reasonable to assume, in the spring of 1968, that the project might be continued. But the opposition had already begun work on the final blow which eventuated in the U.S. Senate Subcommittee hearings in the summer.

The Washington hearings, conducted by the Permanent Subcommittee on Investigations of the Senate Committee on Governmental Operations, chaired by Senator John McClellan of Arkansas, provided the final occasion for the convergence of all the forces opposed to the project. A variety of interests meshed. Senator McClellan was interested in discrediting the Poverty Program and showing that it wasted money and contributed to social disorders. There is no evidence that he was at all interested in the Woodlawn project as such. The Chicago political leaders were primarily interested in showing that federal programs that bypass City Hall end in failure. They did not share McClellan's antipathy to OEO spending, only to spending for organizations independent of City Hall control. The Police Department's Gang Intelligence Unit was primarily interested in discrediting First Presbyterian Church, the home of the Rangers and one of the centers in the TWO project. The Church, more than the TWO project, was perceived as the major hindrance to the GIU program of destroying the gang. The press was interested in selling newspapers. With these conditions the McClellan hearings were not so much an investigation as a political lynching, an occasion for the release of stored up fury and irrationality.

The convergence of these forces was not accidental. In the winter, investigators from the Senate Subcommittee had visited Chicago. They were originally interested in finding whether a case could be made that federal funds were being used to instigate or foment riots and urban disorders. They found no leads worth pursuing. But they did not go back empty-handed. The GIU provided the investigators with material that would serve the subcommittee purposes just as well—scandalous stories about the Woodlawn gangs, TWO, and First Presbyterian Church. The investigators returned and in partnership with the GIU began to develop the case.[43] Out of this mix of interest came the hearings which began on June 20, 1968. The police provided witnesses to testify. McClellan provided the format at which testimony could be given without cross examination and with immunity from libel suits. The press, the key to the McClellan-GIU-City Hall strategy, gave front-page cover-

[43] Robert Novak, "How Ranger Probe Started," *Chicago Sun Times*, July 12, 1968, p. 1.

age to whatever was said. The major part of the hearings was directed at First Presbyterian Church and its staff rather than at TWO. Relying on testimony by the police, particularly Captain Edward Buckney, head of GIU, and by two major witnesses secured by the police, ex-Ranger George Rose and Ranger mother Mrs. Annabelle Martin, the hearings featured sensational charges of gunrunning, pot parties, and sex orgies in the church, all of which were front-page material for Chicago newspapers. That no legal action has been initiated against the Church for these serious crimes for which the police claimed to have evidence is only one indication of their lack of substance. A thorough examination of the credibility of witnesses at these hearings, later conducted by a blue-ribbon committee of the Chicago Presbytery,[44] confirms the interpretation shared by the Rangers, TWO, and First Presbyterian Church that the GIU was using the immunity of the Senate hearings, the passions of Senator McClellan, and the services of the press to continue its program of seeking to discredit and undermine the work of the Church and TWO with the youth.

Even though the hearings spent little time examining directly the TWO Manpower Project—or, perhaps, because they never examined the project—the hearings served their purpose. The project, which was closed down at the end of May, was not refunded. Captain Buckney's comment to the press on hearing of the news was, "I really hadn't expected OEO to do it."[45] What appears to the observer as a case of overkill was apparently deemed as necessary by the opponents of the TWO program. That such a concerted and

---

[44] "Report to the Presbytery of Chicago from Its Committee Investigating Allegations of Wrongdoing Made Against the Reverend John Fry, Mr. Charles LaPaglia and Miss Ann Schwalbach of the Staff of First Presbyterian Church, Chicago," presented to the Presbytery of Chicago, September 16, 1969, pp. 43-77. A model of investigative thoroughness, even with the limitation of complete noncooperation from the Chicago Police Department, the report failed to find any evidence in support of the charges against Fry or the Church.

[45] *Chicago Tribune*, August 1, 1968, p. 7.

concocted final attack through the McClellan hearing was regarded as necessary to kill a program which had already been undermined repeatedly is a kind of negative evidence that even a crippled and harassed project might have been regarded as sufficiently effective to warrant continuation.

The positive evidence of the merits of the Manpower Project was provided in the final evaluation submitted to OEO in February 1969, by Dr. Irving Spergel, project director of the evaluation team from the School of Social Service Administration of the University of Chicago. The evaluations recommended continuation of the project.

> On the basis of available evidence there was no strong programmatic reason for termination or failing to extend the life of the project. Modification of design elements, especially staffing patterns, was entirely feasible and already planned. The elements of a more effective demonstration were at hand and needed only more time, more professional staff and more sophisticated development.[46]

The evaluation, itself hampered by lack of police cooperation and by two Senate subpoenas of research records, was unable, because of the brevity of the program, to test most of the demonstration features. It did conclude, however, that the gang structure provided "a natural and logical mechanism" to recruit and select staff and participants, and also that TWO was an appropriate agency to administer such a program.[47] According to the evaluation

> The key accomplishments of the project were: 1) the probable reduction of delinquency and crime in the area, 2) the placement of a significant number of ghetto youths on jobs, and 3) the prevention and control of riots.[48]

The reduction of crime in Woodlawn was not only clearly documented in the police statistics but also readily appar-

[46] Spergel, *Evaluation*, p. 345.
[47] *Ibid.*, p. 338. [48] *Ibid.*, p. 345.

ent to the Woodlawn residents. The evaluation report concluded that

> The presumption of a connection between the effects of the Youth Manpower Project which served a great many delinquents and the decline of crime in District 3 (Woodlawn) therefore, remains strong.[49]

The job placement activity, although hampered by adverse publicity, was termed moderately successful. In the brief period of the project 634 youth participated formally in some aspect of the project. Of these, 62 were employed as subprofessionals in a part- or full-time capacity. By the end of the program between 83 and 107 of the trainees had been placed on jobs. The evaluators' conclusions were that

> The TWO Youth Manpower Project did as well, if not better than most programs. No other youth manpower program probably ever reached so relatively large a pool of hard-core male delinquent youths.[50]

The evaluation also indicated "definite evidence of the reduction of community tension by the Blackstone Rangers and the East Side Disciples in relation to three major riot potential situations."[51] The most noticeable instance, and one that received local recognition, was the determined "cool" in Woodlawn following the assassination of Dr. King. Comparison of police statistics in black areas of Chicago during April 1968, reveals that something was happening in Woodlawn to distinguish it from other neighborhoods.

There were, of course, a number of basic weaknesses in the project, many of which were in the process of being corrected. Other observed weaknesses were the result of outside interference. The basic conclusion of the evaluation was that the project was progressing as anticipated, that it was "reasonably successful" in its first year, "that a pioneering approach to youth manpower development in the

---

[49] *Ibid.*, p. 344.   [50] *Ibid.*, p. 343.   [51] *Ibid.*, p. 66.

TABLE 1. COMPARISON OF CRIME STATISTICS
(April 1968 in comparison to April 1967)

AREA	SERIOUS ASSAULTS	ROBBERY
Chicago (as a whole)	Up 19%	Up 19%
Monroe District	Up 155%	Up 62%
Fillmore District	Up 84%	Up 64%
Wood District	Up 16%	Up 55%
Grand Crossing District (Woodlawn)	Down 14%	Down 49%

SOURCE: From transcript of WBBM-TV (Chicago) report by Walter Jacobson, broadcast June 21, 1968.

ghetto has been offered,"[52] and that it should be continued so that the success or failure of the approach might be measured. In light of the encouraging progress, the termination of the project led the evaluators to point out that

The inescapable conclusion was that there were issues, other than those of program effectiveness, which must have accounted for the policy decision that the project was a failure. These issues, we believe, were essentially political and interorganizational. It is clear that many powerful groups and organizations acted in such a way as to encourage failure of the project. *The fact that the program had positive results is remarkable in view of the extraordinary opposition to it.*[53]

For TWO the youth project was much more than an occasion for demonstrating and testing innovative concepts in job training. The project represented a major step toward an emerging concept of community control. Under federal guidelines TWO was directly responsible for the administration of a project which showed promise of addressing some of the root causes of youth alienation and gang violence. TWO had an opportunity to demonstrate that a people's organization that commanded the respect, trust, and support of the neighborhood was more able than the tradi-

[52] *Ibid.*, pp. 339, 346.   [53] *Ibid.*, pp. 345-346, italics added.

165

tional youth-serving agencies to develop relationships with the youth, identify the root causes of poverty and powerlessness, and administer a program that would deal realistically with this situation. In addition, this project enabled TWO to demonstrate that some of the existing cleavages within the black community, between old and young, middle class and poor, in-school and drop-outs, employed and unemployed, could be overcome. The significance of the project went far beyond the testing of the numerous innovations in the program design.

What went wrong? Was it that the youth themselves are hopeless criminals as the police-press interpretation suggests? Was it the lack of MA type professional leadership, trained teachers, and tight classroom controls as some of the agency youth-servers suggest? Was it the inability of a community organization to administer its own program as the political leaders seem to suggest? The TWO interpretation, which was privately held by those close to the project and was publicly shared in Woodlawn after the *Tribune* crusade, was that the project was killed, and that it had been in the process of being killed since before it began. The original proposal was opposed by nearly all of the mayor's advisors. Daley, however, found it politically difficult to veto the project. Therefore, according to TWO's interpretation, he approved the project for the sake of making it fail so that when it failed the burden would be placed on TWO, and the city administration could argue that this is what happens when independent organizations get federal help to administer their own programs without the expertise and guidance of city agencies. Whether the continuous attack on the project was centrally orchestrated, or was the result of a mutual convergence of forces each acting independently out of its own self-interest, is not clear. It would be difficult to prove an official conspiracy. What is clear is that the activities of the police, CCUO, the press, and the political leaders interlocked in undermining the project.

It was not simply lack of support, but rather active intervention, that crippled and finally torpedoed the project. Police harassment in and around the training centers intimidated the youth. Strategic arrests of leaders provided the press with material. The press campaign against the project seriously curtailed the job placement opportunities. The almost continuous series of investigations diverted top staff energies. TWO was placed on the defensive from the beginning. There is some evidence that without the concerted attack and harassment the project would have been a demonstrable success. But that is conjecture. More certain is the fact that without the GIU-inspired Senate hearings the project would have been continued. The inescapable conclusion is that the termination of the project was the direct result of the activities of those who wanted TWO's Youth Manpower Project to fail—the police, the agencies, and City Hall. Among these, the role of the police deserves particular attention.

The police, especially the GIU, were hostile because a successful demonstration project would have directly challenged their guiding assumptions. These assumptions were that (1) the gangs as such are evil and must be broken up, (2) any positive image portrayed or program developed is a deceptive cover for illegal activities, and (3) the city and the Police Department badly need a "super-sleuth" unit like the GIU in order to identify and deal with adult individuals and organizations that encourage or support the existence of youth gangs.

GIU Commander Buckney's approach was initially very simple. "By lopping off the head of the gangs, the gang itself will wither and die."[54] The basic operation of GIU was, as he explains, TV stuff:

We expect to be involved in "super-sleuth" activity, tailing various individuals, keeping tabs on people's activi-

[54] Edward Buckney, recorded in Oral History Collection, Chicago State College, 1967.

167

ties, going to various meetings to see what they have to say and pursuing the general line of activity that is seen in the spy movie or on television. The kind of things which are generally accepted by people as being detective activities. . . .[55]

The initial failure of this approach led not to a reassessment of the method and the assumptions, but rather to an elaboration of the GIU ideology and the development of what Charles LaPaglia calls "the Ranger Myth."[56] In the GIU elaborations, alternative approaches to dealing with gang activity, such as those harbored by First Presbyterian Church, along with any other independent programs dealing with gangs, were apparently included among the "heads" that had to be "lopped off." In an article on the Rangers, reporter Lincoln Richardson summarized his dialogue with Buckney this way:

> If First Church is doing the wrong thing, then how can concerned churches work with gangs? They can't.
> How can other social agencies and groups work with gangs? They can't.
> Then who can work with gangs? The police.
> How can churches and other groups help the police work with gangs? They can't.
> Of the many different efforts now being made in Chicago to deal with gangs, which have been the most helpful to the police? The formation of the Gang Intelligence Unit.
> What can be done about gangs? They must be broken up.[57]

Buckney reiterated this same conviction to Senator McClellan at the hearings: "We feel, for example, if the Rangers

---

[55] *Ibid.*

[56] Charles LaPaglia, "On 'Gangs,'" unpublished paper on file at First Presbyterian Church, Chicago, 1969, p. 5 (mimeographed).

[57] Lincoln Richardson, "The Blackstone Rangers," *Presbyterian Life,* February 15, 1968, p. 18.

were divorced from the First Presbyterian Church and from that kind of influence, that the police could very well deal with them in the street."[58]

Much of the attention of the GIU was directed against those organizations who acted out of an alternative perception of the gang phenomenon, who viewed the gangs as potentially constructive community organizations. It was this alternative perception that apparently was most threatening to Buckney. If programs based on that perception proved successful, it would tend to invalidate the GIU "Ranger myth" and therefore the wisdom of the GIU approach. There existed a head-on clash between two approaches to the gangs. The SCLC peacemaking overtures were regarded as ominous signs by the police. The GIU was formed in March 1967, when it became apparent to the city agencies that the OEO proposal might be funded. In November 1968, after the Rangers participated in anti-Daley political activity, the GIU was increased from 38 to 200 men. It appears that nonviolent gang activity was interpreted as more threatening than violent activity. On several occasions intergang conflict was stimulated by GIU officers, and gang members were lured into violent confrontations so that they could be picked up by the police.[59]

The basic point is that the GIU, during the life of the TWO project, had a twisted vested interest in violence in Woodlawn. The TWO project posed a threat simply because it was able to reduce the crime rate, ease community tension, and avert riots where the police had previously failed. In order to justify its existence, to say nothing of its expansion, the GIU needed to have alternative approaches fail. And they used their resources to that end. The existence of this special unit was threatened more by

[58] "Report to the Presbytery of Chicago," p. 76, from testimony at U.S. Senate Hearings, p. 2486.

[59] Numerous accounts of police-stimulated violence are given by LaPaglia, "On 'Gangs'"; Grant, A Report by University Church; and Hyde Park Voices (Chicago), Special Supplement, February 1969.

the possible success of alternative programs than by the failure of their own. Therefore, the GIU was less concerned with contributing to law and order than they were with making certain that no competitive approach could attain order. The project staff interpreted the hostility of the GIU

> as mainly a means of developing its own position in the Police Department. The Unit had to justify its existence both by demonstrating that a serious gang problem existed and that it could more effectively deal with it than any other unit within the police department or organization in the community at large.[60]

The service agencies were threatened by the project in a similar way. Competing for the limited resources in the youth-serving field, a multitude of agencies tended to regard the TWO project as an enemy. TWO was not simply entering the youth-serving business as a friendly competitor. It was testing a program which could alter radically the whole youth-serving enterprise. The success of the project would have dealt a blow to the professional domination in these agencies, and it would have exposed the years of wasted programs in the past. Many people, in TWO especially, had regarded the Urban Progress Center as a total waste of money simply because its resources never reached the community. TWO's program, if continued, would have presented a sharp contrast to the Progress Center operation. And if the TWO model were duplicated elsewhere, the poverty bureaucracy would have been shaken. The termination of the Manpower Project assured the Urban Progress Center professionals that future OEO programs would remain safely in their hands.

As mentioned before, a demonstrated success in a directly funded community program would weaken the political control so jealously guarded by the Cook County Democratic Organization of which Mayor Daley is chairman. The

[60] Spergel, *Evaluation*, p. 224.

170

flow of federal funds has helped sustain a patronage system and a favors system through which the Machine has been able to secure the votes of the black community. If a directly funded program had been allowed to succeed, City Hall might have been progressively denied a major source of political control, the monopoly on the allocation of federal funds. Fifth Ward Alderman, Leon Despres, viewed the termination of the project as "a complete victory for Mayor Daley."

> He actually prevented a meaningful program from being conducted. I think it has great implications. It shows that as County Chairman of the Democratic party, Daley can and will block any independent group from accomplishing anything.[61]

President Brazier's interpretation, shared by TWO's active constituents, supported by the evaluators of the project, and revealed by the observable actions of the established agencies, was that

> The project was killed because the political establishment could not tolerate an independent community organization such as TWO receiving federal funds that were not controlled by the Establishment itself. The project was killed because white society refused to permit indigenous leaders in the black ghetto to deal with problems of alienated youth—a problem that white society by its indifference and racism has forced on the ghetto.[62]

In the brief history of this community-controlled project, TWO elicited a counterresponse from Chicago officialdom the magnitude of which it had not previously seen. The explanation for this delayed and decisive response to TWO can be seen in terms of "slack" in the political system. Any group with skill and determination can marshal and pyra-

[61] *Chicago Tribune*, August 1, 1968, p. 7.
[62] Brazier, *Black Self-Determination*, p. 125.

mid these unused resources and increase its influence within a political system without incurring significant resistance. TWO had been able to build and organize around previously unused resources, primarily the time and effort of citizens. It also built the organization around issues and programs that did not basically challenge the power arrangements of the city. TWO enhanced its bargaining position, but the mayor and the city agencies were still the ones with whom TWO had to deal. When TWO began to move beyond a pressure group and sought to assume functions previously lodged in centralized city bureaucracies, it directly threatened the sovereignty of City Hall. In other words, when TWO developed sufficient power to move toward community control, the "slack" in the political relationship between TWO and City Hall decreased and what social scientists refer to as a zero-sum situation was approximated. If TWO wins, City Hall loses and vice versa. In this head-on situation the city had far more unused resources it could draw upon than had TWO. This "slack" theory of power accounts for TWO's relative success in building an organization as well as for the difficulty it faced in pursuing community control. TWO could pyramid its resources, develop programs, and negotiate with appropriate city officials as long as it did not threaten the life blood of the dominant political machine. TWO would receive a "bigger piece of the pie" as long as the city controlled the "baker."

When TWO was in a position to think in terms of controlling public funded programs and of experimenting with approaches which contradicted the traditional programs sanctioned by the city, the "slack" was gone. It was either TWO or the city of Chicago, and no amount of support from federal officials or the University of Chicago could deliver TWO from the hands of an angry mayor.

The Youth Project was finished, but the Rangers continued. The escalation of police efforts to break them up was matched by their own determination to survive. Under a new name, the Black P Stone Nation, the organization

172

worked with several community groups on a variety of projects including a concerted effort to open up the building trades unions.

Not all was peaceful, however. The calm that existed during the Manpower Project was broken by increased incidents of gang violence and police-gang clashes. One resident, not previously active in TWO, came to the steering committee and with anger in his voice demanded to know what TWO planned to do about the increased gang violence in Woodlawn. Brazier replied, "Why don't you go to the Urban Progress Center? See Captain Buckney or take your problem to the mayor. We tried. We brought peace to this community and for this we have been maligned across the country."[63]

Gang activity increased. Police crackdown was intensified. Only through a major defense effort was the freedom of a majority of the Stone leadership preserved for several years, and police efforts to eliminate them stymied. However, the investigations initiated during the Manpower Project continued to haunt the Stone participants. Jeff Fort, the leader of the Nation, faced, in addition to numerous other charges, a one-year contempt of Congress jail sentence for his refusal to testify before Senator McClellan without the right of cross-examination. In April 1971, three years after the termination of the project, twenty-three Stone leaders, eight of whom were already in jail, were indicted and arrested on 132 counts of conspiracy to commit fraud, forgery, and misrepresentation in connection with the short-lived project. Certain unanswered questions were raised by these indictments: for example, that they should be presented three years after the project which was, at the time, under constant police surveillance, audited by a nationally reputable company, and scrutinized closely by the General Accounting Office and the OEO; that they should be served after intense police efforts to jail top Stone leaders had been of limited success, and after the State's Attorney's office had

[63] Brazier to steering committee, September 16, 1968.

173

been criticized for its method of dealing with the Stones and the Black Panthers. This time the police succeeded in their ongoing campaign to put Fort and other Stone leaders behind bars. Fort received, in May 1972, a five-year sentence and four of his colleagues lesser terms. It is ironic that the youth leaders were trapped through the one major effort in which they worked cooperatively with the adults in Woodlawn.

Yet the Nation, its image tarnished in the black community, its leadership in jail, avenues for legitimate activity blocked, its resources "dried up," still continued to grow and, by 1972, claimed an affiliation of thousands of young people and adults in all parts of Chicago and several other cities across the country. The gangs were now Mayor Daley's problem. However, the conditions that produced them were still Woodlawn's problem.

CHAPTER IV

The Attempt to Control:
TWO and the Public Schools

THAT the inadequacy of the school system is the major factor in youth alienation might be contested. Few would argue, however, with the contention that the schools in Woodlawn were failing. Research carried out by the staff of the Woodlawn Mental Health Center showed that seven out of ten first-graders in Woodlawn were not adapting to the student role and the school situation.[1] The majority of Woodlawn children were "in-school dropouts" at age eight. Later research revealed that more than half (51 percent) of the students who completed eighth grade did not finish high school; only 20 percent of those who did finish received what the researchers considered a high school education. Ninety percent, then, either dropped out of school or were "in-school" functional dropouts.[2] That the youth gangs were made up of school dropouts and pushouts was not the primary reason for TWO's concern about the quality of the public schools in Woodlawn. The schools were simply inadequate by any standard.

In trying to bring about change in the situation TWO had, between 1961 and 1967, spent more effort with less success than in any other area. At first the issues were *de facto* segregation and the personality and administration of School Superintendent Benjamin Willis. Boycotts, pickets,

[1] See Sheppard G. Kellam and Sheldon K. Schiff, "Adaptation and Mental Illness in the First-Grade Classroom of an Urban Community," *Psychiatric Research Report 21* (American Psychiatric Association, April 1967), pp. 79-91.

[2] "Woodlawn Experimental Schools District Counseling Program to Prevent Dropouts," January, 1969, on file at WESP, p. 2 (mimeographed).

175

mass meetings, hearings, and a variety of other Alinsky-inspired tactics accomplished little. Willis withstood widespread pressure to resign and *de facto* segregation increased. In 1963, 87.8 percent of black students went to schools that were at least 90 percent black. By 1965, the figure rose to 90.2 percent.[3] After several years of frustrating experiences, the intense efforts gave way to despair and sporadic activity. But TWO was not alone. A major study of the Chicago school system, the Havighurst Report, the first since 1932, was released in 1964. The report, commissioned by the Board of Education and supported by the press and many citizen groups, received no attention from Willis or from the school bureaucracy. Its recommendations for both the integration and upgrading of the public schools were not implemented or, in most cases, even considered by the Board.[4]

By the time Willis finally resigned in the spring of 1966, segregation was no longer an issue in Woodlawn. Brazier, in his annual state of the community address, said:

> We aren't forgetting about integration but we aren't waiting for it either. We want quality schools now. It is an insult to tell me that there have to be white kids in my school before it can be a good school. We want good black schools now.[5]

TWO was much more clear about what it wanted than about how to get it. Unlike most institutions in Woodlawn, the public school system seemed impermeable.

While TWO was struggling with the deteriorating situation in the Woodlawn schools, the University of Chicago was developing a proposal to the federal government for an Urban Education Laboratory to be located in the South

[3] Christopher Chandler, "Increased Segregation Reported in City's Public Schools," *Chicago Sun Times*, September 27, 1966, p. 18.

[4] Lois Wille, "Chicago Schools Get an 'F,' " *Chicago Daily News*, October 8, 1966, p. 3.

[5] Brazier to delegates meeting, January 9, 1967.

Campus area of Woodlawn. The proposal, prepared during 1965 by a University committee on urban education, called for the construction of a research and development center for urban education to be funded under Title IV of the Elementary and Secondary Education Act of 1965.

It was not until a May 4, 1966, site visit by federal officials that TWO received and examined the proposal. After studying it, the chairman of the TWO schools committee and President Brazier were alarmed not only because this project was planned unilaterally by the University without any consultation with TWO, but also because the content of the proposal was seen as inimical to the interests of Woodlawn.

Among other things, the proposal called for the construction of an experimental school, the development of specialized research centers, and the creation of an experimental school district to provide freedom for the University to do its research.

This laboratory will provide opportunities for the study of problems related to urban education; the dissemination of the findings and the implications of that research and the demonstration of model programs and techniques developed in the laboratory and tested in experimental classrooms. . . .

The independence of the laboratory as a function of the University of Chicago will be maintained to permit research scholars maximum freedom and adaptability during the course of their basic inquiry. . . .

The model for the Urban Education Laboratory and Experimental School is the teaching hospital. . . . The experimental school views its students in part as means toward the end of constructing better curricula, more effective teaching techniques and improved climates of learning.[6]

[6] "Proposal for an Urban Education Laboratory," submitted to the U.S. Commissioner of Education (Committee on Urban Education,

TWO was as much disturbed by the University concept of "service" as by its plans for using Woodlawn as a laboratory for research.

> Here, for perhaps the first time, the experimental district is visualized as a multi-dimensional sociological unit within which educational, physical and mental health, social and legal research is conducted and services are provided for the youth and adults of the district. Research scholars from various disciplines and their professional counterparts, practitioners in the community, will find common purpose in working with the total population to provide unified research and improved service to individuals and families.[7]

A central component of the proposal was the development of what was called Neighborhood Research Centers, presumably to provide the University laboratory staff closer access to the "disadvantaged, low-income sections of the Experimental district."[8]

> The center could serve as a town hall, adult education center, and consulting service to the neighborhood. Activities for adults will give the teaching staff a chance to know them and to recruit helpers for educational purposes. Of special importance is the way such activities for adults will be used to develop leadership in the Negro community; for it is such indigenous leadership from within that will determine the rate of accommodation of the Negro community to its new legal rights.[9]

To the TWO leaders, this proposal posed a threat both to the organization and the community. If successful, this $10 million center would house and accommodate research agencies working in Woodlawn, using Woodlawn as a laboratory, yet totally controlled by the University. TWO

University of Chicago, October 15, 1965), pp. 2, 6, 18 (mimeographed).

[7] *Ibid.*, pp. 29-30.   [8] *Ibid.*, p. 30.   [9] *Ibid.*, p. 32.

178

regarded this as a clear attempt by the University, having failed in more direct methods, to control and pacify the area under the guise of research. The University's actual motives may have been nothing more sinister than to enhance its own prestige, attract faculty, and secure research grants for graduate students. But to TWO it appeared as an act of arrogance. Both in the content of the proposal and in the way it was developed, the existence of TWO, block clubs, and indigenous Woodlawn leadership had been ignored. More threatening still, it appeared that the University might be seeking to develop the equivalent of a competitive federally funded community organization. After consulting with the schools committee chairman, Brazier agreed that TWO had to intervene forcefully. The organization would insist on major alterations of the proposal and on a major voice in the revision, development, and control of the project before TWO would support or even permit such a proposal to be implemented. TWO did not wish to oppose categorically the idea of an Urban Education Center because such a center might provide the organization with a way of addressing in a total way the critical situation of the schools in Woodlawn.

On May 16, Brazier wrote a ten-page letter to Dean Roald Campbell of the University's Graduate School of Education, with a copy to Ward Mason, Director of the Research and Development Centers Program of the U.S. Office of Education, outlining the specifics of TWO's objections. In the concluding pages Brazier argued:

> TWO and the University look at Woodlawn in two different ways. TWO regards the community as people seeking dignity, justice and self-determination; the University sees the community as a convenient laboratory.
>
> There may be, and undoubtedly are, areas in which our two points of view overlap. However, these areas of joint cooperation will not be found if proposals such as this are developed unilaterally by the University *for* the Woodlawn area. . . .

179

It seems odd that the proposal is in such advanced stages of development without consultation in depth on these matters with The Woodlawn Organization. It appears that the University is really proposing a mammoth, federally-financed community organization, with an emphasis on research, run from the top down. For the proposal speaks of developing "indigenous leadership," "town halls," "of bringing the Negro into the mainstream of American society" without ever asking the people of Woodlawn whether they want the kind of leadership the University would develop, the "research centers" the University would supervise, or "the mainstream" that the University has decided should be our goal. The Woodlawn Organization has developed, and will continue to develop leadership for our community. We will choose our own leaders and define our own mainstream.

It is strange that a scholarly community concerned with human development should be so awkward in dealing with its neighbors to the south. The researchers ask, "what are the causes of alienation in the ghetto?" "What are the causes of low self-esteem among the people?" One cause of alienation and low self-esteem is being treated like objects, without being respected or consulted by the large bureaucracies that are supposed to be trying to "help" them. Oddly enough, the University may now be trying to study what it may be helping to create—alienation. . . .

The Woodlawn Organization proposes that collaboration on the proposed program be on the basis of respect for the self-determination of the Greater Woodlawn Community. TWO's feeling in this regard is based on our history, with which the University is in large part familiar, and on our conviction that research without the willing, close participation of the indigenous community will be ineffective and false research.[10]

[10] Letter from Brazier to Dean Roald Campbell, May 16, 1966, on file at TWO.

The response was quick and a meeting was arranged. It is not insignificant that, in sharp contrast to earlier relationships between TWO and the University, the meeting was at the TWO office. Dean Campbell, Julian Levi, and Bruce McPherson sat uncomfortably in the small, hot 63rd Street office while Brazier and two members of the schools committee demanded an explanation. Campbell apologized for the lack of communication and tried to explain the University's position. Levi, having had far more experience in dealing with Woodlawn than Campbell, finally interrupted Campbell's awkward presentation saying, "If we want this proposal, we are going to have to work with and through TWO." Brazier confirmed this and added, for Dean Campbell's benefit: "TWO is the only community organization in Woodlawn and there are parts of this proposal that we don't like." Levi again facilitated the discussion by suggesting a community policy board to iron out problems TWO had with this proposal and, perhaps, to serve as a permanent policy board if the Center were funded. Campbell argued that the faculty involved might not accept this. Brazier assured him that such a board would be essential if TWO were to support the project in any way. Aware that a copy of Brazier's May 16 letter was in Washington, the University's immediate concern was that Brazier send a second letter to the U.S. Office of Education endorsing the proposal and indicating that differences with the University had been worked out. TWO made it clear that such a letter could be sent only after it was certain that the organization had significant control over the project. Working sessions to negotiate a policy board and revise the proposal were scheduled to prepare for a June 7 meeting between TWO and University representatives. By the time the meeting was held, however, University President George Beadle had already received a letter from Washington indicating that the University proposal could not be funded at this time. Among the reasons given was that "the cooperation and

181

participation of local community groups had not been secured."[11]

The June 7 meeting became the occasion for a consideration of a variety of alternatives: (1) revise the proposal for later funding, (2) seek Title III funds through the Chicago Public Schools, (3) abandon the project completely. Brazier indicated that TWO would welcome continued discussions with an eventual goal of a funded proposal in which Woodlawn residents were deeply involved. In light of the Office of Education recommendation it was agreed that future discussions should include representatives from the Chicago public schools system.

Meetings were held throughout the summer to work out an initial relationship between the University, the Woodlawn community, and the Chicago public school system. District 14 Superintendent Curtis Melnick at first insisted that other groups than TWO should be included to represent the community. Levi, who had earlier refused to include several Woodlawn agency representatives in the discussion, responded forcefully that as far as the University was concerned TWO represented the Woodlawn community. The University's insistence on this point was understandable. Since it was only TWO that was able to effectively stymie the proposal, only TWO had to be dealt with. Furthermore, procedures would be simplified if the negotiations were limited to the three major parties.

On the surface this appeared an unlikely three-way relationship. The University of Chicago had been a longtime critic of the Chicago school system. Any relationship between the two institutions was certainly strained by the widely publicized evaluations of the Chicago schools by University of Chicago professors Hauser and Havighurst. The TWO-University relationship had, at best, moved from open hostility to mutual suspicion. The ties between TWO and the school system were virtually nonexistent. TWO had

[11] Letter from Ward Mason to Dr. George Beadle, June 3, 1966, on file at WESP.

organized school boycotts, picketed the district superintendent's home, campaigned against General Superintendent Willis, and was generally regarded by school officials as negative and uncooperative.

Two factors opened the door for communication: the appointment of a new General Superintendent of Schools and the lure of federal funding. Former Superintendent Willis had been a block to any top-level University-public schools discussions and a primary point of contention between many community organizations and the schools. His successor, James Redmond, understandably anxious to convey a new image, encouraged a variety of exploratory discussions with institutions and organizations previously estranged from the public schools bureaucracy. The major factor, however, was the possibility of federal funding under Titles III and IV of the Elementary and Secondary Education Act.

The interests of the three participating groups were evident at the outset. The University wanted the $10 million research center and all the enhancement possibilities that would have come with it. But in order to get this "plum," the University had to secure the support of TWO and the cooperation of the public school system. Superintendent Melnick could see the advantages of having such a center in his district. The resources it would provide and the further possibilities of Title III funds channelled through the Board of Education outweighed his reluctance to get tied up with TWO. TWO, realizing that its support was deemed essential by the federal government (and therefore by the University) and that Superintendent Redmond wanted to develop friendlier ties with the black community and their organizations, saw this three-way exploration as an opportunity to develop leverage in an area in which previously it had only slight influence. Representatives of these three institutions met throughout the summer to work out the beginning of a structured relationship.

After five negotiated drafts a proposal for a Woodlawn Community Board for the Research and Development Center in Urban Education was prepared and ratified by the three component institutions. The primary function of the Woodlawn Community Board (WCB) was "to review and approve (and in some cases initiate) all proposed policies and activities of the Research and Development Center in Urban Education which will directly affect the children, adults, community or community organization of Woodlawn." Two provisions were of special significance for TWO:

> It is recommended that seven (7) representatives be selected by each of the component institutions for the organization of the Woodlawn Community Board. Decisions relating to the replacement of each component group will be the sole responsibility of each component group.
> Decisions of the Woodlawn Community Board must have concurrent approval of the three component institutions represented. Each component group will make a separate determination in caucus of what constitutes the position on any question before casting a single vote.[12]

In a month of negotiations TWO had secured a virtual veto in the development and administration of the proposed project.

As the 21-member board began to meet in the fall of 1966, a concern about the variety of possibilities that could emerge from this tripartite relationship became more important than the question of the Research and Development Center and the content of the original proposal. With WCB support the University then submitted to the Office of Edu-

[12] "Woodlawn Community Board for the Research and Development Center in Urban Education" (final draft), June 28, 1966, included as Appendix A in Willard Congreve, *Final Report: Institutional Collaboration to Improve Urban Public Education with Special Reference to the City of Chicago* (Washington, D.C.: U.S. Department of Health, Education, and Welfare, Office of Education, Bureau of Research, Project No. 7-0346, March 15, 1968).

cation a proposal for a development project, the primary purpose of which would be

> To create an organizational structure and a sustained forum for analysis of the basic question: What organizational forms, programs and designations of roles and relationships can be determined by the Chicago Public Schools, the University of Chicago, and The Woodlawn Organization to facilitate a collective approach to the improvement of research, development, demonstration, dissemination, and training programs and practice in the public schools.[13]

This developmental project would permit the three institutions to explore ways of working together, develop a process for doing so, and create proposals for future funding.

The Office of Education rejected this relatively modest $94,000 developmental proposal. This rejection, more than anything else, served to bring the three constituent groups on the Board closer together. The Board approved a threefold recommendation at its December meeting:

> (1) re-open discussions with the government at the highest levels; (2) at the same time pursue opportunities to receive funding from private sources; and (3) open up all other avenues for acquiring assistance for our collaborative work.[14]

The first course of action proved successful. With prodding, University President Beadle and General Superintendent Redmond intervened with HEW Secretary John Gardner and Commissioner of Education Harold Howe. In funding the developmental project, the Office of Education indi-

[13] "Institutional Collaboration to Improve Urban Public Education with Special Reference to the City of Chicago," proposal submitted to the U.S. Commissioner of Education (Graduate School of Education, University of Chicago, October 12, 1966), p. 8 (mimeographed).

[14] Minutes of Woodlawn Community Board meeting, December 7, 1966.

cated that federal resources for program implementation after the developmental period would have to come through Title III, which is handled through the existing public school bureaucracy. Although TWO representatives on the Board were extremely skeptical of Title III funding, they agreed that the developmental period should be used to examine all alternatives.

The developmental grant provided the Board with an opportunity to become very serious about the possibility of collaboration. The project staff represented the three major parties. Willard Congreve of the University served as Director, with Anthony Gibbs of TWO and Miss Lorrain LaVigne of the Board of Education as Associates. Although drawn together around a common concern to improve education, it was clear that the three institutions had their own particular interests and purposes and their own perceptions of what was necessary to improve the schools.

The spring discussion at the WCB meetings about "The General Statement of Purpose and Procedure of the Developmental Project" is illustrative. The statement identified the three distinct interests of the participating groups. The purposes and contributions of the University and the Chicago public schools in the project were relatively clear. The University was interested in "research and training." The school system was interested in "upgrading school programs by applying research findings and experimental evidence" and by "improving the pre-service and in-service education of school personnel."[15] It was the role and particular interest of TWO that became the occasion for controversy. The original drafts prepared by the project staff identified TWO's particular interest in changing the educational program so that "it will be geared to the special needs of the youth of the community."[16] The TWO representatives ob-

[15] "General Statement of Purpose and Procedures" (revised draft), April 20, 1967. Included as Appendix B in Congreve, *Final Report.*

[16] "General Statement of Purpose and Procedures" (tentative draft), March 17, 1967, on file at WESP (mimeographed).

186

jected sharply to the description of TWO's interest. The implication of the term "special needs," Brazier argued, missed the point. TWO was not particularly interested in compensatory programs addressed to what educators might regard as "special needs" of Woodlawn youth. Brazier indicated that TWO wanted a fundamental change in the educational system in Woodlawn. The revised statement of TWO's interest in the project read as follows:

> The Woodlawn Organization is primarily interested in building leadership for the redevelopment of the community and in changing the basic educational program and the allocation of resources so that the educational system will be geared to the needs of the youth and the community.[17]

At the following meeting several school principals on the Board wanted clarification, particularly of the phrase "changing the basic educational program." They were told that it was TWO's view that the schools in Woodlawn were simply a failure and needed to be radically changed and, furthermore, that TWO wanted its position to be clearly stated at the outset.

Three distinct interests were involved in this project: (1) research and training, (2) upgrading the system, and (3) overhauling the system. While it might have been evident that all three could not be served equally, it was not clear which, if any, would prevail. With this clarification of the different contributions and perspectives, the WCB agreed that the project staff should address itself to four major questions:

1. What are the educational problems as perceived by citizens and the community organization; by school personnel; and by the scholars of the educational process? What are the educational problems as revealed by the already available data?

[17] "General Statement" (revised).

2. What ideas can be identified and developed to help solve the problems which have been revealed?

3. What new ways of working together can be established so that these ideas can be implemented?

4. How can such programs be financed?[18]

In response to the first question the staff engaged in an assessment survey of conditions, attitudes, problems, and perceived possibilities in East Woodlawn. Their report to the Board in June, based on 164 interviews with students, teachers, parents, and school administrators, was grim. The conclusion was that the system of public education in Woodlawn was not working well at all. Physical conditions were bad. Relationships were bad. Certainly the educational achievement outcome was not good. Teachers blamed parents. Students blamed teachers. Nearly everyone blamed administrators. Superintendent Melnick and some of the principals were defensive and charged that "self-fulfilling questions" had been asked in these interviews. TWO representatives on the Board assured Melnick that the perceptions reported by the project staff were mild in comparison to the perceptions shared by TWO.

The manner in which the staff addressed the other questions was largely determined by their assessment of the problems and needs. TWO's contribution to the process of assessing and interpreting the school situation in Woodlawn was a partially submerged factor which had significant impact on the future development of the project. If the assessment phase had been carried out solely by the school system, it would presumably have pointed out the need for more resources, training, and programs. The University might have pointed out the need for further research. Largely because of the way the assessment process was conducted, the particular perspective of TWO became the informing perspective of the project staff. The final report of the developmental project director indicates this direction:

18 *Ibid.*

During the months of June and July, the Project staff struggled to try to find the key to answering the major questions about experimental program intervention and collaborative working relationships. As soon as the data from the assessment were assembled it became apparent that limited interventions similar to the compensatory programs would not work. What was needed was a major overhaul of the entire social system of the school and new administrative structural relationships which would insure the meaningful participation and collaboration of parents, community, and University personnel in the efforts of the schools.[19]

Once it was committed to a general goal of basic structural change of the school system, the staff and Board faced the fundamental problem. How do you change the existing system? Resolution of this problem was complicated by the fact that major funding to bring about the change would probably have to come through the existing system. Should the staff design a program and then seek the support of the three participating institutions, or should the staff be more concerned about developing the administrative process through which the participating institutions could collaborate in program development? The perspective of TWO on this matter again prevailed in the staff. The project report summarized it this way:

The Project staff was urged on several occasions by both University and public school personnel to spell out in detail the program of intervention before becoming concerned with structure. However, having once determined that a major overhaul of the social system of the school was essential if success were to be realized, the staff found that prior to determining more specific program dimensions the implications for such an overhaul in terms of the organization and control of the schools needed to be made explicit. Therefore, major staff effort was di-

[19] Congreve, *Final Report*, p. 3.

189

rected toward developing an administrative plan that would permit this overhaul.[20]

The project staff had visited New York and Washington for a firsthand look at experimental school programs and became convinced that the weaknesses in these experiments were, in large measure, "because the essential collaboration had not been securely formed and maintained."[21] Perhaps of greater influence on the project staff was TWO's not-so-hidden agenda of pressing for increased community control of the schools. TWO was much more concerned about the mechanism of control and administration than about the details of program innovation.

TWO representatives on the Board were encouraged by the progress and direction of the developmental project. What had originally started as an autonomous Research and Development Center and later had the possibility of becoming a remedial or compensatory program was now committed to seeking fundamental changes in the roles, rules, and relationships within the existing school system in Woodlawn.

For the September 1967, meeting of WCB, the staff prepared a working paper which became the basis for the subsequent program design. The document, "Toward the Creation of an Experimental School District in East Woodlawn," dealt with the problem of converting a cluster of schools "from one basic plan of operation to another, from one basic philosophy of teaching and learning to another."[22] Two strategies were considered. In what was termed "the self-renewal" method, all the existing personnel related to the schools would be involved in determining overall direction and philosophy. The second approach, called the "acceptance-of-focus" method, was recommended by the staff.

[20] *Ibid.*, p. 32.   [21] *Ibid.*, p. 27.

[22] "Toward the Creation of an Experimental School District in East Woodlawn," Discussion Paper No. 3 presented at the Woodlawn Community Board, September 27, 1967, on file at WESP, p. 7 (mimeographed).

In the second method, a small group of individuals who have the time and additional resources, as well as a commitment to bring about change, develops an initial focus or thrust which the personnel of the schools to be renewed are asked to accept. . . . People presently in the school who feel they cannot commit themselves to the focus are given the opportunity to withdraw.[23]

The "acceptance-of-focus" method was endorsed by the Board as the best way of utilizing additional resources, securing the necessary cooperation and support of the participating schools, and, above all, locating strategy and program development in the new collaborative administrative structure.

The working paper identified the primary focus of a proposed intervention program by the simple phrase, "people helping people." The staff saw the basic problem in Woodlawn schools as the breakdown of cooperative relationships between parents and teachers, teachers and administrators, school and community, students and teachers, and students and community. The goal of the intervention program would be to develop the structure and processes whereby a mutuality of effort and support could be encouraged. Through a variety of mechanisms involving reallocation of roles and responsibilities, parents, teachers, administrators, students, and community groups would share in the development of a new community educational system.

The staff recommended that this intervention strategy be carried out in three Woodlawn schools comprising a kindergarten through twelfth-grade stream which would be designated as an experimental school district. Initial opposition to this recommendation came from public school representatives, who wanted the additional funds spread around more, and TWO representatives, who doubted that the TWO constituency would accept this limitation. However, the staff sustained the point that, to demonstrate the possi-

[23] *Ibid.*, p. 8.

bility of change through this strategy, the project must be held to a reasonable scale.

Far more difficult than securing agreement on general strategy was the creation of the administrative design. From TWO's perspective, some alternative to the present centralized administration bureaucracy of the school system was mandatory. The Board considered four alternative administrative designs presented by the staff.

In one plan the 'Board of Education would retain complete control of the project. The Board would develop a special district, contract with the University of Chicago for research and training, and invite TWO to develop an advisory board. Although this would be the simplest plan to implement, it was immediately rejected by the TWO component because it would not satisfy the primary criterion of "active, meaningful, and honest involvement"[24] of the community. It was also felt that the Board of Education control would limit the freedom to experiment. A second plan would place control of the project in a nonprofit-making community education corporation. Teachers would have to take a leave of absence from the Board of Education and become employees of the corporation. It was agreed that with such a structure the project would find it difficult, if not impossible, to secure public funds or Board of Education support. In the third plan, the University of Chicago would contract with the Board of Education to operate and administer the special district. Here, also, the limitations were greater than the advantages. TWO, with its past relationship with the University, could hardly be sold this structure. Each plan failed to meet essential criteria. The WCB supported a fourth plan which would retain the tripartite collaborative arrangement under which the developmental project was being administered. The Board of Education would be asked to establish an experimental district, and then turn over the administration of

[24] *Ibid.*, p. 15.

that district to the WCB and the administrative staff it would hire.

Both the project staff and WCB were encouraged by the conclusion of the October 2 meeting of the Woodlawn Community Board. A strategy and structure had been approved and the staff could proceed to develop the content of a major intervention proposal. It was left to the three co-chairmen of the WCB, Dean Campbell, Superintendent Melnick, and Reverend Brazier to work out the details of a memorandum of agreement which would legalize WCB as the administrator of the proposed school district.

This proved to be no simple matter. WCB, perhaps over-confident and not fully aware of what it was doing, had delegated to the three chairmen the task of preparing what turned out to be the single most determinative document in the project, a legal agreement that would stipulate the rights and responsibilities of the Woodlawn Community Board. The basic point of contention was the degree of autonomy granted the experimental district. The Board of Education would insist that any agreement conform to the Illinois School Code which places sole responsibility for administration of Chicago public schools with the general superintendent and the Chicago Board of Education. TWO, in the middle of its youth project which was being severely handicapped by limitations placed upon it by an agreement with the mayor and OEO, was not enthusiastic about par-ticipating in still another program that would be subverted by bureaucratic and political interests. Project director Wil-lard Congreve worked with the three chairmen throughout October developing a memorandum that would, on the one hand, be acceptable to Brazier and, on the other hand, be approved by the Board of Education. By November 3, after several drafts in which Congreve toned down the originally clear and explicit demands of autonomy, a memorandum was sent to the Board of Education for approval at its December 13 meeting. In the meantime, Congreve was in

193

contact with General Superintendent Redmond. Although Redmond supported the concept of the project, he was of the opinion that the memorandum as it now stood would not be approved by the School Board. Redmond's assessment was correct. Upon the advice of Board attorney James Coffee, the School Board deferred action and requested that the memorandum of agreement be rewritten so that it would be legally acceptable under the Illinois School Code.

This setback was critical. The deadline for submission of a proposal for Title III funds was January 15. A prerequisite for submission was the acceptance of an administrative design legalized by a memorandum of agreement with the Board of Education. The WCB staff now had to rewrite a memorandum which was acceptable to the three participating institutions and have it in the hands of the Chicago School Board by December 22 for their December 27 meeting. The prospects were not encouraging. Congreve revised the memorandum on Thursday, December 14 to satisfy the Board lawyer Coffee. This document, which would have made WCB merely an advisory body, was acceptable to Melnick and Campbell. Congreve told Coffee and Melnick that he doubted that Brazier would "buy it." As Congreve recalls, the reply of the school officials was, in effect,

> He will have to if we are going to have an experiment. The law will not permit us to do anything else, so the best we can do is to proceed in good faith that the director will involve the community and the collaboration will continue.[25]

Brazier rejected the revised memorandum. TWO would not participate unless there were guarantees that the director of the experimental district would be held responsible to the Woodlawn Community Board. The following Monday, December 18, the TWO steering committee voted unanimously to reject any agreement which would not require

[25] Congreve, *Final Report*, p. 46.

the project director to deal directly with WCB and to obtain WCB concurrence in all policy and program matters. Caught in the middle, Congreve developed still another draft, this time reflecting Brazier's position. The same day that TWO's steering committee rejected the School Board-approved draft, Coffee and his downtown staff rejected the later revision. The Friday deadline approached. Melnick would accept whatever Coffee approved. Campbell would accept anything. Brazier would accept an agreement only if there were clear guarantees that the project staff would be responsible to the community. Congreve called Julian Levi, whose skill with words and knowledge of legal technicalities had helped the project staff before, and together they arranged a meeting on Tuesday between Coffee and Brazier. The impasse was finally overcome by a collaboration of legal minds and political wisdom. They developed a memorandum sufficiently ambiguous to be tolerated by all parties. The minimal assurance Brazier demanded was included in the agreement.

The Board of Education agrees that the director of the experimental district is required to obtain the advice, counsel, recommendations *and concurrence* of The Woodlawn Community Board prior to making any recommendations related to personnel, organization, programming, administration, finance or any other matters concerning the experiment, to the General Superintendent of Schools and the Board of Education.[26]

But it was also made clear that control of the project remained with the Board of Education:

The concurrence, or lack of it, of the Woodlawn Community Board will not bind the General Superintendent

[26] "Memorandum of Agreement Among the Board of Education of the City of Chicago, The Woodlawn Organization, and the University of Chicago," Board of Education Report No. 67-1214 (amended), December 27, 1967. Included as Appendix N in Congreve, *Final Report.*

195

of Schools in directing the performance of this experiment or of making any recommendations to the Board of Education . . . nothing in this agreement will be construed to limit the authority of the Board of Education to control and manage the schools in the experimental district in accordance with the administrative and decision-making powers of the Board of Education contained in the laws of the State of Illinois.[27]

The accepted memorandum was a good political document. Brazier felt that TWO could live with it. Coffee thought the Board would pass it. Congreve could now submit the Title III proposal.

That such an agreement was ever secured was no small achievement in light of the December deadlock between TWO and the School Board. December was a hectic month for TWO. Embroiled in a youth project which was being undercut and facing the possibility of being bypassed in planning for participation in the federally sponsored Model Cities program, TWO was in no mood to accept a meaningless agreement with the Board of Education. To Brazier and the TWO steering committee the acceptability of the memorandum of agreement hinged on the word "concurrence." The director was required to secure the concurrence, not simply to seek the advice, of the Woodlawn Community Board on all matters concerning the experimental district. TWO, with a veto on WCB, had a point of leverage from which it could develop a strategy for working within this new administrative structure. The concurrence clause was central because it provided for the maximum degree of autonomy that the Board of Education would allow and the minimum that TWO would accept.

Several members of the Board of Education apparently felt that the memorandum gave away too much to TWO. Prior to the December 27 Board meeting, the *Chicago Tribune* began its crusade against the TWO youth project. With

[27] *Ibid.*

196

sensational front-page stories about TWO's relationship with gangs, some members of the Board of Education had second thoughts about entering into any agreement with TWO. Partly on the basis of strong support from Dean Campbell and Superintendent Redmond, however, the memorandum was adopted by an eight to three vote.

The School Board had little reason to worry. The experimental district was clearly under their jurisdiction. The powers of the Woodlawn Community Board were very limited and one major point, prominent in early drafts of the memorandum and the key to WCB's "acceptance-of-focus" strategy, was deleted from the final agreement. Earlier drafts stated that

> faculty members in the schools will be invited to express an interest in continuing as members of the faculty. Those who do not wish to remain will be granted transfer to another school without prejudice.[28]

Under the final memorandum the experimental district would not have the authority to have recalcitrant teachers transferred.

The memorandum of agreement was a compromise document and an ambiguous one. But it brought to a successful conclusion the developmental program, and led to the establishment of the first Chicago experimental school district in which a community organization would participate on a policy-making and administrative level.

A variety of factors, including the lure of federal funds, a new general superintendent, the skill of lawyers, and luck, contributed to the final settlement and the formalization of a tripartite relationship. Three factors appeared to be of particular significance.

The successful outcome of the feasibility project was at-

[28] "Memorandum of Agreement" (fourth draft), December 18, 1967. Included as Appendix M in Congreve, *Final Report.* See also Appendix J (first draft), October 3, 1967 and Appendix K (second draft), November 3, 1967.

tributable in no small part to the existence and recognition of TWO as the spokesman for Woodlawn. The project director in his final report recognized TWO's participation as the key ingredient:

> Where a strong community organization like TWO does not exist, we doubt if the wisdom and integrity of the professionals alone will do the job. We come to this conclusion not only from the experience of our study, but also from examining several local reform efforts which have attempted to go forward without strong relationships with a community organization (Roxbury in Boston, Adams-Morgan in Washington, D.C., and the New York University Bedford Stuyvesant Project). Further, we would hypothesize that where a community organization does not exist, one of the first things that a school system and/or a university interested in local educational reform should try to do is to help create such an organization with the full knowledge that it will eventually create conflict with the very institutions which helped it to come into existence.[29]

Progress in the developmental project was clearly facilitated both by the early recognition of TWO as the representative of the community, and by the way in which TWO exercised that role. The recognition was, of course, secured originally by the organization's capacity to obstruct the University's plan for a Research and Development Center. However, early in the discussions the University saw the advantage of having one group capable of negotiating on behalf of the entire community.

As important as the fact of recognition was the manner in which TWO carried out its spokesman role. During the two years from May 1966, until the major intervention project was funded in the summer of 1968, TWO exercised its spokesman role in what can be called low-visibility, private negotiations. Although there was nothing to be

[29] Congreve, *Final Report*, p. 50.

secretive about in this developing tripartite relationship, it was simply not widely publicized within TWO or the Woodlawn community. The steering committee was aware of the developmental project and supported it. But the issues raised at the Woodlawn Community Board were seldom discussed at TWO meetings. The major reason for this relatively quiet approach was that as long as TWO was already recognized as spokesman for Woodlawn, the TWO staff did not have to politicize the issue and mobilize support in order to secure such recognition. The absence of vehement and vocal community interest in the early negotiations provided Brazier with greater latitude as a negotiator. Given the prevailing hostility within TWO's active membership toward both the University and the public schools, unnecessary visibility of this exploratory relationship would serve no useful purpose. Supported by a relatively quiet constituency on this issue, Brazier could assure the schools people and the University both that TWO would function cooperatively in a collaborative effort and that TWO had undivided community support. At the same time, TWO could avoid stimulating either premature hopes or premature controversy within its constituency. The seven TWO representatives on the Woodlawn Community Board represented Woodlawn interests without specific mandates or pressure from TWO's broader constituency. It was only after the memorandum of agreement, after TWO had secured the maximum advantage from its recognized spokesman role, that it found it wise and necessary to publicize its involvement, "socialize" the controversy, and mobilize support around specific issues confronting the Woodlawn Community Board.

A second factor leading to a formal settlement was the priority given to the development of a collaborative, administrative relationship. Had the priority been given to the specific content issues and program development, the predictable controversies, similar to those most vividly revealed in the Ocean Hill-Brownsville experience in New York,

199

would have most likely prevented any structural relationship. The Woodlawn experiment was able to develop and legalize mutual commitments prior to the escalating of controversy over the content and direction of the project.

Finally, the tripartite relationship served to soften the polarization that often accompanies two-party negotiations. Although the initial antagonists were the University and TWO, it was soon apparent, as the negotiations developed and as the most likely source of funding was under Title III rather than Title IV of ESEA, that TWO and the Chicago public schools were the major parties in the project. In this tripartite relationship the University often served as a buffer. The University with an immediate interest in developing working relationships with TWO and with a style that was congenial to the schools' representatives, was able to facilitate the negotiations on numerous occasions by re-interpreting TWO's concerns in language acceptable to the schools and vice versa. On the only occasion where a special caucus of the three was necessary, the University sided with TWO, thus placing on the school component the onus of being obstructionist if they did not concur. The University, as a kind of middle component in the tripartite structure was able to provide a competent director for the developmental project and later for the experimental program, who was acceptable to both the school system and TWO. The presence of the University from the beginning provided a way for both the schools and TWO to avoid a crisis confrontation. As McGeorge Bundy, President of the Ford Foundation, wrote to Julian Levi, after reading the memorandum of agreement, "I can see that someone has done a very neat job of reconciling the interests of the parties concerned."[30] The University's role was not at all that of a passive moderator. Julian Levi's effectiveness as a lobbyist in Washington and his access to top officials in HUD and HEW gave weight to his judiciously chosen words at critical moments in the life of the project.

[30] *Ibid.*, p. 52.

200

Congreve concluded the final report on the developmental project with this perceptive summary:

In one sense, we have accomplished much. In another sense, we have done nothing. To be sure, feasibility to move ahead has been established. The administrative framework has been created. The experimental plan is ready for implementation. But all could vanish overnight. Collaborative agreements are perishable. They depend on mutual trust, which is always fragile in situations such as these. Unless something concrete happens in East Woodlawn soon, all we have done these past eighteen months will have been for naught. Even worse, the entire effort could be viewed as another one of the white man's parlor games.[31]

The memorandum of agreement paved the way for Title III funding. Although the grant was not secured immediately, the project staff forged ahead with a clear expectation that the proposal would be funded by the summer of 1968. The proposal was refined by the staff, reviewed by WCB, negotiated through the centralized bureaucracy at the Board of Education, and submitted to the U.S. Office of Education. A two-part proposal was finally funded at a level of $1,350,000.

The first and major part was for an intervention program in the two Wadsworth schools located in the heart of Woodlawn. The federal funds would raise the per capita expenditure for the 1,852 Wadsworth students from $546 a year to $1,262. The general goal of this Experimental Schools Project was stated as follows:

The objectives of our proposed program emanate from the needs of highest priority—to restructure the school as a social system in terms of its community through mutuality of effort, and to improve the quality of teaching and learning in the schools through mutuality of ef-

[31] *Ibid.*

201

fort. The objectives and subsequent interventions will have two foci: (1) roles and relationships of persons acting largely within the school: teachers, administrators, other school personnel, and children, but not excluding parents; and (2) roles and relationships of persons acting largely in the home and community: parents, but not excluding teachers, administrators, other school personnel, and children. We believe it is important to think of change in terms of how people work together as well as which people work together.[32]

The project would have two major components. The central feature, in what was referred to as the community component, was a staff of thirty school-community agents who were to be recruited from the community. They were to organize parents and facilitate their active participation in the planning and programs in the experiment. The staff of the in-school component was to be primarily concerned with teacher training, curriculum development, classroom innovation, and experimentation.

The second part, attached as a supplement to the elementary school operation grant, was for a planning grant "to provide teachers, administrators, parents, and students of Hyde Park High School with an opportunity to plan the operational phases of the high school program at the same time the elementary program is becoming operational."[33] In the high school phase of the program it was considered "imperative that the method for planning as well as a process for change come from 'inside' rather than 'outside.'"[34] Therefore, the major task at the high school level was two-

[32] "Operation Grant: Woodlawn Experimental Elementary Schools Project," a proposal for funding under Public Law 89-10, Title III, January 1968, on file at WESP, p. 5 (mimeographed).

[33] "Planning Grant for High School Component: Woodlawn Experimental Schools Project," a supplement to Operation Grant, April 1968, on file at WESP, p. 5 (mimeographed).

[34] *Ibid.*, p. 16.

fold: the development of a planning approach and the actual designing of a program. The goal of the first year was simply for the students, parents, teachers, and administrators to ascertain how they could plan together and then to determine what kinds of programs they wanted.

With the prospect of funding in July, the staff was hectically meeting deadlines and the WCB members were flooded with mimeographed revisions to approve, administrative procedures to adopt, and personnel hiring processes to initiate. The schools project had entered a new phase. The University and the public schools representatives on WCB were enthusiastic about the prospects. The TWO representatives frequently made it clear that celebration was premature and that the major problems had not yet been faced. One member of the Board put it this way at the February meeting:

I feel that the relationship is far more fragile than many on the Board have wanted to admit. This was apparent at the December Steering Committee meeting in which TWO unanimously opposed a contractual arrangement in which the WCB and thereby TWO would merely serve an advisory role. Whether the new agreement, to which we have consented, provides a more significant place for TWO remains to be seen. It will depend partly on how we interpret and use the power we do have on the WCB. TWO is not interested in participating in a project which is merely intended to "soup up" the school system as it is. TWO takes the stand that public education in Woodlawn is a tragic failure and in need of basic and radical revision. It is our opinion that the original proposal expressed this view. But now there have been a variety of qualifications. If this project begins to die the death of a thousand qualifications, we predict that TWO's support will be withdrawn. We strongly support the efforts thus far in the Developmental Project. We merely suggest that the

major difficulties and explosive issues are ahead of us and
have not been settled by the establishment of an initial
working relationship.[35]

The primary value of the contractual agreement between
the three participants was that it enabled the Woodlawn
Experimental Schools Project (WESP) to be funded. It did
little, however, to clarify the lines of authority and the
decision-making powers within the Board and project staff.
In other words, although WCB was legalized and could
administer a program, the precise authority of the Board
had yet to be tested. This ambiguity in the memorandum
of agreement led TWO to a new strategy in its relationship
with the project and also gave rise to a series of critical
issues within the project itself.

Now that the Board was legalized and TWO's role in the
project was designated, at least in general terms, the organization's influence in WESP depended upon its skill in exer-
cising leverage within the limits of the agreement. The point
of leverage was the concurrence clause. Since many people,
from Superintendent Redmond down, wanted this project
to succeed, the director would want to avoid being in a
position of telling the Chicago School Board that he could
not get concurrence on this or that matter. It would simply
reflect a weakness in the experiment and its director. And
since the University representatives were frequently in support of TWO's specific requests on the Board and since the
public schools' representatives were hesitant to be the one
to veto a particular decision, TWO had a position from
which to exert influence within the project. TWO's strategy
was revealed in three incidents during the spring of 1968,
when the project was being prepared for implementation.

1. TWO sought and secured virtual control of the community component. In the original plan the thirty commu-
nity-agents and the sixty indigenous teacher aides were to

[35] Statement to the Woodlawn Community Board, February 7,
1968, on file at TWO (typescript).

be recruited, screened, and trained by a University task force. It was also stipulated that the associate director for the community component have a Master's degree. While the TWO representatives recognized that proposals are usually written with a particular audience in mind (federal officials), they made it clear that in practice the community component belonged to TWO and that TWO would provide the personnel for it. Organizing was TWO's area of expertise. Anthony Gibbs, who had doubled as acting director of the youth project and associate director in the developmental project the previous year, became the associate director of the community component. Two former organizers for TWO, Sol Ice and Lelia McClelland, also went on the WESP staff. They in turn recruited, trained, and supervised the school-community agents.

2. In an administrative change initiated by Redmond, District 14 Superintendent Melnick was elevated to an associate general superintendent for all South Side schools, and Hyde Park High School principal Donald Blyth became District 14 superintendent. The principalship of Hyde Park was vacant. TWO and the Woodlawn Pastors' Alliance mobilized a campaign to secure a black principal: not any black principal, but a particular one, Mrs. Anna Kolheim, who had been a gadfly during the Willis regime. Melnick indicated that because of her past attitudes she was not only low on the list but was unacceptable. Brazier and Congreve, working informally, and several committees from TWO, acting directly, informed Blyth, Melnick and Redmond that if Mrs. Kolheim were not appointed, WESP would be in jeopardy. By June the central administration announced her appointment.

3. After the funding was confirmed in late May, WCB proceeded to recruit staff for the project. It was clearly anticipated that Willard Congreve who had ably negotiated the rapids of the developmental project would continue as permanent director. Through the past two years, the TWO representatives, and Brazier in particular, had learned how

205

to work with and upon Congreve. TWO had hoped his appointment would be done quietly and quickly. However, Congreve, in preparation for the project, had met with a variety of teacher, parent, and student groups and his leadership was becoming an issue. With the formalization of the project a wider public was becoming concerned about the experiment and was attending the regular WCB meetings. To Brazier's dismay Congreve had let it be known that if the community wanted a black director he would step down. This put TWO on the spot. As the representative of the community, TWO simply could not support Congreve over a black candidate even though Brazier and the TWO representatives preferred to continue with Congreve. When the issue was considered at the June 5 Board meeting, sentiment in support of a black director was expressed by several nonvoting participants. When the vote was called for, TWO's delegation abstained and Congreve was approved nine to two. Dean Campbell, chairing the meeting, interpreted TWO's abstention as lack of concurrence. TWO's spokesman argued that "we are not opposed to Mr. Congreve but we do not want to go on record in support of this motion."[36] When pressed by a caucus vote and the procedural requirement for concurrence, TWO altered its position and cast a unit vote for the appointment. This strategy served several purposes. Congreve's appointment was secured. TWO representatives kept faith with a constituency that was demanding black leadership. And most important, it was becoming clear, even though never explicitly stated, that the rest of the project staff would be black.

With the formalization of the administrative structure and the initiation of the experimental project, TWO assumed a new relationship with WESP which was based less on private negotiations and cordial collaboration and more on organized pressure, visible community support, and the more characteristic TWO tactics of confrontation. The very structure of the new administrative arrangement encour-

[36] Minutes of Woodlawn Community Board, June 5, 1968.

aged this new approach. The authority of WCB and the project staff was not clear. Furthermore, TWO was a minority even though it had veto power on the Board. In developing further influence in the project, TWO relied less on the persuasive powers of its seven Board members and more on organized and visible community support. The burden of raising issues for WCB to consider and of influencing the Chicago public schools and the University delegates was carried more by community pressure organized through TWO than by the official delegates representing TWO. This enabled TWO officially to continue cordial collaboration at the Board level and, informally, to increase pressure upon that collaborative administrative structure.

There were other factors that gave rise to this strategy. When WCB became a quasi-public agency and the project had received a grant of one and a third million dollars, community interest in the project rose rapidly. Where earlier meetings were attended almost exclusively by fifteen to twenty official Board members, meetings in the spring and summer of 1968 began to draw twenty to fifty observers. TWO, now operating in public, was increasingly conscious of the need to develop a broad base of support so that it would be apparent to the other members of the Board and to the nonresident observers that TWO not only claimed to be the spokesman of Woodlawn, but did, in fact, represent the expressed interests of the community.

An early example of TWO's increased attention to constituency support centered around the initial exploratory program at Hyde Park High. Congreve's initial contacts with some Hyde Park teachers were not favorable. The more militant black teachers became suspicious of the entire project and of TWO's motives in getting involved with the University and the Board of Education in the first place. Representatives of the Black Teachers' Caucus expressed their criticism at a private meeting with Brazier and demanded representation of their caucus on WCB. The discussions were evidently fruitful for TWO. At the July meet-

207

ing of WCB Joseph Montgomery, a Hyde Park High teacher, read the following letter from Bobby Wright, president of the Black Teachers' Caucus:

> The Black Teachers' Caucus recognizes the Reverend Arthur M. Brazier as being the leader of the Black people of Woodlawn. Therefore, any attack, no matter what form it takes, against the Rev. Brazier becomes an attack against the Black Teachers' Caucus. Therefore, no education program involving Black teachers will be successful in Woodlawn unless the Reverend Brazier is satisfied himself that it protects the best interests of the Black people of Woodlawn. Any attempt by the Board of Education or any of its agents to circumvent this program will have far reaching consequences in the Black schools all over the City of Chicago.[37]

Mr. Montgomery, a member of the Caucus who was active in the preliminary discussions, later became coordinator of the planning project at Hyde Park High School.

The public nature of WCB meetings, instead of hampering TWO's spokesman role, provided the key to the new strategy. The school-community agents organized parents not only to become involved in the schools but also to attend the regular Board meetings. Beginning in the fall of 1968 and continuing throughout the life of the project, the Board meetings were attended by between 100 and 200 people, most of whom were parents, students, and teachers of the participating schools. In one way TWO was organizing pressure upon itself. That is, TWO through its influence in the community component brought pressure to bear on TWO as an official segment of WCB. The importance of TWO control of the community component was soon apparent. It not only provided the organization with thirty paid community organizers who could, in addition to their

[37] Appendix A of minutes of Woodlawn Community Board, July 25, 1968.

208

duties in WESP, organize parent groups for membership in TWO, but it also provided the manpower by which TWO could mobilize support for increasing community participation and influence in (if not control over) the total experimental schools project. This innovative collaborative administrative structure posed problems for the WESP staff once the project was operational. The administrative authority of WESP was ambiguous in the memorandum and was never clarified. The purpose of the intervention program and the strategy for change were made clear, but the instrumentality for effecting that purpose was fragile. The major objective of the project was to create a "new social system" in the school, characterized by "a mutuality of effort" involving parents, students, and community residents as participants in the shaping of the new system. "The basic hypothesis undergirding this project," Congreve pointed out, "is that this new social system will facilitate the development of an education program involving both the school and the community which, through relevance and expertise will meet the needs of the children of Woodlawn and significantly increase their educational attainments, their self images, and their abilities to achieve success upon graduation from high school."[38] Simply put, this hypothesis was: If you want to increase academic achievement, you have first to change the system so that those most immediately affected by the educational process have power to influence that process. The problem facing the WESP staff was that it did not have the clear authority to implement a strategy of intervention which could test the hypothesis. The quasi-official status of WESP within the school system as a whole posed the basic problem. It was never made clear precisely what power the WESP staff had in relation to the three experimental schools

[38] Willard Congreve, "Report of Activities of the Woodlawn Experimental Schools District Project for the Period February 1, to June 30, 1969," memorandum to Dr. Curtis C. Melnick, June 26, 1969, on file at WESP (mimeographed).

or the Board of Education. Further, internal lines of authority within the project itself were never settled.

Given that ambiguous authority relationship, much of the time and emphasis of the project staff was devoted to testing and trying to establish its own power and/or warranty. A series of authority-testing crises and confrontations marked the history of the project from 1968 to 1970. It was through this process of crisis and confrontation more than through the variety of in-school programs that the primary objective of the experiment, the creation of a "new social system," was served. Although the goal of "mutuality of effort" was often strained in these crises, the goal of parent, student, and community involvement was facilitated by them.

Because of its ambiguous quasi-official status WESP became more like a community organization than a public agency. Without clear authority WESP developed its base of power and supplemented its vague legitimacy by relying more and more on its source of community support. TWO and the WESP staff were drawn closer together because they shared the same weak authority position in relationship to the existing school structure. In its struggle with participating schools and with the Board of Education, WESP found its major ally in the community component. Thus, while WCB had all the appearances of a cooperative public agency board, the WESP staff began to look more like an arm of TWO. The first year evaluation in June 1969, included this observation: "The WESP administrative staff, unlike the Woodlawn Community Board, uses a 'conflict, confrontation, resolution' method of facing issues and solving them."[39] Congreve reported the same point in different terms:

On occasion the project director felt powerless to deal with staff selected through The Woodlawn Organization.

[39] "Report of the Research and Evaluation Component for the Year Ending June 23, 1969," on file at WESP, p. 17 (mimeographed).

210

As a result, he occasionally found himself in the role of puppet leader, rather than a director. At times he was used as a scapegoat.[40]

The major crises of the first year revealed the basic problem of authority and the strategy of the WESP response.

The relationship between the project staff and the existing personnel in the three schools was a point of contention from the beginning. The Wadsworth teachers were divided on the issue of parent involvement. Some found the school-community agents abrasive, the director of the community component "dictatorial," and the classroom teacher aides threatening. A hard-core group of seven teachers aligned themselves against the project. Because the formal memorandum of agreement did not give the project director authority to have teachers who would not accept the program focus transferred, the WESP staff had to work around the obstructionists. Four of the teachers continued the attack and brought charges against the project directly to the Board of Education. Even though their action received no official School Board or teacher union support, it hampered the effectiveness of the in-school program. It was only after months of workshops, trial experiments, discussions, and hassles that a solid majority of the Wadsworth faculty began to accept and, in some cases, appreciate the contributions of the parents and teacher aides and the intervention of WESP itself.

The same problem emerged in a more specific form at Hyde Park High School and consumed the major part of three consecutive WCB meetings during the first fall of the project. One concrete instance of faculty resistance to student participation in planning sessions triggered the issue. The students came to the October Board meeting claiming that they had been kicked out of a planning session. Specific charges of insulting behavior were leveled at a particular white teacher, Edward Szkirpan. An investigating

[40] Congreve, "Report of Activities."

211

committee supported the student charges at the following meeting which was fortuitously chaired by Rev. Brazier. The students, at this crowded meeting of over 150 people, came with 688 signatures on a petition for the removal of Mr. Szkirpan from Hyde Park. After two hours of heated discussion and direct confrontation with Mr. Szkirpan, in which he said he would not defend himself without legal counsel, the Board unanimously approved a motion that Mrs. Kolheim give Szkirpan a leave of absence effective immediately. The Board also approved as policy

> that where it becomes evident to the Woodlawn Community Board that any member of the staff no longer cares to participate in the WESP, whether voluntarily or involuntarily, that immediate steps be taken to effect an administrative transfer.[41]

The issue became sticky. The students, with vocal committee support, full support of the WESP staff, and the votes on WCB, wanted Szkirpan out. But, Szkirpan well realized, a teacher cannot be compelled to accept an administrative transfer against his wishes without a lengthy set of hearings and investigations. Levi and Congreve were afraid of precipitating a confrontation with the teachers' union similar to the chaotic Ocean Hill-Brownsville struggle in New York. Szkirpan simply could not be removed by WCB vote. The Board did not have this authority. Szkirpan stayed and the tension increased. The following meeting Brazier urged that the Board test its authority and recommend, under powers stipulated by the memorandum of agreement, an administrative transfer. After caucus, the public schools delegation vetoed this motion apparently in fear of the precedent it would establish, if successful. A weaker, but eventually effective, motion to "use any means or remedy available" was approved. The case was quickly settled "out of court." Szkirpan was gone and WCB was never informed how it happened. In any case, a show-down

[41] Minutes of the Woodlawn Community Board, October 24, 1968.

with the union, on the one hand, and the Board of Education, on the other, was avoided and the student-community demand was satisfied.

But the basic issue remained. Many teachers felt that they were being judged and accused by nonprofessionals. Staff members and many of the parents felt that some of the teachers were trying to sabotage the project. After one teacher expressed opposition to the project, saying that she could not "swallow the philosophy," Brazier, acting as chairman, responded, "We don't expect teachers to swallow anything whole. But we do expect teachers to stop throwing road and body blocks into this project. There is a lot of footdragging that is slowing down this joint effort."[42]

The structural problem of the WESP administration was that it had no authority over its classroom staff. In fact, participation in the project was, in practice, optional. The director, in a bi-monthly report to WCB and the Board of Education, stressed the implications of this problem:

Most people (teachers and administrators of the schools) see two agencies—the usual Chicago Public Schools, and the Woodlawn Experimental Schools Project. If they choose to respond to WESP, they may; but if they choose not to respond to WESP, they feel fully protected within the Chicago Public Schools structure. . . .

Thus, the ambiguity is taking its toll. Everyone knows that decisions made with the project staff are not binding. Even when teachers and principals are involved in the decisions, when the going gets tough in implementing these decisions, the regular staff can by-pass the project director and the Woodlawn Community Board and deal directly with those who are officially their supervisors.[43]

It was problematic whether the experimental schools district was a district at all.

[42] *Ibid.*
[43] "Bi-Monthly Report of the Project Director," Woodlawn Community Board Report 2-4-69, February 13, 1969, on file at WESP, p. 4.

The relationship between WESP and the centralized downtown schools bureaucracy was even more problematic. The Title III resources were channelled through the regular Board of Education offices. WESP was clearly a low priority item with the middle management level downtown. Whether this was a deliberate strategy of harassment or the regular inefficiency of an oversized and overorganized army of clerks is not certain. However, at every WCB meeting the same issue arose. Supplies were delayed for months. The staff operated without desks and typewriters. Salaries were held up. Job descriptions were reclassified and salary schedules altered to fit preexisting categories (i.e., the Board of Education had never hired a community organizer). Continued inability to communicate with the central administration and the regular failure to meet the payroll was demoralizing, especially to the indigenous community agents.

Furthermore, the special district, although designated as an experimental program, was granted no exception from uniform system-wide policy regarding teacher-pupil ratios, teacher qualifications, and assignments. The project simply had no weight downtown. The evaluators of the first year observed that "Higher levels of the Board of Education can ignore if they wish the requests of the WESP staff, since the WESP authority structure is only partly—and not authoritatively—within the Board of Education structure."[44] As it turned out, action on the part of the centralized office was secured less by the appeal of the project director than by the organized pressure of the growing community component. A January salary tie-up was overcome only after the teacher-aides and school-community agents demonstrated at the Board of Education. Since the authority of WESP was never clearly established in the line and staff processes of the Chicago public schools, the WESP staff had to rely more on the methods characteristic of TWO than on the usual line and staff channels of a public agency.

[44] "Report of Research and Evaluation," p. 17.

214

The physical situation at Hyde Park High School became the occasion for an extended controversy between the Woodlawn community and the Board of Education. For two years the educational program at Hyde Park had been disrupted by a remodeling program. Ushered in with high hopes, the renovation project soon became a symbol of the insensitivity and inefficiency of the central bureaucracy. The history of the renovation program dates back to the 1965 decision to build a new school in nearby Kenwood. As a consolation, Hyde Park was to have major rehabilitation through what was termed a unique program, "new life for old schools." The $2 million renovation was to be staggered and funded through yearly allocations from the regular maintenance budget of the Board of Education. For three years workmen were in the building, classes were juggled and, at various times, the gym, library, and auditorium were closed down. The principal was expected to cope with the internal problems and coordinate the process. For the staff and students the situation became intolerable. Schedule deadlines were not kept, tension between white workmen and black students was increasing, and the morale within the school was deteriorating. The classroom teacher had no voice in the design of the facilities they were to use. The new principal, Mrs. Kolheim, had no access to the top where the decisions affecting her school were made. Beyond this, the $2 million renovation had already run to $6 million and estimates for completion were over $9 million, the approximate cost of the two new high schools which had recently been completed in the neighboring communities of Kenwood and South Shore.

Pressure from students and teachers at Hyde Park was mounting. Frustrated both over the disruption caused in the school and her inability to get any satisfaction through regular channels, Mrs. Kolheim, supported by students and faculty, brought the matter to the Woodlawn Community Board. The Board investigated and found the situation critical. Congreve recommended that

215

> In keeping with the Memorandum of Agreement, the Woodlawn Community Board requests that the processes of developing working drawings, writing specifications, letting contracts, and consummating purchases, which up to this time have been held exclusively within the purview of the Central Office Staff, be placed in control of a community contractor.[45]

WCB argued that since the modernization process at Hyde Park High was inextricably bound with WESP and directly affected the success of the experimental project, and since the central office seemed unable to do an adequate job, all further developments in the modernization process should be under the supervision of staff secured by and responsible to WCB.

The Board called a special meeting at which Dr. Edwin Lederer, Associate Superintendent for Operation Services, the top man responsible for the Hyde Park modernization, was invited to respond to the residents' complaints and the Board's request. Over 150 parents and students attended. For twenty minutes Dr. Lederer talked about how the School Board's only concern was for the students, teachers, and parents of Hyde Park High, and how difficult things were all over, and how money was not available to speed up the project, and how if we are to move forward together we all need patience and cooperation. Then he turned to the architect and project coordinator who set up maps and diagrams and talked about what had been done, what was planned, and why it was all so difficult. The parents and students finally exploded with a volley of heated observations:

> Conditions at Hyde Park are ridiculous. We want something more than pictures on the wall at this meeting.

[45] "Modernization of Hyde Park High School," Woodlawn Community Board Report 1-69-1, January 9, 1969, on file at WESP, p. 4 (mimeographed).

There are rats, roaches . . . white workmen insulting black girl students.

We want to know when the school will be finished.

You need to resign if you can't get the job done.

You can do it for the white schools, but not for the black schools.

Haven't you ever taken a look at the atrocities being done to the black students at Hyde Park High School?[46]

After an extended shouting match most of the audience, on cue from the director of the community component, walked out of the meeting. Somewhat stunned, Dr. Lederer then heard the recommendation from the Board.

The way was then clear for Mrs. Kolheim, Rev. Brazier, and Julian Levi to intervene with top level staff of the Board of Education. An agreement was reached in which Andrew Heard of the Black Architects Collaborative was hired by WESP as a professional link between the project and the central office.

Through the efforts of Mr. Heard and TWO, black subcontractors secured bids, and trainees from the TWO job-training programs were employed in construction. In addition, Heard, working in close cooperation with the Hyde Park High staff, initiated major changes in the design of the final phase of renovation. Even though many of the problems of inconvenience, delay, and lack of funds persisted in the renovation program, the frustration and tension were reduced.

WESP was led into successive confrontations with various levels of the existing school system in order to establish its own position *vis-à-vis* the regular authority structure. Having only limited support from the Board of Education and mixed participation from the existing school staffs, the project was drawn closer to the community for its own survival. TWO's strategy, exercised through its control of

[46] Minutes of Woodlawn Community Board, January 30, 1969.

the community component, its influence on WESP staff appointments, and its direct participation on WCB, was to facilitate the movement in this direction. There were several clear indications of this movement toward increased community involvement and influence in WESP.

The activities of the school-community organizers had a decisive impact upon the project. The twenty-four community residents organized twenty parent councils with more than 500 active participants. These parents became both the base of support for the project in its struggles with the school system and also a source of criticism of the project.

Largely because of the organizing activities of the resident community organizers, the regular WCB meetings soon became crowded, sometimes chaotic, and clearly community-oriented. These meetings were the largest community meetings in Woodlawn (with the exception of the more irregular gatherings of the Black P Stone Nation), much larger than the Model Cities, Urban Progress Center and other agency-spawned community meetings and larger even than TWO delegates meetings. In fact, attendance at WCB, the quasi-official board for three schools, was comparable to the citizen attendance at the meetings of the Chicago School Board. In the Woodlawn Board, unlike the Chicago School Board, audience participation became a factor in the meetings. It was also a factor in TWO's strategy. When between one and two hundred parents, students, and residents began to attend, the Board occasionally found it difficult to conduct business. The chairman was often on the spot. If he recognized non-Board members, the meetings could get out of hand. If he refused to recognize non-Board members, the parents would interrupt anyway claiming that this was a community board and that they should be heard. TWO, through Brazier, was able to offer a solution. While, on the one hand, Brazier as a Board leader and TWO President would state from the chair that "We have to have orderly meetings," TWO organizers encouraged vocal parent involvement and, on at least one occasion, disruption.

218

Brazier could then say to the Board, "Something clearly has to be done to preserve the effectiveness of the Board." Soon Brazier offered a proposal. At the December 1968, meeting he introduced his recommendation with these remarks:

Now each of the three components has a veto and each has seven members on the Board. Often it is extremely difficult for parents to understand the significance of the veto. It looks to them like the community is outnumbered 14-7. And indeed we are, in the discussions of the Board. People in the community would feel that their participation was much more important if arrangements regarding numbers on the Board were revised so that the community would have a majority of Board members.[47]

What he did not mention, but was a definite factor limiting the credibility of the Board in Woodlawn, was that the racial make-up of the Board was thirteen white and eight black.

Brazier proposed that the University and schools members drop from seven to five each and that TWO membership increase from seven to eleven. This opened up a discussion about the constituency of the Board that continued through the winter. Students, teachers, and the teachers' union all wanted membership. Arguments were presented that the University should not be involved at all and that whites should not be members. In the spring the reconstitution of the Board was agreed upon. The final outcome was that the University reduced its membership to four (which included two black faculty), TWO increased to ten, and the Chicago public schools included two students and four teachers. Twelve of the new 21-member Board lived in Woodlawn and all but three on the Board were black.

In the spring of 1969 the Board changed the time and place of meetings from late afternoons on the edge of the University campus to evenings at a church in the center of East Woodlawn. This both facilitated and symbolized the

[47] Minutes of Woodlawn Community Board, December 5, 1968.

movement toward increased community involvement and influence.

A more significant change was the appointment of a new project director. Congreve had done an outstanding job and was a central factor in bridging the many components and constituencies in the initial year. If he was to be judged by how he facilitated the transition from a University-initiated proposal to a community-led operational project, he would be rated high, at least by TWO leaders. However, it was apparent to Brazier as well as Congreve, that he had served his basic purpose in establishing the project. The day after the Board of Education approved the second year continuation grant ($1,636,256), Congreve announced his resignation to the Board. TWO was not unprepared for this occasion. Following Congreve's announcement Brazier spoke:

> On behalf of TWO and the Community Component, I want to say that we feel Dr. Congreve has done a tremendous job under great handicaps in bringing the project to its present position. Many of us knew that at some point in time he would step down. As a result, TWO was constantly in search for someone to take his place if and when he made such a decision. . . . We have found a person we fully recommend. She has high intellectual capacity. Her integrity as it relates to the education of black people cannot be questioned. In some circles she may be controversial. I recommend to the Woodlawn Community Board the name of Mrs. Barbara Sizemore as Project Director. This suggestion is the result of a unanimous vote of the monthly TWO delegates meeting, and we hope this Board and the Board of Education will also appoint her as Project Director.[48]

Mrs. Sizemore, formerly a principal at a Chicago high school, a doctoral candidate at the University of Chicago, writing a dissertation on community control in education, a very outspoken critic of the Chicago public schools sys-

[48] Minutes of Woodlawn Community Board, April 10, 1969.

tem, had been a consultant and friend of TWO for several years. There was no doubt that she was the community's choice for project director. There was, however, some doubt that she would receive Board of Education approval. In June, after the Woodlawn Community Board unanimously recommended Mrs. Sizemore, Melnick, chairman of the personnel committee, was told by several of the more vocal parents to tell the Board of Education that the Woodlawn community will not accept anyone other than Mrs. Sizemore. The School Board approved Mrs. Sizemore by a split vote, six to three.

During the second year of the project, it was clear that WCB and WESP belonged to the community. TWO had located and secured a popular director. The community presence dominated the Board meetings. But the basic problem of authority remained. While it might be said that the community controlled WESP, it was still problematic as to what, if anything, WESP controlled. At her first Board meeting Mrs. Sizemore identified several aspects of this basic problem that were still unresolved:

> When I undertook this task I was advised that the WESP would be a failure if the achievement scores of the students of WESP did not improve significantly. I was also advised that the teachers should not be antagonized. This posture seems somewhat inconsistent if one assumes that teachers have something to do with raising the achievement scores. . . . This shortsighted though important goal statement of higher achievement scores disregards the stated objectives of our proposed programs which emanate from the needs of highest priority—to restructure the school as a social system in terms of its community through mutuality of effort. . . .[49]

After reaffirming the original project goals and strategy of improving educational achievement through structural

[49] Barbara Sizemore, "Director's Report to Woodlawn Community Board," July 24, 1969, on file at WESP, p. 2 (mimeographed).

changes in the processes of decision making and control, Mrs. Sizemore identified two areas which continued to limit the project: lack of support from the Board of Education and lack of control over in-school staff. The specific form of these two problems centered on the emerging plans for Model Cities in Woodlawn and the procedures for teacher evaluation. Mrs. Sizemore recommended that "teachers and principal evaluations should be the direct responsibility of the Director of WESP" and that "Model Cities educational programs for Woodlawn be channelled through the Woodlawn Community Board."[50]

The WESP conflict with Model Cities was part of a larger controversy which is dealt with in the following chapter. The issue in WESP centered around the three-way relationship between Model Cities, the Chicago Board of Education and WESP. When the Woodlawn schools experiment was funded under Title III, it was the major component of what the Chicago Board of Education called "The Chicago Comprehensive Project." This project was sold to the U.S. Office of Education partly on the grounds that it would dovetail with the federal Model Cities program. Julian Levi had, early in the planning stages, reported to WCB that "it is now accepted procedure in Washington that priority in processing and funding will be given to all programs located in Model Cities areas."[51] Superintendent Redmond's summary of the Chicago Comprehensive Project, issued in May 1968, made use of the Model Cities Administration's concern for concentration and coordination of resources. The Comprehensive Project summary states:

> There are four geographical areas in Chicago which can be rightfully labeled inner-city hard core and have been identified as target areas for the Chicago Model Cities Program to which the Chicago Comprehensive Project

50 *Ibid.*
51 Minutes of the Woodlawn Community Board, January 3, 1968.

relates. These are: Woodlawn, Lawndale, Uptown, and Grand Crossing Boulevard. The Board of Education would be pleased if sufficient funds were available and plans were completed to initiate concentrated programs in each of these areas immediately. At the moment, however, such funds are not available.

We have chosen to begin our thrust in Woodlawn, where an Experimental District has already been created and the University of Chicago and The Woodlawn Organization are ready to begin a collective venture with the Chicago Public Schools. By beginning in Woodlawn, Chicago does not relinquish responsibility for or intentions of establishing programs in the other three model city areas. We intend to do this as soon as possible. *We do expect, however, that our experience in the Woodlawn Project will guide us and accelerate our efforts in the reconstruction of the other areas.*[52]

The Chicago Board of Education had led the federal government to believe that WESP would be a prototype for the educational component of Model Cities efforts. Certainly the capacity to elicit citizen participation, to develop a collaborative administrative structure, and to initiate innovative and effective programs qualified WESP to be the "model" for the Model Cities implementation. However, by the time Chicago's Model Cities program was funded for $38 million in the spring of 1969, the Board of Education had apparently decided to use part of its share of $11 million to develop a competitive "experimental" program in Woodlawn. The central Model Cities agency in Chicago developed a standard plan for all four Model Cities areas without differentiating activities in each area to relate to existing programs and organizations. The fact that in Wood-

[52] James F. Redmond, "Chicago Comprehensive Project, Title III, Elementary and Secondary Education Act," May 22, 1969, on file at WESP, p. 1 (mimeographed), italics added.

lawn a federally funded Board of Education-endorsed project had already made significant progress was ignored by Model Cities planners.

The issue came to a head when District Superintendent Donald Blyth, a member of WCB and also a participant in Model Cities planning for the city, announced the specifics of Model Cities at the first WCB meeting under Mrs. Sizemore's directorship. Blyth's report triggered a heated discussion and unanimous support for Mrs. Sizemore's recommendation that all Model Cities programs for Woodlawn be channelled through WCB. Brazier and several other TWO representatives argued that the Model Cities program was being used by those who wanted to divide the community and to undermine WESP. Julian Levi, in a passionate speech reminiscent of, but in sharp contrast to, a 1961 exchange between him and TWO, said "I don't believe in citizen participation. I believe in community control." He went on to argue that the U.S. Office of Education has too much interest in Woodlawn to allow it to be subverted by this "divisive and extraordinarily unfortunate program in Model Cities."[53] Upon Levi's recommendation, Brazier, Sizemore, Campbell, and Melnick were directed to meet with Redmond to work out an agreement and develop the mechanism whereby WCB would become responsible for Model Cities education efforts in Woodlawn. The recommendation, presented in writing to Redmond, was that in order to eliminate waste and competition the "co-plus" school (Tesla School) be included in the experimental district, and that WCB be the citizen-participation structure for decision making in the Model Cities education program for Woodlawn. Redmond replied to the special WCB committee on August 19 saying that a meeting would not be productive "because certain rights and responsibilities have been assigned by the U.S. Department of Housing and Urban Development to the Model Cities Program in the

[53] Levi to Woodlawn Community Board, July 24, 1969.

Office of the Mayor and through it, to the local Model Cities Council."[54] Any ideas WESP has for Model Cities, Redmond suggested, should be directed to Irwin France, the mayor's deputy assistant for Model Cities. WCB regarded this reply as unacceptable on the grounds that the Board of Education and not the mayor's office was responsible for WESP, its boundaries and responsibilities, and that the Board of Education had not transferred to the mayor's office decision making for the educational program in Woodlawn.[55] Redmond chose neither to exercise the authority stipulated in the memorandum of agreement nor to continue in the direction indicated in the Chicago Comprehensive Project proposal.

The educational component of Model Cities in Woodlawn was not brought under WESP. Conflict continued on the local level. At the September WCB meeting, several parents who were active in the WESP parent councils charged that they were excluded from participation in the Model Cities parent group at the Tesla co-plus school and that meetings were controlled by school employees. The Model Cities parent chairman called the TWO parents "spies." Brazier, chairing the meeting, observed that this outburst of Woodlawn parents attacking each other was "an example of what has been designed by the power structure of the City."[56]

WESP and Model Cities continued on separate paths. It was no consolation to WESP staff and WCB that the Model Cities school effort in its first year failed to develop either significant citizen participation or an effective program and, therefore, provided no experimental alternative. What was lamentable was, on the one hand, that the Model Cities resources were not available to the collaborative structure

[54] Minutes of Woodlawn Community Board Model Cities Committee, September 11, 1969.

[55] Minutes of Woodlawn Community Board Model Cities Committee, September 18, 1969.

[56] Brazier to Woodlawn Community Board, September 11, 1969.

which already had community support and was funded with the understanding that it would become the channel for Model Cities schools planning; and, on the other hand, that the Board of Education had failed to support WESP at this critical moment. It was evident not only that the Woodlawn Experimental Schools Project was peripheral to the major interests of the Board of Education, but also that the Board was supporting programs in Woodlawn that worked at cross purposes with WESP. During the first year of WESP it was possible to attribute the difficulties with the central office to the inefficiency of middle-level bureaucrats. Now it became apparent that the Board of Education at the very top level regarded WESP as neither a high priority program in itself nor a model for future Board of Education experiments.

Mrs. Sizemore indicated in her initial report that if the Experimental Schools Project was to succeed, the director must have a measure of control, at least comparable to that of a district superintendent, over the principals and teachers of the experimental district. The project staff had argued that since WESP was a special program, the collaborative administration should be given special consideration in recruiting and securing teachers for the three schools and, furthermore, that the responsibility for teacher evaluations should likewise be a collaborative task so that the classroom teacher could be evaluated in terms of the project goals. In pursuing these ends WESP found a strong adversary in Mrs. Edna Hickey, central office Director of Personnel.

Mrs. Hickey defended her "rules" on teacher assignments, according to Mrs. Sizemore, on the grounds that they were necessary to get teachers to work in ghetto schools. WCB argued that the project did not want teachers who came only to avoid financial penalty. Furthermore, the project staff had indicated that the experimental district found no problem in attracting teachers. The only problem was in getting them through Mrs. Hickey's rules.

The centralized control of teacher assignments could not

be overcome. The Board of Education faced a variety of pressures at this point. The teachers' union wanted the seniority system maintained whereby increased freedom of choice in placement accompanied longevity. In this situation Mrs. Hickey had the most control over the least experienced. WESP wanted to intervene in the assignment process so that it could secure the faculty it wanted. This would be a faculty that was almost completely black and committed to the project. The federal government, which poured an increasing amount of funds into the Chicago system, was demanding action on a plan for integration, particularly in public school staffing. Any integration plan would necessitate increased centralized control of personnel, a move that was opposed both by the union, because it limited their freedom of choice, and by WESP, because it limited their freedom of recruitment. Although there were a variety of ways the WESP staff could seek and recruit teachers, they would have to do so within the restrictive limits of Mrs. Hickey's "rules." It is ironic that the argument of integration, which for years had fallen on deaf ears, would now become the Board of Education's major weapon in maintaining centralized control and the Board's source of justification for limiting the emerging aspirations of the black community as expressed in WESP.

Mrs. Sizemore made it clear in assuming the directorship that a revision of the process of teacher and principal evaluation was of top priority. If WESP was to succeed, teachers would have to be evaluated in terms of the goals of the project and under procedures established collaboratively by participants in the project. It was Mrs. Sizemore's assessment "that effective use of the teacher evaluation procedure and due process would eliminate much of the poor teaching in the East Woodlawn schools."[57]

Efforts to assume responsibility in teacher evaluation brought Mrs. Sizemore and the WESP administrative staff into direct conflict with the Hyde Park High School princi-

[57] Sizemore, "Director's Report."

227

pal, Mrs. Kolheim. Mrs. Kolheim was caught between her immediate superiors in the school system, her teachers, and WESP. Neither the WESP staff nor the teachers liked the existing teacher evaluation process which was handled exclusively by the principals. For the teachers, the ratings influenced access to summer employment as well as promotion. WCB agreed that a new process of evaluation must be developed. Upon recommendation by Mrs. Sizemore and with the obvious support of the teachers, WCB voted in April 1970, to give all Hyde Park teachers a "superior" teacher efficiency rating. The Board directed Mrs. Kolheim to submit such ratings to the central office. In this move the Board sought not only to express their confidence in the existing high school faculty but also to challenge the existing centralized process of evaluation. The move backfired. Mrs. Hickey voided the "superior" ratings and insisted that the building principal and not WESP was responsible for rating teachers. The controversy was drawn. At the May 14 WCB meeting the usual crowd of over 100 parents was supplemented by more than thirty Hyde Park High School teachers who were using this opportunity to express a variety of grievances against their principal.

Mrs. Kolheim's position was clear. If the WESP staff or WCB wanted to make the evaluations, then the staff or Board should sign them and submit them. But she could not and would not accept the responsibility for evaluations she was not asked to make. WCB was on the spot. They could not force Mrs. Kolheim to sign their blanket "superior" ratings for all teachers. They could not submit them directly to Mrs. Hickey. Without evaluations many teachers could not secure summer employment. Julian Levi recommended that the Board reconsider its April directive. Now the teachers became vocal. Their argument was also simple. Is WCB bona fide or not?

> As teachers we can't afford to straddle the fence. What we want to know is this: do we follow the dictates of the Board of Education or do we follow the WCB? If the

WCB stands its ground on evaluations we will support the community Board and put our summer jobs on the line. If the WCB reverses its position we will know that the experimental project is merely a game and we will crawl back in line with the Board of Education policies.[58]

WCB was not merely caught in a struggle between Mrs. Kolheim and her teachers, a conflict which WESP had helped stimulate. The Board was caught with a decision it could not implement. The Board either had to admit its weakness in front of the teachers and parents or continue on a course which would lead to a more damaging defeat later. The Board was immobilized. A motion to reconsider the April directive passed nine to eight and then, on recount, was defeated ten to six. Finally, to avoid further embarrassment, the Board adjourned to a closed session where it was determined that two sets of evaluations would be submitted, one by WESP and one by Mrs. Kolheim. The compromise was a face-saving gesture. Edna Hickey and the standard evaluative procedures prevailed.

The continuing uncertainty about WESP's authority in the three participating schools and within the Board of Education structure contributed to internal dissension among various participants. The uneasy relationship between Mrs. Kolheim and Mrs. Sizemore continued. The dispute between Mrs. Kolheim and the teachers erupted in a teacher boycott which closed down the school for several days in June 1970. When a settlement was reached, the teachers, who found they still had to deal with the central office and not with WESP to negotiate grievances, became resistant to the in-school activities of the parent organizers and the WESP staff.

The "Woodlawnization" of WESP in the second year of the project did not lead to community control. Although TWO became increasingly influential within WESP, the in-

[58] Spokesman for Hyde Park teachers to Woodlawn Community Board, May 14, 1970.

fluence of WESP within the Chicago public schools did not increase. In fact, if anything it decreased. In 1968-69 the white leaders of the collaboration, Congreve, Levi, Campbell, Melnick, Perlin, and Blyth could intervene with the Board of Education as well as with the state and federal agencies to secure special consideration. It mattered little that these men had no enthusiastic support from the community. When, in 1969-70, the project developed a local base of support, secured a black director, restructured WCB, and became more responsive to the community, the problematic character of the authority relationship negotiated in the memorandum of agreement became more apparent. Without the authority to initiate change and restructure relationship within the school system, WESP became more like a community organization and less like a city agency, more the educational division of TWO and less the Board of Education's demonstration project. The greater influence of the community component within WESP, the more WESP appeared to be an abandoned child of the Board of Education.

The results of WESP after two years were mixed and the future uncertain. There were many impressive accomplishments both in the classroom and in the community. The most favorable in-school results were seen at Wadsworth Elementary School. A reading readiness program involving teacher aides, individualized instruction, flexible curricula and scheduling, new techniques, in-service training for teachers and parents, and cooperative planning contributed to a rise in academic achievement. The director's report of the results of the Metropolitan (Reading) Readiness Test was used as evidence in one area (see Table 2). The reduction of teacher attrition and the increased support of the project by the teachers was also encouraging.

It was in the community component that the impact of the project was most visible. Prior to WESP there was no effective channel for parent or community participation in the schools. Parents were discouraged, sometimes even prevented, from visiting schools. PTA's, where they existed,

TABLE 2. COMPARISON OF READING READINESS
(in percentages)

	READY TO READ	PROBABLY READY	NOT READY
Wadsworth, 1964-65	29	34	36
Wadsworth, 1968-69	62	34	4
Chicago, 1968-69 (City-wide)	52	35	13

SOURCE: Peter Negronida, "Pupils Show Gains in Woodlawn Tests," *Chicago Tribune,* February 25, 1970, p. 10.

were seen as puppet groups. School buildings were locked up at 4:30 p.m. every day. In the first two years of WESP, thirty-five parent councils were formed. Parents were hired as organizers and teacher aides. Others volunteered service for a variety of in-school functions. Through the community education program Wadsworth was open for adult courses and special programs almost every evening. The parents and community residents had access to the schools, the teachers, the WESP staff, and, most clearly, to the governing Board of the project. The old lament of school administrators and teachers that parents in neighborhoods like Woodlawn are not interested in their children's education and their own further education and will not participate in the schooling process is demonstrably false. WESP provided an atmosphere of enthusiasm and hope.

The problem of authority, however, continued to limit the project. Progress toward the expressed goal of revising and restructuring the roles, rules, and relationships of the educational enterprise was hampered by the status of WESP in the Chicago school system structure.

The increased community control of WESP did not lead to WESP control of the schools within the project. The project was granted freedom within limits. This included the freedom to develop supplemental programs, spend supplementary funds, elicit teacher and principal cooperation, and include parents, students and residents in planning and car-

231

rying out all these supplementary activities. The core of the school system and the hierarchical structure of authority in that system was not altered. WESP did from time to time test its leverage within the basic structure of the school system, but it always avoided, bypassed, or backed away from head-on conflict over such basic issues as union negotiations, teacher certification and assignment, staffing patterns, Edna Hickey "rules," and Model Cities. The enabling memorandum of agreement provided leverage for TWO to shape WESP, but it provided far less leverage for WESP to restructure the school system. In contrast with the early vision and rhetoric of overhauling the system and restructuring relationships, TWO and WESP had to settle for supplementary programs and increased parent involvement.

During the final year of the project, Mrs. Sizemore became more vocal in her advocacy of community control. Under her leadership, the development of the CAPTS model involving the community, administration, parents, teachers, and students in proposing, implementing, and evaluating program and curriculum generated enthusiasm. The parent councils were beginning to mobilize support for a proposal to continue the experiment beyond the termination of federal funding in June 1971, and to expand the size of the district and increase the autonomy of the Woodlawn Community Board and WESP. The proposal, submitted to the Chicago Board of Education in January 1971, called for the creation of School District 28 to include the twelve Woodlawn schools with a student population of 10,600. Central to the proposal was the designation of the Woodlawn Community Board as the authoritative governing board for the new district with clear powers to hire and fire teachers and to develop curriculum and shape programs. Within Woodlawn support for District 28 was growing. There was, however, little evidence that the Board of Education, facing serious financial problems and wary of the Woodlawn experiment, would either grant greater autonomy to WCB or provide major financial resources ($800,000 of additional funds was requested) for the project. The signs pointed the other way. Growing tensions and controversies within WESP, between the community component and the administrative staff, between teachers and parents, between Mrs. Kolheim and Mrs. Sizemore—tensions borne partly out of frustration with WESP's limited role—were used by the Chicago Board of Education as evidence that the experiment did not warrant continuation.

In April 1971, while the community hearings in support of District 28 were eliciting community support and while the Board of Education was still, at least officially, considering the proposal, the internal tension in the project erupted into open controversy. The ongoing conflict between WESP director Mrs. Sizemore and Hyde Park High School principal Mrs. Kolheim escalated, resulting in charges and counter-charges and finally the boycotting and closing of Hyde Park High School. The controversy was hopelessly complicated by a variety of factors: tensions within WESP itself, teachers' anxiety about parent interference, union rights, evaluation procedures, and the lack of clear lines of authority within the project. A minority group of teachers siding with Mrs. Sizemore triggered massive student support in boycotting classes and demanding the resignation of Mrs. Kolheim. Many parents, disturbed with the militant teachers, supported Mrs. Kolheim. TWO, a supporter of both women, tried to steer a middle course, but with little success. Area Superintendent Melnick's intervention, removing Mrs. Sizemore from jurisdiction over the one high school in the special district and granting Mrs. Kolheim a leave of absence, solved the immediate crisis but made the continuation, to say nothing of the expansion, of WESP doubtful.

Recognizing that both Mrs. Sizemore and WESP would not be around in the fall, the parent councils, the Community Board, and TWO, in a final demonstration of community influence, secured the return of Mrs. Kolheim to Hyde Park High. WESP was finished. This internal controversy was not the cause of WESP's demise. It was rather the final agony of a community control project whose termination was apparent.

There are contrasts between the Youth Project and the Schools Project, particularly in TWO's strategy. The final outcomes of the two projects were not, however, dissimilar. In the Youth Project, TWO secured funding directly from Washington and worked outside of, and often at odds with, the existing youth-serving and youth-controlling agencies. In the Schools Project, TWO's strategy was to change the school system from within by cooperating with the Board of Education. This strategy was, of course, influenced in large part by a realistic assessment of funding possibilities. The conduit for Title III funds had to be the Chicago Board of Education. Within this limitation TWO's influence over the development of the project was impressive. After years of ineffectiveness in dealing with the public schools, TWO parlayed its resistance to a University Research and Development Center into a major community-oriented project; negotiated an agreement with the Chicago Board of Education in which a community organization was granted a limited but still unprecedented role in administering a schools program; and through control of the community component of the project expanded its influence on the Woodlawn Community Board and the WESP staff.

In spite of these accomplishments WESP was severely limited by a variety of constraints imposed by the prevailing authority structure of the school system. These limitations had the same effect on the Schools Project, over a longer period of time, that the more swift counterresponse of the police-politician-press complex had upon the Youth Project. That is, the intent to demonstrate possibilities of community control was subverted. In different ways the Youth Project and WESP suffered the same fate. Both programs were experiments in community control. Both were popularly supported. Neither project had the authority to circumvent or overcome the limitations placed upon it. Both were undercut by the institutions they were trying to change.

234

CHAPTER V

The Limits of Control:
TWO and Model Cities

THE federal government began in the 1960s to provide substantial resources to deal with mounting urban problems. Lyndon Johnson's landslide victory in 1964 seemed to provide him with a mandate to solve domestic problems, even though the national budget was beginning to be drained by the Vietnam war. The Model Cities program emerged as the new federal response to urban decay. At least the designers argued that it was new. Developed primarily under the leadership of MIT professor Robert Wood, then Undersecretary of Housing and Urban Development, the Model Cities concept, like many other programs, grew out of a sense of failure with past government programs. It was to incorporate a new strategy of initiating and coordinating social change. Woodlawn provided a good case. The federal government had been pouring a considerable amount of money into Woodlawn, some through TWO projects, but most through city agencies—the Youth Project (OEO), the job-training programs (Department of Labor), WESP (Office of Education), the Urban Progress Center, the Woodlawn Mental Health Center, Vista, Job Corps, Title I (ESEA) Projects in the public schools, urban renewal projects, and many more. There was no pattern, no coordination, no overall strategy in the use of federal funds. Past programs tended to be faddish, political, fragmented, and overlapping. The Model Cities concept was going to correct this.

Many past programs, originally designed to coordinate the previous efforts, soon became competing agencies themselves with fullblown administrative bureaucracies and particular interests to protect. The result had been a pro-

235

liferation of agencies, a fragmentation of authority, and a jurisdictional jungle. There would be no Model Cities bureaucracy. Rather than add a new structure Model Cities would try to coordinate the existing federal, state, city, public, and private programs and resources in a given target area.

Past programs had been based, as Peter Marris and Martin Rein pointed out, on a "circular" theory of poverty:

> The theory allows for a very flexible strategy, since it sets no order of priority. If the causes of poverty are circular, then intervention at any point may be effective, and the more the better. At the same time, neglect of any one aspect of the problem is excused by the indirect influence upon it of action elsewhere.[1]

This meant that each agency could justify itself in terms of its point of intersection in the poverty cycle and could interpret the whole problem from its vantage point. Model Cities was based on an understanding of the interdependence of various aspects of poverty. It was not sufficient merely to have a variety of fragmented interventions. Thus, the Model Cities program guide stated, "The program for action at the local level should encompass all of the deep rooted social and environmental problems of a neighborhood."[2] In contrast to its predecessors, the urban renewal legislation of the 1950s, the President's Commission on Juvenile Delinquency in 1961, and the Poverty Program in 1964, Model Cities was supposed to be comprehensive.

Past programs, once established and fully bureaucratized, tended to become conservative—protecting and expanding

---

[1] Peter Marris and Martin Rein, *Dilemmas of Social Reform* (New York: Atherton Press, 1967), p. 39.

[2] U.S., Department of Housing and Urban Development, Model Cities Administration, *Program Guide: Model Neighborhoods in Demonstration Cities*, HUD PG-47, December 1967 (Washington, D.C.: Government Printing Office, 1968), p. 3.

236

their own enterprise. In Model Cities the new magic word was "innovative." Priority was to be given to imaginative and innovative proposals. "Cities should look upon this program as an opportunity to experiment."[3]

Another failing charged against past federal programs was that the resources were often spread too thin to have a telling impact on any one community. Model Cities was going to concentrate sizeable resources in limited areas. No more than 10 percent of the population of the larger cities could be included as Model Cities target areas. And the original idea was that the federal government would limit the new effort to ten or twelve cities.

The new words were "comprehensive," "coordinated," "innovative," and "concentrated." The Demonstration Cities and Metropolitan Development Act of 1966, termed Model Cities because some congressmen thought the term "demonstration" carried ambiguous overtones, was heralded by the President as a program "to build not just housing units, but neighborhoods."[4] If it had come at a later time its slogan might have been, "Model Cities puts it all together."

With this general goal of redirecting and coordinating the hodge-podge of existing programs, Model Cities faced what Marris and Rein call the dilemma of social reform: in our society no one has the authority to coordinate. In guarding against the abuse of power we have diffused and fragmented authority so that no level of government has a clear right to coordinate all levels and no center has the power to coordinate other centers. The federal government cannot take over and run the cities. Less formal means must be found to coordinate social reform. In the Model Cities program the federal government would have to rely on the usual form of inducement—money. HUD, for example, could not force cities to do a better job but it could make it profitable for cities that cooperated. The federal government, according to the grand design of Model Cities, would

---

[3] *Ibid.*, p. 4.   [4] *Ibid.*, frontispiece.

supply much needed money to cities that developed plans that met the federal guidelines and used the new words. Model Cities was enthusiastically received. With such enthusiasm, especially from politicians, it was necessary to delete the original limitation on the number of cities that could benefit. Everyone wanted to participate, and after two years more than 150 cities were enrolled, including Eagle Pass, Texas and Smithville, Tennessee, the home of the chairman of the House Subcommittee that approves the HUD budget.[5] Such compromises were apparently regarded as the price that popular programs must pay.

The dilemma of federal social reform was soon apparent. The legislation included two essential requirements which appeared, at least in Chicago, as incompatible: final control of the program by the existing city governments and "widespread citizen participation" in all phases of planning and implementation of the program. The record of controversy in Chicago seemed to indicate that it was difficult if not impossible to have both. The federal government could support an independent community project without city agency support or it could aid city programs without citizen support, but it could not do both. The Model Cities program, however, claimed that here too it could succeed where others had failed. The intent of the legislation was to help cities solve their problems. The federal government would not develop a Model Cities bureaucracy to implement the programs. Nor would they contract directly with designated target areas. After protest from the mayors over past citizen action programs of OEO there would be no more bypassing of City Hall. Instead, the money strategy would be used. Although the elected governments of the cities were fully

[5] When asked why Smithville was selected a HUD official was reported to have remarked, "Smithville is a very small place, but there are those who love it." See William Hamilton, "The Cities vs. the People: Citizen Participation in Model Cities," *Everyman's Guide to Federal Programs Impact! Reports*, Vol. I, No. 2 (Washington, D.C.: New Community Press, Inc., 1969), p. 4.

responsible for applying, planning, approving, and implementing the Model Cities program, "widespread citizen participation" was mandatory in order to receive the money. Midwest Regional Director of HUD, Alan Goldfarb, made it clear that one of the major goals of Model Cities was to develop and strengthen community organizations and institutions at the neighborhood level so that the residents of model neighborhoods would have a clear stake in the program.[6] The Model Cities program guide interprets the citizen participation clause this way:

> The implementation of this statutory provision requires: (1) the constructive involvement of citizens in the Model Neighborhood and the city as a whole in planning and carrying out the program, and (2) the development of means of introducing the views of area residents in policy making and the provision of opportunities to area residents to participate actively in planning and carrying out the program.[7]

The strategy, at least on paper, was clear. The federal government was telling city halls, "You work out an authentic partnership with target area organizations and residents and we will give you a few million dollars for programs." Of course, the city was clearly the senior partner, being responsible for determining the partnership structure which would fulfill the performance standards. The only leverage that residents in Model Neighborhoods had was the HUD requirements that made it "mandatory" for cities to provide "the means for the Model Neighborhood citizens to participate and to be fully involved in policy-making, planning and the execution of all program elements."[8]

By the time TWO became alerted to Model Cities, the record was not encouraging. December 1967 was a critical month for the organization. The Youth Project was under

[6] Presentation to Seminar at University of Chicago, Public Affairs 291-2, October 2, 1968.

[7] *Program Guide*, p. 20. [8] *Ibid.*, p. 21.

attack. The tripartite Woodlawn Community Board nearly collapsed when the Board of Education ruled that the community could assume only an advisory role. In the midst of all of this Brazier briefed the TWO delegates on the Model Cities picture. He had met with Mayor Daley on December 19 to discuss Model Cities and he was alarmed at the prospect. Thus far, it appeared to be a repeat of the Poverty Program style of citizen participation. While TWO had been tied up in a Youth Project and with planning for an experimental schools program, the City had moved ahead with its own Model Cities planning for Woodlawn.

The City of Chicago submitted an application on May 1, 1967, proposing a method for developing and implementing Chicago's Model Cities program. Conceived and developed without consulting the neighborhoods involved, it proposed a planning process which was in further violation of HUD requirements. The Community Legal Council documented these violations:[9]

1. The model area residents were not involved in developing the Chicago application. In fact, Model Area Councils, the citizen participation structures, were appointed more than a year after the Chicago application was submitted. HUD required that "the development of an effective application should include, from the beginning, the involvement of a cross-section of public and private groups and neighborhood residents."[10] The Chicago application was developed by the staffs of city agencies. The Citizens Advisory Committee, supposedly representative of the people, had no chairman, made no reports, and made no policy decisions. Of the forty-three members, eight lived outside of Chicago, only four were black, and none were residents of Model Cities target areas. Chicago's application was unique in that it designated four model neighborhoods. HUD preferred

[9] Community Legal Council (Chicago), "Citizen Participation in Chicago's Model Cities Program: A Critical Analysis" (Chicago: Community Legal Council, May 15, 1968) (mimeographed).

[10] *Program Guide*, p. 33.

that each city have one model neighborhood in order to concentrate efforts and to facilitate the relationship between the neighborhood citizen structure and the City Demonstration Agency (CDA). Though the Chicago application indicated that each model neighborhood would have a citizen council, there was no citizen group from the four areas which would enter into partnership with CDA, the city agency responsible for the development and oversight of the program. According to Community Legal Council research, "Chicago's proposal was prepared by city personnel from information compiled in the Department of Development and Planning's 1966 *Comprehensive Plan for the City of Chicago.*"[11]

2. The HUD standards stipulated that

there must be some form of organization structure, existing or newly established, which embodies neighborhood residents in the process of policy and program planning and program implementation and operation. The leadership of that structure must consist of persons whom neighborhood residents accept as representing their interests.[12]

In the Chicago proposal the mayor would appoint all persons to serve on the citizen participation structures, the four Model Area Planning Councils. The proposal suggested using persons from the existing community conservation councils and the Urban Progress Center Advisory Boards (both of which are appointed by the mayor) as a base. Furthermore, it was not proposed that the mayor limit his appointments to people who lived in the target areas. Each target area was surrounded by a designated "study area" which included a more affluent population. The mayor could appoint anyone within the study area.

3. The HUD program standards required that

11 Community Legal Council, "Citizen Participation," p. 2.
12 *Program Guide*, p. 21.

in order to initiate and react intelligently in program matters, the structure must have the technical capacity for making knowledgeable decisions. This will mean that some form of professional technical assistance, in a manner agreed to by neighborhood residents, shall be provided.[13]

The Chicago proposal made no provision for technical assistance to Model Area Planning Councils. The plan apparently was to be developed by the existing professional planners within the city agencies.

It had become apparent to TWO leaders that if Model Cities were controlled by the existing political apparatus, it would be an expanded version of the Poverty Program. Despite the rhetoric and the federal guidelines, Model Cities would merely become another means of channelling federal funds into the planning, service, and control bureaucracies of the city. The elements of the "Chicago style" of federal programs were already present. Millions of dollars of federal money was to flow in to maintain Chicago's political-governmental apparatus. Existing community organizations that were independent of, and usually in opposition to, the established agencies of service and control, were bypassed if they could not be coopted into the city's plan.

In December, amidst the controversies around the Youth Project and the Schools Project, Brazier criticized the city's proposal:

We will not be planned for. We will not be bulldozed out or rehabilitated out. We will not stand for another Urban Progress Center type program. We are through with plantation politics. Those days are over. But just saying so won't make it true. We must close ranks and get the kind of Model Cities program we need. We have put too much into this organization not now to stand up for self-determination.[14]

[13] *Ibid.*
[14] Brazier to TWO steering committee, December 18, 1967.

TWO had fought with the city administration on the Urban Progress Center and had lost. They learned from that experience. Brazier said to the delegates at the December meeting, "We win some and we lose some, but we are not going to lose the same way twice."[15] Brazier suggested, and the delegates endorsed, what was the beginning of a new strategy. TWO decided to assume the initiative in Model Cities planning; it did not wait for the mayor to establish his "citizen participation" structure. TWO was determined to form a community-wide planning council, seek technical assistance, and develop a Model Cities plan adhering as closely as possible to the intent and guidelines of the Model Cities legislation.

The major obstacle to this strategy was that TWO had no authority to develop such a plan. The federal government would deal only with proposals and plans approved by the City Demonstration Agency and the Chicago City Council. TWO's strategy was directed toward HUD because its only leverage with the CDA in Chicago was the HUD requirements. TWO was hoping to make a strong case: that its planning council, and not the group appointed by the mayor, consisted of persons whom the neighborhood residents accepted as representing their interests; that its plan conformed to the statutory requirements of the legislation while the city's plan was in clear violation; and that its plan was superior to that of the city in quality, vision, and potential effectiveness. It was a long-shot strategy. But an assist from HUD could put TWO in a strong bargaining position with City Hall.

Throughout the winter and spring the issue of Model Cities was raised at every delegates and steering committee meeting. The frequent discussion of this issue served to rally community support and cultivate a determination to resist the city's approach at a time when TWO and city agencies were locked in controversy over the Youth Project. Model Cities was held up as a "do-or-die" issue for the organiza-

[15] *Ibid.*

tion. TWO was being prepared for what was interpreted at the time as the most significant struggle in its history. The feeling expressed by many of the TWO leaders was "if the city wins this one we can pack up." In the spring of 1968 the TWO meetings were lively and the rhetoric was exciting.

The strategy began to take shape. An exploratory session with Chicago Model Cities director Irwin France and Deputy Mayor Dave Stahl confirmed the suspicions TWO leaders had about the process the city was establishing. The city was hoping to select some TWO members for the official Woodlawn Model Area Planning Council but would not allow TWO to have the majority voice. Through intermediaries TWO leaders received assurance from Walter Farr, HUD director of the Model Cities Administration in Washington, that it would be inconceivable for HUD to fund a Model Cities program in Woodlawn which did not receive the support of TWO. With this indirect assurance TWO was ready to initiate an independent Model Cities planning process. Unable to secure sufficient planning funds to hire technical assistance, TWO approached the University of Chicago. Conversation with the University had been opened and new relationships with particular faculty members had been developed through work on the Youth Project, the Experimental Schools Project, and the Woodlawn Mental Health Center. Under the direction of the Center for Urban Studies a group of faculty, who had already been meeting in a colloquium on the University's programs in relation to Woodlawn, agreed to help develop a means of providing technical assistance for TWO's Model Cities planning.[16]

By summer TWO was ready. An open-ended planning council of more than 200 residents, many of whom were not previously active in TWO, had met twice. A faculty-student

[16] See William Swenson, *The Continuing Colloquium on University of Chicago Demonstration Projects in Woodlawn* (Chicago: University of Chicago Center for Urban Studies, November 15, 1968).

task force from the University was available. The active constituency of the organization, angered by the city's attack on the Youth Project, was eager to make an issue out of Model Cities planning. The signals from HUD were encouraging.

The mayor's office, a full year after submitting its application for Model Cities planning funds, had not appointed the four Model Area Planning Councils. In Woodlawn the process was being held up by TWO's resistance. Irwin France had requested TWO to submit a list of names so that the mayor could proceed with his appointments. TWO refused to submit any names unless the mayor would make a written commitment about the size and constituency of the Model Area Planning Council (MAPC). TWO insisted on 51 percent membership as a condition for participation claiming that, although it did not represent all of the interests in Woodlawn, it did represent the vast majority of organized interests of the target area. France claimed that the Model Cities legislation, as he interpreted it, would not allow the City to permit TWO or any organization to have a majority on the Council. Unable to get names from TWO, the Model Cities staff of the City approached TWO members directly. The steering committee of TWO, at a special meeting on May 25, 1968, voted to urge all TWO members to refuse to accept an appointment to the mayor's committee. Although they could not prevent members from serving on the City's council, this corporate action, coupled with the alternative planning process being developed by TWO, was sufficient to prevent what TWO regarded as "defection" to the enemy. Two homeowners who were members of the steering committee pleaded that if they refused to participate on the mayor's committee they would be subject to harassment which they could not afford. In all, five residents who were identified with TWO, three of whom had been active in the organization, accepted initial invitations to serve on the mayor-appointed committee of twenty-three for Woodlawn. The steering committee of TWO in a heated

245

meeting decided that they should be divested of any offices or committee leadership in TWO. The argument prevailed that since there were two parallel and competing planning processes, these five should not be allowed, because of a possible conflict of interest, to maintain leadership in both TWO and MAPC.

TWO inaugurated its active planning process at an all-day community conference at St. Cyril's Parish Hall on June 22. Over 250 residents met with the University faculty-student task force in plenary sessions and workshops. In the absence of President Brazier, who was in Washington for the Senate hearings on the Youth Project, staff director Leon Finney explained the advisory relationship of the University task force. Julian Levi reemphasized this supportive role. "You are going to decide," he told the group, "not the City and not the University, what kinds of solutions to Woodlawn's problems you are going to propose."[17]

The planning process posed some problems. How could the process be structured so that the professionals would not dominate, residents would have ample opportunity to contribute, a plan could be developed in three to four months, and the federal guidelines would be followed? Was it possible, within a limited period of time, to have significant citizen participation and utilize to the best advantage the skills of the professionals? The suspicions Woodlawn residents harbored toward the University was one barrier. The task force's technical language, professional style, and lack of experience in relating to Woodlawn residents was an additional barrier. Rather than establishing a series of subcommittees on the various segments of the Model Cities Program, the TWO steering committee voted to use its existing standing committees as a base for Model Cities planning. The one disadvantage of this move was that these committees, even though they had always been open to anyone in the community, would not attract those residents

[17] TWO Model Cities Council meeting, St. Cyril's Parish Hall, June 22, 1968.

who were not supporters of the organization. This was outweighed by the many advantages of using the existing committees. The standing committees had a history of dealing with the multiplicity of problems in Woodlawn. They also had experienced leadership. By expanding on this base, TWO could best provide the accumulated skills and insights of the past both in developing the problem analysis, the initial task in Model Cities planning, and in guiding and controlling the University task force. With slight alterations in areas of responsibility, the eight active standing committees of TWO covered the areas stipulated in Model Cities guidelines. For each committee there was a corresponding faculty-student team and a TWO staff member. The experience of these planning committees was uneven. Attendance ranged from five to fifty. By mid-August a process was developed which would both encourage citizen participation and utilize the skills of the task force.

> Task force members would not passively come to meetings to receive requests or instructions, since in that way their special abilities would not be fully used. Instead, each task force began to prepare proposals prior to each meeting and would then present them as possible alternatives for action, as goals, or as problem formulations. Committee members would each receive a copy of the proposals, and could comment immediately or study them for a week and then respond. Many of the Task Force proposals were criticized mercilessly by the committee members and were shown to be full of holes. Very rarely did a Task Force member think the criticism unjustified or wrong, and the consensus was that the committees could operate best when they had proposals to respond to. . . . This method proved very productive and became the central device for developing the Model Cities plan. It also fulfilled the HUD requirements for Model Cities planning and the structure of the final document.[18]

[18] Swenson, *Demonstration Projects*, p. 118.

247

The work of the social welfare committee is illustrative. The committee, most of whom were ADC mothers, identified major problems such as low grants, invasion of privacy, and insensitivity of social workers. Each Friday evening the task force would bring a cumulative summary which was regularly revised. The primary difficulty came in developing recommendations. The community participants talked about particular case workers and particular problems that affected them in real life. The task force had to translate these particularized suggestions into program recommendations. They then revised these recommendations until the committee was satisfied that the task force really understood them. The task force chairman, Harold Richman, said later, "The community people kept us honest, especially our treatment of their ideas. It was a good experience, because every Friday night we knew we were responsible to them."[19]

After segments of the plan were developed, at least in outline, to the satisfaction of the various committees, the revision, coordination, and write-up of the total plan was handled by relatively few people. TWO had formed a ways and means committee made up of the standing committee chairmen and TWO officers to oversee the final development. It was this committee that provided many of the unifying principles and established the priorities for the final draft. Most of the writing, however, was done by a coordinating committee of the task force. The TWO staff, with advice from black consultants, made revisions and sent parts of the document back for several rewrites.

Hundreds of copies of a 144-page summary draft were prepared for review by the general Woodlawn public. Brazier presented the plan and interpreted major sections of it to the large Planning Council on November 11, 1968. Several community hearings were then held in various parts of Woodlawn. In the Essex area, over 100 residents had an extended discussion over various aspects of the document,

[19] Presentation to seminar at University of Chicago, Public Affairs 291-2, November 20, 1968.

particularly the educational component. In December, over 300 residents convened to approve any revisions that came from the area meetings. The University task force was not invited to participate in any of these review sessions. This was TWO's way of saying that the University's task was done. This was Woodlawn's plan and it did not need to be interpreted or defended by white professionals. At a follow-up meeting the Planning Council approved the revised plan and recommended that it be pursued as Woodlawn's Model Cities plan.

It is difficult to assess the character and quality of citizen participation in the development of this Model Cities plan. The top leadership in the organization, the officers, staff, and ways and means committee played a central role in representing the community in the final development of the plan. There was some resentment that in the most significant stages of the planning, only a relatively few were actively involved. TWO maintained that the few who were involved represented the community through TWO, and were, as the federal guidelines require, "Persons whom the neighborhood residents accept as representing their interests." The TWO leaders and the staff that the organization hired assumed a spokesman role in the planning process. They were instrumental in setting priorities, maintaining a working relationship with the professionals, and editing the final document. It can be argued that through participation in the varied activities of TWO and because of a trust many residents have had in TWO, many people who did not actively participate in the TWO Model Cities planning regarded the plan as their plan, as a plan in which they participated. It can also be argued that "they," the constituency of TWO, did indeed participate in the planning process because it was through the corporate capacity of their community organization that the independent planning venture was made possible.

In a more direct way a large number of Woodlawn people were involved in some aspect of the planning process. More than 200 residents participated in the committee work with the task force during the initial stages. In addition there were six general community meetings and a number of area meetings, the total attendance of which exceeded 1,400. It would be safe to estimate that at least 500 Woodlawn residents participated in some phase of the process.

It is appropriate to compare this TWO style of planning not with some idealized model but with the planning process developed by the city. The Model Area Planning Council for Woodlawn and the three other target areas were appointed by the mayor in the summer. Mrs. Jean Himes, the deputy director of the Woodlawn Council had been with the Commission on Youth Welfare. Of the twenty-three original appointees to the Woodlawn MAPC, ten, including the chairman, did not live in the target area. Few of the members represented any organized constituency. Indeed, they were told that they were on the council as individuals representing Woodlawn as a whole and not as representatives of particular groups or organizations. The primary task of the nine subcommittees was to prepare a "problem analysis" of the needs of Woodlawn. The MAPC meetings during the summer and fall were attended by the appointed members, resource persons from a variety of city agencies, and only a handful of community residents. One student who attended MAPC meetings regularly in the fall reported that, by his count, only rarely did the community residents outnumber the agency personnel among the non-council participants. It was clear that MAPC was not developing a plan but was merely supposed to identify "problems" which the planners would consider. After this continued through the fall months, there was growing dissatisfaction within the Model Area Planning Councils. In December, Joe Sander, the chairman of the Uptown Council resigned with several of his members. Sander had a long list of complaints. The Uptown Council, like the other three, received no money for technical assistance. The Council's decision to add new members was repudiated by the City

Demonstration Agency. What disturbed Sander most was that the actual planning was done downtown by the agencies. All that MAPC was to do for five months was to "define the problem which anybody could do in fifteen minutes."[20] The Council was simply not involved in planning at all. They received a plan from CDA which they were to approve without study because CDA hoped to submit the plan to Washington before the Nixon administration took office. Sander was quoted as saying, "If we exist just to comply with a law in order to bring money into the city, then they will have to find other patsies and not come around asking me for my good name."[21] In the Grand Boulevard area the MAPC co-chairman, the Rev. Curtis Burrell of the Kenwood-Oakland Community organization also resigned. Burrell's analysis was even more harsh:

> Serving in the capacity of co-chairman, I was able to gain firsthand knowledge of how the city of Chicago really operated and how the federal government said they should operate. Seeing the contradiction, I resigned my membership on the council in September. The Council is stacked against the interests of the people in favor of other interest groups. There is not "widespread participation." The technical advisors are people who work with city departments and they see to it that the pre-planned city programs are proposed. . . .
>
> Thus, the paternalism of the city and the defeatism of the council under a program titled "Model City" is the highest insult to the human dignity and self-respect of black people. For, in essence, the city is saying that the same old genocidal plantationism of this racist society is the model for this city, for us.[22]

[20] Donald Schwartz, "Ex-Model Cities Unit Chief Tells Why He Quit," *Chicago Sun Times*, December 13, 1968, p. 50.

[21] Betty Washington, "Daley Hit as 3 Quit Uptown Plan Unit," *Chicago Daily News*, December 12, 1968, p. 3.

[22] Curtis E. Burrell, Jr., "KOCO Head Exposes Model Cities Program," *True People's Power* (Chicago), April 1969, p. 1.

251

Leaders in both of these MAPC's were charging that the councils were merely "window dressing," a front group for centralized city planning. This internal dissension was less evident in Woodlawn's MAPC primarily because the most vocal source of opposition, TWO, was never part of the Woodlawn Council. While the Woodlawn Council faced little internal controversy, it also generated little community support.

After TWO announced its own Model Cities proposal, Brazier, at a press conference in December 1968, observed that "Chicago's Model Cities program does not represent the ideas, efforts, or desires of the Woodlawn residents,"[23] and requested that no plan be submitted to the City Council that did not have the support of a target community. Brazier went on to point out the two basic flaws of the official Model Cities planning procedure in Woodlawn:

> 1) Area residents have played no part in planning or developing the organizational structure through which citizen involvement was to be obtained. . . . 2) The council has no staff other than that which the city provides and has no funds with which to hire the professional and technical assistance necessary to perform a planning and development function.[24]

TWO cast its planning procedure, its use of professional assistance, and its participation structure in sharp contrast to the poorly attended, agency-dominated Model Area Planning Council. The most significant contrast was in the content of the two plans themselves. The city had no plan in December but there was evidence that, since it was being developed by the existing staffs of city agencies, it would reflect the prevailing presuppositions, programs, and policies. Nothing new was emerging.

The TWO plan, on the other hand, was developed out of alternative basic principles. From TWO's perspective, the

[23] *The Observer,* December 18, 1968, p. 1.
[24] *Ibid.,* p. 2.

252

city agencies were failing in Woodlawn and the remedy could not be found simply by having more of the same. Three basic concepts lay behind the TWO-University plan.

1. *Citizen Responsibility.* TWO argued that it was not sufficient merely to have various residents participate in the planning process. A structure had to be devised through which the primary responsibility for the implementation and administration of the program would be in the hands of the community. An adequate plan would, if based on this premise, encourage the development of local institutions through which citizen responsibility could be exercised. In city programs the local citizens are passive beneficiaries of services planned and implemented by others. The TWO plan asserted that

> the failure to recognize the critical role of *citizen responsibility,* exercised through accepted and recognized community organizations, may account largely for the frustrating failures of public programs which deal with the problems of the inner city, and the inability of professionals to use their knowledge in any effective way in the inner city. Government programs, public agencies and departments, and professionals cannot by themselves or in combination guarantee that social change will be effected in ways which are acceptable either to the inner-city resident or to society at large.[25]

2. *The Whole Man.* The TWO plan maintains that "this concept dramatizes the need to treat community and personal problems as a whole and not in terms of conventional categories of educational, medical, social welfare, or legal approaches."[26] Traditional programs have been too often centered around and influenced by the professional and institutional enhancement needs of the agencies that developed them. Each agency tends to interpret the basic prob-

[25] The Woodlawn Organization, *Woodlawn's Model Cities Plan* (Northbrook, Ill.: Whitehall Company, 1970), p. 26.

[26] *Ibid.*, pp. 26-27.

lem of the inner city in terms of its professional interests and to develop elaborate administrative mechanisms parallel but unrelated to a vast array of other agencies. The citizen with a problem is confronted by a bewildering variety of agencies that are vertically related to his community. By focusing on its specialty rather than on the needs of the citizen, the agency often deals with only one facet of a complex situation and thus is unable to break the cycle of factors that create and maintain the ghetto.

3. *Decentralized Centralization.* The existing arrangement of governmental agencies can be characterized as "centralized decentralization." On the one hand, the agencies are decentralized in the sense that they are relatively free from public control through regular political channels. At the same time, they are centralized internally and are therefore insulated from neighborhood influence. These "new machines," as Theodore Lowi calls them, have become islands of autonomous power, internally centralized and split off from public control. The TWO proposal points toward an alternative arrangement which might be termed "decentralized centralization."

> We seek also in this document to give conceptual and programmatic content to the central issues of decentralization. The basic thrust is that there is a real and fundamental difference between decentralization, a desired goal, and fragmentation, which would merely continue present weaknesses. In order to achieve effective decentralization . . . it is essential to develop centralized community-wide facilities. Consequently, decentralization of operations requires centralization and consolidation of many technical, professional, and support functions.[27]

The TWO plan proposed a level of neighborhood government through which the existing fragmentation and distance of professional services would be overcome.

[27] *Ibid.*, p. 29.

The most important part of the TWO plan was the outline of this new governmental arrangement which would alter both the way in which services were provided and the quality of those services. The proposed local governmental institutions would be responsible to a governing board of 100 which would serve as a neighborhood legislature. A "convenor," elected by the board, would be the equivalent to a neighborhood "city manager." In TWO's proposal forty of the governing board would be elected by the community-at-large and sixty would be elected by the TWO constituency. Governmental functions would be carried out through a wide variety of community-based agencies, all with citizen boards.

The most innovative aspect of the structure was the system of "outreach centers" called "pads." A brief summary of the plan described the pad system this way:

The Outreach System will consist of a network of facilities, each serving a two- or three-block area of the community. Community agents will contact residents to inform them of available services, to discover problems, and to actually deliver needed services. The facilities will be located in stores, basements, apartment buildings, houses, etc., and would multiply as needed. The "pad" would have four primary functions:

a) stimulating community organizations,

b) providing easy access to facilities, services and institutions,

c) giving early diagnosis of all sorts of problems,

d) doing prevention and early treatment work.

Pads will be manned by staffs of nonprofessionals who are residents in the immediate neighborhood, and are known by their neighbors. They would be intensively trained by all of the participating professions in the basic knowledge and skills necessary to provide primary services to citizens. These "community agents" would perform many of the non-specialized tasks that doctors, social workers, lawyers, teachers, and other professionals have had to perform in the past, but for which no great training or professional skills are necessary.

Professionals will not control the pads, but will be called upon from backup facilities in the Core and other systems as the community agents decide is necessary.[28]

The pads provided the basic link between residents and the service facilities. They would serve as multipurpose centers in which the variety of services are brought together at the most immediate level.

The Plan also outlined a variety of substantive programs: a comprehensive community health system coordinating under one program the multitude of existing health services; an experimental financial assistance program which would provide a guaranteed minimum income twice the amount of the existing system, with work incentives and virtually no administrative red tape; a legal program including a neighborhood law firm, a conciliation council to settle intra-Woodlawn disputes, and a legal aid bureau; and an elaboration of the existing Woodlawn Community Board for education to cover a wider range of activities. Although many of the components of the plan revealed imaginative ideas, the heart of the TWO plan was the administrative structure through which the residents would have a major voice in defining problems, shaping policy, implementing programs, and evaluating results.

A sense of accomplishment and an aura of confidence were evident in the TWO meetings in December 1968, and early January. TWO had a Model Cities plan. It received informal support from several HUD officials who regarded it as a model of the HUD "vision" of a "comprehensive," "coordinated," "concentrated," and "innovative" plan. Julian

[28] "The Model Cities Plan of the Woodlawn Organization—an Abstract," in Eddie N. Williams (ed.), *Delivery Systems for Model Cities: New Concepts in Serving the Urban Community* (University of Chicago, Center for Policy Study and Center for Urban Studies, 1969), Appendix, pp. 81-82.

Levi was prepared to exercise his considerable influence with the Washington officialdom. Senator Charles Percy responded favorably to the basic concepts in the plan. In addition, the community enthusiasm which was clearly evident in September continued throughout the fall. Attendance at TWO meetings was high. The hearings on the TWO plan generated widespread community support. TWO had pledged to fight "all the way" for this plan. Brazier proclaimed that "for the first time in history the black community has an opportunity to develop and adopt a 'People's Plan' for their community."[29] Few people at the hearings raised the political question. It seemed to be assumed by many of the residents attending the final meetings that this was *the* Model Cities plan.

Many things were happening within TWO which stimulated this growing confidence and enthusiasm. The ground breaking for Woodlawn Gardens on December 3 was an occasion for community celebration. The outcome of six years of negotiations and struggle, Woodlawn Gardens was to be, as Brazier put it at the ceremony, "the beginning of what might be called the renaissance of the Woodlawn community."[30] The Woodlawn Experimental Schools Project was beginning to have an impact and the constituency on the Woodlawn Community Board was being revised to include a majority from the community. In addition, TWO secured a new and expanded On-Job-Training program for paramedical training; a $60,000 grant from the Citizens Crusade Against Poverty (CCAP) for training organizers was renewed and increased to $100,000; and TWO received a $65,000 grant from the Community Renewal Society to secure technical assistance in planning. With half of this grant the organization secured the services of Whitley and Whitley, a black architectural and planning firm based in Cleveland, to help develop a physical environmental plan for Woodlawn. Finally, discussions with the University of

29 *The Observer*, November 20, 1968, p. 1.
30 *The Observer*, December 4, 1968, p. 2.

257

Chicago, New York Life Insurance Company, Connecticut General Life Insurance Company, Zenith Corporation, Campbell Soup, the Urban Coalition, and others led to several proposals for housing rehabilitation, job training, new housing developments, and economic development projects. All of these projects dovetailed and gave private-sector support to the overall TWO Model Cities concept.

TWO not only had a Model Cities plan, it also had a solid constituency backing, federal encouragement, private-sector assistance, and University of Chicago support. TWO had all the pieces together except the big one: City Hall approval. Here was the dilemma. TWO had a plan and it had citizen support, but it had no authority. CDA and the Woodlawn MAPC had the authority, but they had no plan, as yet, and no significant citizen participation. The city process was behind in its timetable. Two MAPC chairmen had resigned in protest over the way the city was developing its plan and there was a growing resistance in all the Model Cities areas to the official Chicago process. While the City Demonstration Agency was having trouble securing citizen support for a plan it was preparing to submit to City Council, TWO had a popularly supported plan and no place to which to submit it. By law, the federal government would receive only the plan that was approved by the Chicago City Council and the City Council would receive and consider only the plan presented by Irwin France and CDA.

The outcome of a year of maneuvering on both sides resulted in a stalemate on the Woodlawn Model Cities plan. To Mayor Daley and the city administration the TWO plan was a direct challenge to municipal sovereignty and a clear threat to the existing system of program planning, professional service, and political control in Chicago. CDA could, and later did, incorporate some of the TWO programmatic ideas into their plan. What CDA could not do was to give up control over the implementation of Model Cities. The city's strategy had been, on the one hand, to secure support from some individual TWO members and, on the other hand, to discredit TWO's capacity to administer federally funded programs. The first approach fell short. Even though a few TWO members accepted the mayor's invitation, the organization made it clear that this in no way signified either TWO or Woodlawn community support. The second approach may have been decisive. Shortly after it became apparent that TWO and the University were cooperating to develop a plan, the McClellan subcommittee, with encouragement from Chicago officialdom, launched the "investigation" of the Youth Manpower Project. The effort to discredit both TWO and the University may well have been, as Brazier charged, directed less at the $927,000 Youth Project than at the potential threat of the multimillion dollar Model Cities proposal that was then in its early stages.

TWO based its strategy, in no small part, on its past experience with OEO and on the HUD standards for Model Cities. The organization had the opportunity and the capability not only to block the city's efforts in Woodlawn but also to provide an alternative proposal which would meet all but one of the basic HUD standards.

These two political strategies resulted in a temporary deadlock. Stalemate was the best for which TWO could have hoped. Since it had always been clear, at least to the TWO leaders, that the Model Cities administration would not receive and fund the TWO-University plan directly, the most that could be expected of TWO's extensive efforts was to stymie CDA in Chicago and to place TWO in a position to negotiate a compromise. It was not surprising that the TWO leaders were willing to compromise. The purpose of developing power has always been for TWO to use it as a basis for negotiation. The major question was, what kind of settlement could TWO secure?

Several factors precipitated the settlement. In early January 1969, Congressman Mikva and the South Side independent aldermen met with Irwin France. The political leaders expressed their support for the TWO plan and

259

urged France to compromise. The basis for an agreement was emerging. If CDA would be receptive to the TWO plan, TWO would participate on the Woodlawn Model Area Planning Council. Additional pressure was coming from HUD. Because the citizen participation aspect of Model Cities was problematic in almost every city, HUD issued a clarifying statement in December. This 27-page document provided a more detailed interpretation of the original performance standards on citizen participation. The document was especially critical of those cities which substituted "the appearance of participation" for the real thing:

> The commitment to participation as ritual is producing signs of trouble in some cities. As residents gain experience with the complexity, the promise and the constraints of public planning, they are less content with situations in which they perceive themselves as ratifying programs which provide more funds for agencies to conduct business as usual.[31]

The HUD document also had advice for community organizations:

> In some cities, militants chose to stand aside because of suspicion of the city's motives. By boycotting Model Cities, militants have been able to create a situation in which their suspicions were self-fulfilling. Their absence from the citizen structure demonstrated for them the unrepresentativeness of that structure. . . . The militant group which offers to participate only if it has control, or an exclusive turf, or a special privileged position, creates difficult problems. They cannot be given these things. . . . The initial militant position, which might be sum-

---

[31] U.S., Department of Housing and Urban Development, Model Cities Administration, *Citizen Participation in Model Cities*, Technical Assistance Bulletin No. 3, December 1968 (Washington, D.C.: Government Printing Office, 1968), pp. 14-15.

marized as "no control, no participation," has been found to be negotiable when cities were willing to specify rights, responsibilities, and guarantees.[32]

These two sections seem to have been written with the Chicago situation partly in mind. The signals from HUD were becoming clear. If TWO continued to boycott the established process, HUD would no longer look favorably on TWO's efforts or motives. If TWO was to be taken seriously by HUD, the organization would have to play by the rules, work out an agreement with Chicago officials and channel the proposal through CDA and the City Council. The implicit understanding, although never spelled out, was that if TWO played by the rules, HUD would insist that the city of Chicago play by the rules. That is, HUD would enforce its own standards on citizen participation.

Brazier was ready to negotiate with CDA and the local MAPC. But first he had to sell this move to a TWO steering committee that was prepared to fight to the end for the TWO plan. Brazier's argument, presented at three January steering committee meetings and discussed thoroughly at a special meeting of the Woodlawn Pastors' Alliance, was twofold. First, he suggested that TWO should rethink its basic strategy. In the early years, TWO had insisted upon being recognized as the sole representative of Woodlawn and also upon having majority representation on all community boards. That strategy, necessary to develop a base of power, was, Brazier maintained, neither necessary nor wise at this point. TWO should think more in terms of community control than of TWO control. TWO, if it controlled Model Cities, would become a governmental agency. This would put the organization in a difficult position. Although it would administer a program, it would not have the real power to determine the course of that program. In addition, TWO, and not City Hall, would become the target for criticism against Model Cities. Brazier raised the question of

[32] *Ibid.*, pp. 19-20.

whether the organization really wanted to become a quasi-governmental buffer between Woodlawn residents and the CDA-City administration complex. Furthermore, Brazier pointed out, government programs do not provide the path toward community control. Even if TWO had not been outflanked in the Poverty Program controversy and had secured a majority on the local OEO council, it was clear, Brazier maintained, that the Poverty Program would have still been a failure. Brazier's approach to the TWO delegates was interesting. He did not say, "Look, we can't get our plan. Let's settle for what we can get," an approach that might have triggered the TWO activists to demand a showdown with Daley and France. Instead Brazier argued that TWO should reconsider whether it wanted to control Model Cities at all.

Coupled with this theoretical argument, Brazier presented several practical arguments for negotiating with the CDA structure at this time. If TWO did not come to terms with the local MAPC, the stalemate would continue with the eventual possibility that there would be no Model Cities program in Woodlawn and the city would allow the neighborhood to deteriorate until it was ripe for massive clearance. If TWO submitted its plan to CDA at this point, France would send it to the Woodlawn MAPC and it would be rejected. Then the mayor could say "the people rejected the TWO plan." If TWO negotiated for representation on MAPC, the TWO plan could be introduced at the neighborhood level. There were signs that many of the MAPC members were getting tired of the city's procedures and would support the TWO plan.

The steering committee authorized a three-man negotiating team to meet with France and H. H. Anderson, the chairman of the Woodlawn MAPC. The outcome, presented to the steering committee on January 27 for approval, was that TWO would have 50 percent of the membership of a reconstituted MAPC. However, and this was the catch, the 50 percent would include the seven TWO members previously appointed by the mayor (before the agreement, MAPC had included two more TWO participants). Under the proposed arrangement the council would be expanded from twenty-three to thirty-two to include nine new members provided by TWO. Brazier indicated that France had assured him that if TWO gave its support to MAPC, the TWO plan would be given a fair hearing. With this fifty-fifty arrangement, Brazier expressed confidence that the TWO plan would have a good chance at least at the local level. There was some doubt expressed at the steering committee whether the seven "turncoats" would return to the TWO position and whether France would ever seriously consider the TWO plan. In spite of these reservations, the recommendation from the negotiating committee was approved and TWO joined the Woodlawn Model Area Planning Council. The nine new members were appointed by the mayor on February 15, dined by Irwin France on February 18 and attended their first meeting the following day.

The city had secured what it needed most in Woodlawn, credible citizen participation. What TWO would secure from the settlement remained to be seen. Having bargained away its strongest lever, TWO would have to rely upon its skill in influencing MAPC, a verbal agreement with France, and the willingness and ability of HUD to interpret and enforce its standards favorable to TWO. The organization did not have to wait long to find out that it had lost the bargain.

The first meeting of the reconstituted council caught the TWO representatives by surprise. In addition to the council members there were thirty-one "resource" persons from various city agencies and eighteen visitors, half of whom were either reporters or University of Chicago students. After welcoming the new council members Chairman Anderson called for the subcommittee chairmen to report on their evaluations of the first-year action plan which had been developed by the city. A 34-page document marked "Draft for Discussion" was distributed and the resource persons from the Chicago Dwellings Association, the Board of Education, and the Police Department answered questions about the projects listed in the document. The chairman asked if it was the "consensus of the council" that this plan be approved and sent to the City Council. It was only then that the TWO members on the council began to realize that they were being asked to approve a Model Cities proposal for the coming year. Noel Alsbrooke and James Grammer, the two major TWO spokesmen on the council, immediately objected. They had just received the draft and had not had time to read it and they would not vote on something they had not examined thoroughly and discussed within TWO. The MAPC staff responded that it was imperative to approve the plan at that meeting in order to meet the deadlines prior to the City Council meeting on March 13. One council member said, "There is nothing too objectional about this plan. . . . Moreover we can change it after City Council approves it." The chairman added, "I'm not going to shove this down your throat, but do you think the community will be served if we delay? Anybody could nit pick and nothing would be accomplished for Woodlawn."[33] TWO members, some of them unaccustomed to this kind of meeting, could hardly believe what was happening. Anderson called for a vote and the city's plan was approved fourteen to eleven. After a brief shouting match the TWO members walked out. The March issue of the *Model Cities Report*, the official CDA newspaper, described the occasion this way:

> The once turbulent community of Woodlawn has cast off its differences as previously critical organizations merged into the Model Area Planning Council.
>
> Joined by many residents who have long criticized the proposed Woodlawn Model Cities program, the Model Area Planning Council has now approved the plan and

[33] Chairman H. H. Anderson to Woodlawn Model Area Council, February 19, 1969.

sent it on to the Chicago City Council for its blessing. . . .

The chairmen of the nine subcommittees gave their reports to the community at a public meeting which drew more than 150 interested residents. . . . As its final action that night, the council voted to approve all nine components of the proposal and send it on its way to the city's aldermen.[34]

The city's strategy had worked. With TWO's presence CDA could claim "widespread citizen participation." TWO had been outmaneuvered. It was clear that despite the claim of 50 percent representation on MAPC, the seven TWO members that were previously appointed by the Mayor were solidly in the CDA camp. TWO could count on only nine out of thirty-two members.

It is difficult to compare the city "plan" with the TWO proposal. In fact, what the Model Area Planning Council had approved was not a plan at all but merely a listing of 137 projects under nine categories, which were to be parcelled out to over forty public and private agencies. There was no mention of a strategy for change, no structure for administration and implementation, no process of evaluation. Apparently this was not necessary because the projects were to be handled and evaluated by the agencies to which they were "awarded." The Department of Streets and Sanitation, the Board of Education, the Chicago Committee on Urban Opportunity, the Chicago Transit Authority, the Police Department, the Board of Health, the YMCA, and many others each got a piece. The charge that the city of Chicago was using Model Cities monies to strengthen and expand existing bureaucracies and traditional programs was

[34] *Model Cities Report* (Chicago), March 1969, p. 1. This monthly newspaper, the official Model Cities publicity organ, indicates that the meeting was attended by "150 interested residents." The minutes of the meeting reveal that there were 101 people present: 41 council or subcommittee members, 36 staff representatives from Model Cities and other agencies, and 18 "others" of whom not more than ten could be termed "interested residents."

265

confirmed. Even funds for a proposed crosstown expressway and curb and gutter repair were included.

The charge that the city's plan was prepared downtown was also confirmed. One undifferentiated "plan" was presented to all four Model Area Planning Councils. Only an occasional note in the margin indicated that a particular project did not apply to a particular target area. According to a HUD staff person, who attended the MAPC meetings in several target areas, the subcommittee reports recommending approval of the plan, reports which were read by indigenous council members, were identical in each of the councils indicating that even the citizens' evaluation had been prepared by central staff.

After MAPC approved the city plan, a mandatory community hearing was held. Over one hundred were present and almost all of them were TWO supporters. One after another the residents said that they had worked on and wanted the TWO plan. One speaker called for the resignation of the MAPC chairman. Another argued that the mayor's appointees on the council, eight of whom did not live in the target area, did not represent Woodlawn. Samuel Huffman, a CDA official, tried to soothe the meeting. He said.

> The city does not have a plan. It has a list of projects. A plan can be developed later and certainly TWO's proposal will be considered and adopted if the community wants it. Nothing will be done, no money will be spent without community support. All we are trying to do now is to tie down the federal funds.[35]

The hearing broke up in chaos with MAPC accusing TWO of purposefully disrupting the meeting and TWO accusing the MAPC staff of engineering the meeting.

Apparently worried about this adverse community response and aware of the agreement that TWO would have an opportunity to present its plan to MAPC prior to the City

[35] Samuel Huffman to the Model Cities community hearing at Woodlawn Methodist Church, February 26, 1969.

Council meeting, MAPC scheduled a special meeting to consider the TWO "inputs." This meeting, on March 10, was only three days prior to the City Council meeting. Obviously the city plan had already been bound and distributed to the aldermen. Nevertheless, TWO wanted to secure MAPC support for its plan so that the record would show that the plan supported by the Woodlawn MAPC was not the same as the CDA plan before the City Council. With the help of members of the University task force TWO summarized its plan in nine brief statements corresponding to the MAPC subcommittees. James Grammer presented the housing proposal and asked that it be substituted in place of the housing section previously approved. The chairman of the meeting indicated that this was not possible. In a surprisingly frank statement he said, "We don't make plans. We just accept or reject plans made for us. We are just a link between the Establishment and the community. We don't originate."[36] Council members argued that the TWO inputs would have to be studied by subcommittees first. After extensive discussion the TWO inputs were received and sent to subcommittee meetings scheduled two days hence. TWO, as much interested in the transcript of the meeting as in the outcome, had hired a court recorder for this and all subsequent MAPC meetings in which it participated. The chairman's attempt to limit discussion, to rule Brazier out of order, to force his own rulings on the council was on record, as was TWO's orderly effort to introduce its plan and Mr. Huffman's assurance that MAPC could alter the plan in accordance with TWO inputs even after the City Council meeting. TWO members turned out for the subcommittee meetings with the result that in all program areas except one the TWO substitute proposals were adopted in committee.

Even though the city's plan had already been publicly announced, presented to the City Council and referred to committee, the local drama in the Woodlawn MAPC continued.

[36] Woodlawn Model Area Council meeting, March 10, 1969.

TWO pursued its efforts to have the local MAPC endorse the TWO plan. If TWO succeeded in this, the city would have to fight MAPC and not just TWO. Then, if CDA prevailed over MAPC, it would reveal to HUD that the local MAPC's were powerless.

The next flare-up centered around the presence of the court recorder. Apparently realizing that such a record might be damaging, MAPC, with encouragement from the staff director, voted to have the recorder barred from the meeting. TWO members, again outnumbered, protested that without this record for their protection and information they could not participate. Once again TWO members walked out.

When MAPC finally accepted the TWO inputs in April the chairman stated that the council does not control the program and that all it can do is to send the TWO material downtown for CDA consideration.

TWO had failed in two of its calculations. It could not secure the support of a majority on MAPC. It could not introduce its plan through the MAPC-CDA process. The one strategy remaining was to play out the scenario for the benefit of HUD officials hoping that the revelations of the powerlessness of the citizens' council, the way it was manipulated by city agencies, and the frequent and flagrant violations of HUD standards, would move HUD to intervene and enforce its guidelines. It was, after all, partly because of HUD encouragement that TWO entered the regular process and began to play by the rules.

The next stage of the process was played downtown. The $38 million Chicago proposal was unveiled March 13, 1969, and referred by the City Council to the Finance Committee chaired by Daley loyalist Thomas Keane. The 34-page document reviewed by the local councils had grown to a 2,300-page, 8½ pound tome. According to committee member Leon Despres, the Finance Committee invited over 1,000 persons to testify at the hearing and the order of the speakers would be determined by the chairman. At the hearing 103 speakers testified and the ratio of supporters to opponents of the city plan was, as Despres had anticipated, three to one. Five TWO spokesmen presented for the record the entire TWO experience and the basic advantages of TWO's alternative plan. Representatives of community organizations in the other target areas also expressed similar opposition. One common grievance was that the 2,300-page document presented to the City Council had never been seen or reviewed by any of the local councils. In the Finance Committee Despres was outvoted sixteen to one, and the plan was sent back to the Council. The three-hour Council "discussion" of the plan at the April 25 meeting is illustrative of one aspect of the Chicago style of politics: discipline. Keane was the first of ten aldermen who extolled the virtues of various segments of the plan. Wigoda then dealt with housing, Derwinsky with education, Burke with law and order, and so on. After each speech, Despres, William Cousins, and Sam Rayner, the three aldermen of the greater Woodlawn area stood up to seek recognition. The mayor, however, referring to his list, continued the rounds, recognizing in one case an alderman who was not even in the room. Only after the TV cameras had gone for the five o'clock news were Despres, Cousins, and Rayner permitted to speak. Despres labeled the Model Cities program "a plan of almost unlimited patronage, limited handouts and massive removal."[37] In addition Despres revealed the contents of a letter from the Midwest Regional Office of HUD which stated that the Chicago proposal was unacceptable and could not be funded in its present form. Despres argued that it was unthinkable that the City Council would approve a plan that HUD had already rejected. The plan was approved forty-one to seven with only the independent aldermen and several Republicans in opposition.

[37] Harry Golden, Jr., "Model Cities Aid Okd by Council," *Chicago Sun Times*, April 26, 1969, p. 1.

It was now up to HUD to determine whether the Chicago plan was acceptable. TWO joined with the major community organizations in the other target areas in urging HUD to withhold funds because of the violations of the federal standards. This strategy appeared for a moment to have possibilities. The Regional Office of HUD had found the City proposal unacceptable at several points. One of the major ones was the lack of clear guarantees for authentic citizen participation. The HUD letter included the following:

> One major concern . . . reflects the necessity for more meaningful relationships with model neighborhood citizens, whose involvement is a major legislative goal of the Program. Widespread citizen participation must be of a quality to gain not only the support of citizens but their direct constructive involvement in decision-making and program execution. Particular attention will need to be focused in this area. . . .
>
> All revisions to the City's Plan in response to the following comments should be the result of the mutual efforts of both City staff and community residents. . . .
>
> The role, responsibility and authority of the MAPC's must be more clearly defined by the neighborhoods and the City, and officially acknowledged by both as a basis for their joint relationship in further development and administration of the program. . . .
>
> The plan should demonstrate how residents gain the capacity to independently initiate and react to proposals, interpret information, and influence policy, planning and program decisions. . . .
>
> It is not evident how the resident structures will have access to decision makers in order to effectively represent the interests of their neighborhoods in ongoing model cities planning. . . .
>
> It is not clear how the City intends to assure that model neighborhood residents will obtain maximum opportunity

for employment on all projects and in the execution of all aspects of the Program, and how their training for career advancement will take place. . . .[38]

This letter also criticized the use of Model Cities monies either for projects outside the target areas, such as the hiring of thirty-five additional planners for the centralized Department of Development and Planning, or for improvements that should be carried out with other resources, such as the repair of curbs and gutters.

CDA, without involving the Model Area Councils (their name had been changed, dropping the word "Planning") as instructed in the HUD letter, prepared a rebuttal contesting the charges against its proposal and offering one structural revision to satisfy the regional office. This one revision would provide for an election by the target area population of 50 percent of the Model Area Councils. Following the election the mayor would appoint the other 50 percent. The coalition of community organizations claimed that this was a totally inadequate response to the magnitude of the issues raised by Regional HUD and that the residents of the communities involved were not consulted in preparing the city's response. The 50 percent election was deemed unacceptable by TWO and the other groups because the mayor, by appointing the other 50 percent would control MAC as effectively as before.

The June MAC meetings in all four target areas were chaotic. In Woodlawn, Anderson was unable to keep the meetings under control. The more he cut off discussion in order to get approval for the CDA defense of the Chicago proposal, the more the meetings degenerated into confusion until on one occasion the police were called in. James Grammer sought to introduce a resolution requesting 100 percent election of the councils. It appeared that a majority of MAC

[38] Federal Regional Model Cities Coordinating Committee, "Initial Response to the City of Chicago's Model City Proposal," mimeo. (Chicago: Midwest Regional Office of U.S. Department of Housing and Urban Development, April 21, 1969), pp. 1, 3, 4, 5.

271

was in favor. However, Grammer was ruled out of order on the grounds that the only item of business was approval of the CDA defense. The staff director, Mrs. Himes, pleaded that if MAC did not approve the CDA revision, then Wood-lawn would not be funded. It was this or nothing because the Chicago proposal had to have Washington approval before June 30. The TWO members and observers were increasingly enraged. Leon Finney, TWO staff director, was refused permission to speak, along with all other nonmembers, at the June 4 meeting. Finney interrupted the meeting saying that the transcripts "we have of this meeting and other MAC meetings will prove that this council is acting under instructions from the mayor and does not represent the people."[39]

At the same time that the city's plan was finally forwarded to Washington, TWO sent to HUD the transcripts of meetings, the sworn testimony of council members, and a detailed list of violations of the federal guidelines. "In this complaint," argued TWO, "we request that before this program be considered for approval, HUD enforce, in regards to the City of Chicago the 'citizen participation' provisions of the Model Cities legislation. That is, we are asking that the law be obeyed."[40]

As was expected, Washington approved the $38 million Chicago proposal. Brazier argued that there was a straight Nixon-Daley trade-off. Nixon's surtax bill passed the House by five votes with last minute support from Chicago Democrats two days after the federal approval of the Chicago grant was announced.[41] A sufficient explanation, however, is found in the shift of federal Model Cities policy under the Nixon administration. It was not simply a matter of the failure of the federal government to enforce the standards.

[39] Betty Washington, "TWO to Take Model Cities Complaints Directly to U.S.," *Chicago Daily News*, June 5, 1969, p. 7.

[40] Affidavit of complaint sent to U.S. Department of Housing and Urban Development, June 16, 1969, on file at TWO (mimeographed).

[41] Brazier's interpretation to TWO delegates' meeting, July 7, 1969.

These standards, ambiguous to begin with, were reinterpreted by the new Secretary of HUD, George Romney, and his assistant for Model Cities, Floyd Hyde. Formerly the mayor of Fresno, California, Hyde was convinced that mayors needed more resources to cope with the problems they faced. In a March 19 letter to the 150 Model Cities mayors, Hyde wrote:

> The Model Cities program is not intended to be a substitute for local institutions. Rather it is intended to make them more responsive to the needs of the community and to improve their capability. Institution building, not institution substitution, is the rule.[42]

Hyde began to talk about "adequate citizen participation" rather than "maximum" (OEO) or "widespread" (early Model Cities). One HUD holdover was reported to have characterized the change this way:

> With that March letter, it became apparent what the strategy of the new administration would be. Instead of repealing earlier guidelines or making a public fuss, the administration would just quietly pass the word to the mayors: just quietly say—"Man, ignore all that stuff. Use this money to strengthen your own position and never mind these new ideas."[43]

In the late spring Romney made it clear that the elected city officials were in complete charge of the program and its administration. In announcing his revenue sharing understanding of Model Cities, Romney was reported by the press as saying "it will be up to the mayors how they spread the money."[44] By late April, when Regional HUD leveled its sharp criticism of the Chicago plan and process, Mayor Daley and Irwin France were already receiving go-ahead signals from Washington. No further deals were necessary.

[42] Hamilton, "The Cities vs. the People," p. 6.
[43] *Ibid.*
[44] *Chicago Sun Times*, April 26, 1969, p. 32.

TWO leaders abandoned any last hopes they might have had for Model Cities. The city clearly was going to have its way. The Poverty Program experience was repeated. The process may have been different. Certainly TWO put up a more sustained countereffort. But the outcome was basically the same. City control of Model Cities was established. CDA had control of the money and the Model Area Councils. There was nothing for TWO to do but to intensify its own activities, consolidate its own strength, and keep a vigilant eye on Model Cities activities. From TWO's perspective the city's Model Cities program was a failure before it began:

> As long as City Hall controls Model Cities and as long as the local citizens are dependent on City Hall experts, Model Cities is just a marriage between urban renewal and the Poverty Program. Both of these programs have failed the Black community miserably.[45]

Having abandoned any expectation that Model Cities would do much good for the community, TWO's primary concern was to keep Model Cities from doing too much harm. The chief threat was that with the millions of dollars of Model Cities resources CDA would be able to use the Model Area Council as a puppet community organization, divide the community, and establish projects that undermined TWO. Therefore, TWO continued a relationship of quiet vigilance interrupted by an occasional flurry of protest activity. One example occurred in October 1969. The program was under way, personnel were being hired and projects were being contracted out. By then even MAC had become upset. They had been assured that they would have a right to "approve or disapprove" of all projects, hiring policy, and contracting as the program went along. The Woodlawn MAC, along with the councils in Lawndale and Uptown, voted to suspend all activity until the rights and responsibilities of the MAC's were clearly stipulated. Irwin

[45] *The Observer*, March 5, 1969, p. 4.

France came out to Woodlawn to talk with the council and quell the minor rebellion. France faced over 300 angry citizens, the result of a TWO organizing effort. France explained that the projects had all been approved by the council last February and by City Hall in April. He conveniently forgot that one of the arguments his staff had used to secure MAC approval at that time was that the program was tentative and could be changed, altered or redirected by MAC at any time. France's defense was not well received.

> Through most of the meeting France attempted to field questions amid shouts and booing and charges that he was being manipulated by the mayor. . . . He was drowned out by such shouted comments as "the city has been double-dealing," "If we don't run this thing you can't have it." "Tell the mayor there will be no Model Cities in Woodlawn."[46]

Although this kind of protest did not alter the Model Cities program, it did serve as a reminder to France that even though he had the funds there were limits to what the community would tolerate.

The election of half of the Model Cities council in April 1970, stimulated renewed citizen activity. TWO saw the occasion more as an opportunity to foster political independence than as a means of influencing Model Cities. There was no way that the Woodlawn residents could gain control of MAC through the election of twenty because the mayor would appoint twenty additional members after the CDA staff analyzed the results of the community election. In any case, it was apparent by now that MAC was merely an advisory board with little or no control over the program. Nevertheless, TWO saw this election as an opportunity for political education. Since TWO could not be directly involved in political campaigns, the Model Cities efforts were carried on by an off-shoot organization named the Woodlawn Peo-

[46] Betty Washington, "Citizens Demand Model Cities Role," *Chicago Daily News*, June 5, 1969, p. 7.

ple's 20. The twenty candidates, with the endorsement of independent South Side politicians and support from the Independent Voters of Illinois organization, conducted a vigorous campaign. With legal help they forced nine of the candidates put up by the regular Democratic organization off of the ballot because of forgeries on the required petitions. Unaccustomed to facing opposition, a number of Machine candidates made the mistake of simply filling in the necessary signatures. The final ballot included eight candidates supported by the Democratic organization, the People's 20, and two unattached. Of the four target areas, only Woodlawn posed a serious challenge to the city. In a very close election seven of the eight Machine candidates won, assuring continued CDA control of MAC. The victory of thirteen of the People's 20 was gratifying but meaningless. The outcome was so close that ballot placement made the decisive difference. The twenty winners were among the top twenty-one names on the ballot. Seven of the People's 20 were listed in the bottom nine names. The mayor appointed his twenty, eight of whom did not live in the target area and none of whom were with TWO. The election procedure increased TWO representation on the council only slightly, from nine out of thirty-two (28 percent) to thirteen out of forty (33 percent). More important, however, was the enthusiasm generated by the campaign, the experience in working for independent candidates and the election of two members of the Black P Stone Nation to public office.

TWO, recognizing that MAC was not a decision-making body and would not usurp the authority of the various agencies they were supposedly coordinating, decided that the best way to deal with Model Cities was through direct contact with the agencies that carried out Model Cities programming, including DUR, the Board of Education, CHA, and police. In short, TWO's best defense against Model Cities was to continue relationships with the implementing agencies. TWO had been more successful with Lew Hill, the head of DUR, than with Irwin France. When Model Cities announced a proposal that would allow the Chicago Housing Authority to buy up vacant land in Woodlawn and develop it through a nonprofit-making corporation whose board would be appointed by the mayor, TWO protested at MAC but made its decisive opposition of this proposal to CHA and HUD directly. The proposal was rejected by HUD. TWO's plan for physical rehabilitation, developed with the professional help of planners Whitley and Whitley, was submitted directly to DUR in the summer of 1970. In the conflict over the Model Cities school program, TWO went directly to the Board of Education, that time without success. Model Cities, TWO had realized, was nothing more than the expansion of existing agencies and existing programs. As TWO hopes for Model Cities were unfulfilled, so its fears were largely unwarranted. Woodlawn would survive Model Cities. While some people may have been disappointed that Model Cities, at least in its first year, did not do much, many others, particularly in TWO, were relieved. The second-year proposals looked like the first. When asked about this at a sparsely attended hearing to examine the second-year action program, the Woodlawn staff director explained that since not much had been done in the first-year action program, the second year would be the same. The City Council, despite Fifth Ward Alderman Leon Despres' contention that the program was marked by "underachievement and overcontrol,"[47] passed a $53 million second-year program indicating that even the cost of doing little was rising. From TWO's perspective Model Cities turned out to be neither as good nor as bad as it might have been. It simply turned out to be all the things that the designers of Model Cities said were wrong with past government programs.

It was not surprising that the TWO Model Cities proposal did not prevail. However, some people were surprised that TWO took this apparent defeat without a full-scale fight. Many Woodlawn residents had invested time and energy in

[47] Harry Golden, Jr., "Council Sets New Rules for Institutions," *Chicago Sun Times,* August 25, 1970, p. 12.

the development of the TWO plan. It would not have been difficult for TWO to organize direct action. Julian Levi and Jack Meltzer of the University, the two most responsible for developing and coordinating the University Model Cities task force, were ready to use their considerable influence at various levels of government. A variety of people, both within and outside the organization, had come to believe that Model Cities was the issue around which TWO might stake its future. In such a struggle TWO could have counted on considerable support within Woodlawn. The controversy might even have, like the 1965 Poverty Program struggle, become a national issue because it would have highlighted the contrast between the TWO and the Chicago plans. The TWO plan was something like what the initiators of Model Cities suggested when they talked about "comprehensive," "coordinated," "concentrated," and "innovative." The city's plan had none of these features. The TWO plan adhered to the federal guidelines on citizen participation and technical assistance. The city's plan violated these guidelines. The issue would have been simple and compelling. TWO was on the side of law and order. The City of Chicago Demonstration Agency was on the side of circumvention of law and the continued disorder of public services and programs.

It appeared to some that TWO was accepting defeat too easily and too calmly. Organizations in other target areas in Chicago, with no plan and far less resources, seemed to be putting up more resistance to the Chicago plan than did TWO. The story was circulated that TWO had "sold out," that it made some sort of deal with the city administration. This was not the case at all. TWO leaders had come to the conclusion that greater control over Model Cities was simply something for which it was not worth fighting. This was the central meaning of Brazier's discussion with the steering committee and the Pastors' Alliance in January. If TWO was ever going to stake its existence on an issue, it would not be the Model Cities program. TWO leaders came to realize that the plan they helped develop, if implemented through the Model Cities administration, would place the organization in a restricted position as a governmental agency. It would have limited administrative authority but it would not have real power to implement a program. It would be vulnerable to intervention, harassment, investigation, and policy changes from above. TWO would be subject to attack from within and without. Federal programs, TWO leaders decided, do not provide the path to community control.

Instead of a direct conflict with City Hall, TWO moved in two less dramatic ways, both of which failed. First, through a negotiated settlement TWO sought to secure a major voice on MAC in Woodlawn so that when TWO came to push and shove over the program and its implementation, it would not be a TWO vs. CDA conflict but rather a MAC vs. CDA conflict. Second, TWO expected HUD to be more rigorous in enforcing its own performance standards, thereby insuring that MAC could secure independent technical assistance and would have significant voice in policy and program planning. Neither of these happened. TWO ended up with a minority voice on a weak council.

There are several reasons why TWO did not seem to be too bothered by this apparent defeat. One, which has already been mentioned, was that while the city's program did not appear to be accomplishing much, neither was it doing much harm. A second was that TWO found that the resources and efforts on the Model Cities planning process opened up possibilities that could be pursued independent of Model Cities resources. The professional assistance from the University, a $65,000 planning grant from the Community Renewal Society, the environmental plan developed with Whitley and Whitley, and a variety of contacts with new funding resources were stimulated by the Model Cities enterprise. TWO's Model Cities effort opened up more doors than the city' rejection of it had closed.

The three major projects with the youth organizations, the schools, and Model Cities were at the center of TWO's attention for nearly three years. This was an exciting period characterized by lively meetings, heady rhetoric, multiple negotiations, frequent press conferences, and, consequently, constant activity. The three projects had some things in common: they were stimulated by the prospect of federal funding; they drew on the resources of the University of Chicago; they addressed some of the systemic causes, rather than the symptoms, of Woodlawn's enduring social problems; and major structural changes in the process of decision making and control of community programs were projected. In each project community control was the central issue. Finally, TWO's efforts were, in varying ways, rejected, undermined, or limited by the countervailing efforts of city agencies.

The tactics, however, by which TWO pursued increased community control differed in each of these projects. In the Youth Project, TWO tried to bypass City Hall and the city controlled agencies. Direct OEO funding supported this strategy. This move toward independence in the planning and administration of a million-dollar program elicited a concerted and forceful counterresponse killing the project. Since funds for WESP were channeled through the Chicago Board of Education, TWO assumed a more cooperative stance and directed its energies toward skillfully maximizing its influence within the constraints of the existing system. The final control of WESP was with the Board of Education. Even though the community exercised increasing influence over the project, or perhaps because it did, the experimental program was terminated when federal funding ran out. Drawing on University resources, TWO developed a Model Cities plan independently of city controlled procedures. TWO had a competitive plan but no market. With a possibility neither of direct funding nor of City Council support, TWO sought to apply pressure on the city from the bottom through the neighborhood Model Area Council and from the top through HUD. Predictably, both efforts failed.

In these different ways TWO challenged the municipal sovereignty of the city. The city's receptiveness to these three projects was inversely related to the degree of community control projected. The TWO Model Cities plan, a clear threat to municipal sovereignty, was never seriously reviewed or considered. TWO's limited control of limited funds in the Youth Project triggered vigorous and decisive opposition. WESP was tolerated largely because it was clear that the Board of Education had ultimate control. When this control was strongly contested, the Experimental Schools Project met the fate of the Youth Project.

The message was clear. For those in TWO who had not noticed it, Brazier spelled it out in detail at steering committee meetings. "The City of Chicago will resist with all its resources any efforts toward community control."[48] Brazier interpreted City Hall's approach to Woodlawn this way: "Help people only if you can control them. If you can't control them, don't help them."[49] In the Chicago political system there are slack power resources that can be mobilized. An organization can, depending on its skill and determination, marshal unused resources and enhance its bargaining power. There is a pluralism in Chicago up to a point. As long as TWO accepted its place in the Chicago political game, it would be recognized as the spokesman for Woodlawn. It was when TWO tried to change the rules of the game, attempted to move beyond bargaining, and challenged the municipal sovereignty of City Hall that the message was made clear: In Chicago, Daley runs it.

Community organizations that develop bargaining power not only help secure for their neighborhoods additional services and resources, but also help maintain, and even enhance, the ongoing governmental agencies. Pressure from organized constituencies is translated into stepped-up agency activity—more programs, more money, more staff, more branch offices, more poverty programs, Title III funds, Model Cities, more jobs per precinct for the political Machine. Organized constituency pressure provides the glue which holds the political-governmental apparatus in Chicago together.

The threat posed by these three TWO projects was clear: control over jobs and money. TWO's administration of a

---

[48] Brazier to TWO steering committee, August 11, 1969.
[49] Brazier to TWO delegates meeting, January 5, 1970.

million-dollar Youth Project, pressure for a semiautonomous school district, plans for a neighborhood governmental structure, are not in the same class with the traditional demands for more goods and services from the centralized city government.

The opposition triggered by TWO's move toward community control did not come merely from the politicians concerned about the future of the Machine and its patronage system. The service, education, planning, and social control bureaucracies have a vested interest in the continuation of a political process which has granted them considerable autonomy and a near monopoly over financial resources in their field. "Helping people" is a fast-growing industry. With money to be made, departments to be expanded, careers to be advanced, research grants to be secured, the established professionals in the "helping" business are not inclined to weaken their control over an expanding market.

One major lesson TWO learned from its efforts toward community control was that it could not count on federal support. It was the lure of federal funding, the substance of federal rhetoric, the content of federal guidelines, and the assistance of federal officials that led TWO into these specific ventures. TWO was soon disenchanted with federal support. The encouragement TWO received from some federal agencies and officials was neutralized or undercut by other federal actions. This situation is attributed not to a duplicity on the part of representatives of the federal government, but rather to the lack of policy and coordination among the multiple levels, agencies, and jurisdictions of federally initiated activity and to the overriding influence of City Hall on federal activities in Chicago.

The Youth Project, initiated with federal encouragement and monitored by federal officials, was finally killed by a Senate investigation. The young men who were encouraged to administer the project were "rewarded" three years later with federal grand jury indictments which probably stemmed less from their innovative and irregular administrative practices than from the police department's determination to rid the community of Stones.

The Woodlawn Experimental Schools Project, financed with HEW money, was weakened by a competitive project financed by HUD. WESP was also indirectly hampered by belated enforcement of desegregation rulings. In the early 1960s when TWO, along with other black organizations, was protesting the planned segregation in the Chicago school system, little or no federal support was forthcoming. With the emergence of black solidarity movements and pressure for community control as well as the increased availability and interest of black teachers for experimental programs, the Chicago Board of Education, under pressure from the federal government, began dispersing black teachers throughout the school system. The federal desegregation rulings were used as grounds for maintaining centralized control of teacher placement.

TWO's Model Cities planning effort was encouraged by HUD officials and favorably reported in a pamphlet published by the U.S. Civil Rights Commission.[50] The middle-level federal reformers could not, however, prevent Mayor Daley from ignoring federal standards or the Nixon administration from revising these standards.

Whenever TWO relied on federal support it found itself a pawn in some larger contest, either between various federal agencies or between federal and Chicago governments. TWO could not move toward community control by direct assault. It was no match against a strong political machine and recalcitrant bureaucracies. Federal support, however well intended, was unreliable. If TWO's initial fight for increasing levels of community control was not defeated, it was at least deferred. In the wake of its experience in this struggle, organizational survival itself became a paramount concern.

[50] U.S., Commission on Civil Rights, *T.W.O.'s Model Cities Plan* (Washington, D.C.: Government Printing Office, December 1969).

CHAPTER VI

The Struggle Is Survival:
TWO Hangs On

TWO's overt efforts toward community control were met with concerted resistance. As a pressure group TWO had faced opposition throughout its history. However, only when the organization was strong enough to assume quasi-governmental functions and to pursue a decentralization of public authority, did it elicit decisive opposition. It is one thing to negotiate with centralized agencies for goods and services. It is quite another thing to challenge the sovereignty of the city of Chicago. On issues where that sovereignty was threatened the corporate power of the established city agencies prevailed, not only over TWO but also over the federal government. Contrary to the traditional adage, you can fight City Hall. What you cannot do is bypass it, split it up, or take it over. One might argue that this was true only in Chicago with its still dominant machine-style politics and a resilient mayor. However, the fact remains that, short of community control, TWO stood nationally as one of the few community organizations even in a position to implement control if it were forthcoming. Perhaps in the future TWO would not need to fight City Hall; City Hall might one day need TWO to sustain its own fight for city control. Community control was an ideal whose time had not yet come.

Faced with the might of established counterresistance and disillusioned with federally funded programs, TWO directed attention to a variety of less threatening ventures in community development. This move toward community development was characterized by increased reliance on nongovernmental resources, an expressed awareness of the limits of power, a disengagement from direct conflict, and intensified pursuit of noncontroversial programs and projects. The motto of the tenth anniversary edition of *The Observer* summarized this development: "TWO—From Protest to Program."[1]

This new stage in the development of TWO was not unequivocally acclaimed. Many people, observers and participants, were quick to conclude that TWO was finished as a people's organization, that it had neither the will nor the resources to persist. It would fight no more. Some observed, without malice, that TWO had tried and failed. Others contended that the organization had "sold out." This negative interpretation appears both premature and simplistic, revealing a tendency to "blame the victim" which is based on imported ideological assumptions and unrealistic expectations.

If one focuses solely on TWO's inability to prevail over the entrenched power of established agencies, then it is true that TWO was not able to sustain the Youth Project against concerted attack, that it could not secure greater support from the public school bureaucracy for WESP, and that it did not receive a hearing for its Model Cities plan. However, the most significant thing to observe about TWO during this period of the late 1960s was not the failure of initial efforts toward community control, but the success of the organization despite this. For, on examination, TWO not only survived the controversies over community control but also utilized the outcome for its own programmatic ends.

First of all, that it was deemed necessary by existing agencies to kill the Youth Project, to negotiate on the Schools Project, and to circumvent TWO in Model Cities, is an indication of TWO's corporate strength. TWO had "taken up the slack." It had reached the point where it could not con-

[1] *The Observer*, September 6, 1970.

tinue further toward community control without threatening, in a basic way, the existing political process. Brazier spoke of this as the "limits of power." To have come to this point is no sign of failure. Few community organizations in Chicago have commanded the attention or elicited the response directed at TWO. Secondly, and more significantly, TWO survived. To engage in major and extended controversies with established agencies and still survive is no small achievement. The Kenwood-Oakland Community Organization and the Uptown Peoples' Planning Coalition, grass-roots community organizations, which, like TWO had worked with youth gangs and had entered into the Model Cities struggle, were in disarray by 1971. When community organizations touch sensitive areas of the body politic, threaten prevailing programs, and elicit concerted counterpressure, survival itself becomes a sign of success. Thirdly, TWO not only survived, it transformed what could have been a series of demoralizing setbacks into new program opportunities for developing organizational resources. TWO's survival impulse led the organization toward possibilities that were being opened, particularly through contacts made and concepts developed, in the Model Cities planning process. The relative longevity of TWO is attributable in no small part to this capacity to milk victories out of defeats. There was much to be milked from the abortive Model Cities effort. "Political actions," William Gamson observes, "must be judged not only in terms of their immediate influence—that is, their effect on the outcome of specific decisions—but by their creation of new resources as well."[2]

If TWO suffered from the setback in its major ventures toward community control, the outward signs were not obvious. It emerged from the 1960s as an established veteran fighter with a possible future as a heavyweight. Like its program, the budget was also expanding. A comparison of the annual reports during the late sixties reveals this growth:

[2] William A. Gamson, *Power and Discontent* (Homewood, Ill.: Dorsey Press, 1968), p. 98.

TABLE 3. Comparison of Annual Financial Reports

Allocation	1967	1968	1969	1970
Receipts to accounts available for general operation of TWO	$ 68,620	$ 83,101	$106,126	$117,964
Receipts to accounts for special programs[a]	216,938	353,946	408,332	481,193

[a] Excluding $817,201 for Youth Project in 1967 and 1968.

Much of the increase came from private sector support: Citizens Crusade Against Poverty ($22,500), Center for Community Change ($68,000), Community Renewal Society ($65,000), and Ford Foundation ($102,000). Since these budget figures include only that money for which TWO had direct administrative responsibility, it does not tell the whole story. Leon Finney estimated that, including the programs administered through agencies and corporations related to TWO, the organization "controls or influences over $30 million in Greater Woodlawn."[3]

The range of activities and programs in TWO from 1968 through 1971 was impressive, probably unmatched by any urban neighborhood organization, black or white. The regular standing committees continued to pursue specific grievances. In addition to this, a wide variety of special projects and programs was maintained or developed.

1. TWO's weekly newspaper, *The Woodlawn Observer*, after lean years with mechanical and management difficulties, had become a valuable part of the overall TWO operation and had potential for becoming the basis for a stable printing and publishing venture.

2. The Early Childhood Development Center, a $100,000 a year OEO-funded Head Start program begun in 1965, continued under TWO administration. The director, in 1971, was a Woodlawn woman whose training had come through participation in the project itself. In addition to the

[3] *The Observer*, September 6, 1970, p. 27.

pre-school educational advantages, the ECDC project was providing opportunities for a number of Woodlawn residents to develop skilled positions that have often been reserved for those with academic certification.

3. In the area of job training TWO received, in 1969, a $119,000 contract with the Zenith Corporation to provide recruiting, counseling, and support services for a program to reach hard-core unemployed. The organization was also a prime contractor with the Illinois State Employment service to recruit and train public aid recipients for paramedical professions. By 1971, after six years' experience in the manpower and job-training field, TWO developed a Career Vocational Institute, a neighborhood-run, multipurpose training center supported by state and federal funds.

4. The Woodlawn Experimental Schools Project showed promise of becoming a model for parent and community involvement in the public schools. TWO, along with the parent organizations and the WESP staff, began negotiating for the continuation of the experimental district, the expansion of its boundaries, and increased autonomy, after the termination of federal funding in June 1971. Although finally defeated, this effort brought together a spectrum of community groups concerned about public schools in Woodlawn.

5. TWO has been increasingly called upon to provide members for advisory or policy boards. In most cases, these boards, although not directly related to the organization, have a majority membership from TWO and report back to the organization intermittently. The Woodlawn Mental Health Center Board has been the most controversial. When the original codirectors, Dr. Sheppard Kellam and Dr. Sheldon Schiff, were made aware, largely through TWO protest, of the distrust between the community and the social agencies, they turned to TWO for help in establishing a community board in 1963. More significant than the creation of the board, often a standard practice through which the semblance of participation becomes a cloak for contin-

ued professional control, was the policy making assumed by the board.[4] Aided by TWO pressure, the Mental Health Center Board, was able, in 1970, to force the removal of Dr. Schiff, with whom there had been a growing mutual antagonism.

In less controversial areas TWO provided membership for the Woodlawn Child Health Center Advisory Board, the Mandel Legal Aid Clinic Advisory Board, and the Woodlawn Drug Abuse Center Advisory Board. The Child Health Center, a free medical clinic supported by a five-year, $1.5 million grant from the Federal Children's Bureau and administered by the University of Chicago staff, handled 43,000 cases in its first four years of operation and was planning to expand its facilities and services. The Legal Aid Clinic utilizing University law students to augment its staff has served TWO committees as well as an average of 160 cases of free legal assistance a week. In addition TWO members have continued participation on the Woodlawn Model Cities Area Council and have secured the chairmanship of several subcommittees.

6. Some of the new opportunities TWO pursued were stimulated by the Model Cities planning effort. The Woodlawn Service Program, a State of Illinois facility, housing and coordinating several agencies under one roof, was seeking to test some of the proposals developed in the TWO plan, particularly the separation of financial assistance from the provision of social services. TWO has a majority membership on the Woodlawn Service Program Advisory Board. Whether major reform in social welfare delivery systems is forthcoming through this pilot program remains to be seen. In July 1970, TWO was awarded a four-year, $315,000 National Institute of Mental Health grant to train lay mental health workers. The proposal was based on the outreach

[4] An account of the development of this policy board is given in Sheppard G. Kellam and Sheldon K. Schiff, "The Woodlawn Mental Health Center: A Community Mental Health Center Model," *Social Science Review*, XL, No. 3 (September 1966), pp. 255-263.

or "pad" concept developed in the Model Cities plan whereby Woodlawn residents would be trained as organizer-subprofessionals to deal with a variety of medical, educational, housing, and legal problems on the block level. The organization acquired VISTA program resources whereby it could provide $50.00 a week stipends for some of its most active participants.

In cooperation with the Chicago Mid-South Health Planning Council TWO has pursued its Model Cities proposal for a comprehensive health care facility in Woodlawn. By the fall of 1970, the Chicago City Council and the Board of Health approved the concept in general and the location on the 63rd Street and Dorchester Avenue site which had been cleared, because of TWO pressure, several years earlier. The Greater Woodlawn Assistance Corporation, supported by a $685,000 federal grant, has the task of developing a working partnership between appropriate public bodies, the insurance industry, the existing health resources, and the Woodlawn residents. The goal is to develop a common health care system and, possibly, a community health insurance plan out of the hodgepodge of existing services and the $6 million-a-year spent for medical care in Woodlawn.

7. Increased attention was given to the need for new and rehabilitated housing. Through the TWO-KMF Development Association Board, TWO was directly responsible for the oversight and policy for the 500-unit Woodlawn Gardens housing complex. With funds from a Community Renewal Society grant for Model Cities planning, TWO hired urban planners Whitley and Whitley to help the organization develop a physical plan for Woodlawn. After a year's work and numerous meetings with the TWO ways and means committee a document[5] was adopted by the organization and in July 1970, submitted to the Department of

[5] For a summary of the plan see Whitley and Whitley, "Policies and Proposals for Improving Physical Conditions in Woodlawn: A Summary Report for The Woodlawn Organization," n.d., on file at TWO.

Urban Renewal. Collaboration with DUR and Model Cities may lead to official acceptance of a revised version of this TWO plan.

In the fall of 1969, TWO entered into an agreement with the University of Chicago, leasing eight acres of land on the South Campus area and securing a $500,000 seed money loan for a second major low-to-moderate-income housing development of 318 units. In addition to this Jackson Park Terrace project, ninety units on the land adjacent to the proposed health center were being planned. TWO directed increased attention to securing and rehabilitating dilapidated and abandoned buildings. First, TWO secured the services of a black consultant firm, Trans-Urban East, to assist the organization in preparing proposals for rehabilitating 251 units and negotiating the proposals through the appropriate governmental channels. In 1971, with the benefits of the federal program, Project Rehab, and with the alarming increase of abandoned and burned out buildings, TWO projected plans for 2,500 rehabilitated units. The Woodlawn Redevelopment Corporation was formed to coordinate and concentrate TWO's efforts to secure assistance in an extensive housing rehabilitation program. Looking forward to the time when TWO would be the owner of an increasing number of housing units, the organization also created the Woodlawn Management Corporation to serve as manager of TWO's housing acquisitions.

8. High on the TWO agenda was the development of revenue-producing programs to make the organization economically independent. In partnership with the Hillman Company, TWO owns and manages a supermarket. Survey research had indicated that this modern market, located next to Woodlawn Gardens, could gross four million dollars annually. Under the arrangements of the TWO-Hillman Corporation, Hillman's would manage the operation for three percent of the gross and receive one-third of the profit. TWO's two-thirds share would, it was estimated, amount to $60,000 annually after three years of operation. This store,

291

opened in November 1970, is located in a mini-mall of eleven shops leased by the TWO-KMF Development Association. TWO also owns and manages a Standard Oil station built adjacent to the shopping plaza. In a small profit-making venture TWO established a watchman service for Woodlawn Gardens. As the demand for its services increased the Woodlawn Security Patrol has been expanded. TWO assumed management of a movie theater adjacent to the shopping plaza and the TWO-Standard station. The TWO-Maryland theater, given to TWO in 1971, soon became a profit-making operation. A Woodlawn Local Development Corporation was established to acquire real estate, fixtures, and equipment for business ventures. The Development Corporation secured a $350,000 loan for the Small Business Association in Washington in order to equip the TWO-Hillman supermarket. Another legal entity, TWO Enterprises, Inc., was formed to oversee the four initial community-owned business ventures, TWO-Hillman, TWO-Standard, the TWO-Maryland theater, and the Woodlawn Security Patrol, and to consider possibilities for new ventures. Finally, a Woodlawn Community Development Corporation, with a board of directors appointed by TWO and Leon Finney as executive director, was established to propose and steer TWO's overall community development strategy and programs.

The sum total of these projects and activities is impressive: over a thousand new or rehabilitated housing units, plans for several thousand additional rehabilitated units, a proposed comprehensive health center, a supermarket, a service station, a movie theater, a coordinated social welfare program, a vocational training center, subprofessional training programs in legal assistance, mental health and education, and a steadily increasing number of other programs along with the week-by-week pursuits of the regular committees.

Thus TWO bore the marks of success. In ten years, the organization had amassed a substantial record of accomplishments. TWO had moved from a noisy protest organization to an established, stable, competent community institution that could attract, develop, and administer programs. Yet these very marks of success contained an obvious ambiguity. Criticism of TWO, especially from some of its supporters, was directed less at what it had accomplished or not accomplished than at what TWO was becoming. TWO in 1971, it was charged, was fat, tame, and accommodating. It was part of the regular political process. It had lost touch with the people. Self-determination had been traded for self-preservation.

Ambivalence about TWO's programmatic achievement is understandable. Clearly, the TWO of 1971 was different from the TWO of 1962, or 1965, or 1968. An outside observer visiting Woodlawn in 1962 would probably have been most impressed, as Charles Silberman was, by the new-found enthusiasm that was evoked by and focused around TWO's protest activity. "Up from Apathy," "Woodlawn: A Community in Revolt," and "The Slum That Saved Itself," were the titles of articles about this "new experiment."[6] "What is crucial," wrote Silberman, "is not what the Woodlawn residents win, but that *they* are winning it; and this makes them see themselves in a new light—as men and women of substance and worth."[7] A similar visitor in 1965 would have been impressed by the organization's determination and ability to mobilize citizen support, to confront city agencies, and to make credible its claim as spokesman for the Greater Woodlawn area. Whether it succeeded or not on a particular issue, TWO had clearly become an organization that had to be reckoned with. In 1968, an observer would undoubtedly have been deeply impressed by the

[6] Charles E. Silberman, "Up From Apathy—The Woodlawn Experiment," *Commentary*, May 1964, pp. 51-58; Georgie Anne Geyer, "Woodlawn: A Community in Revolt," *Chicago Scene*, June 7, 1962, pp. 12-17; Elinor Richey, "The Slum That Saved Itself," *Progressive*, October 1963, pp. 26-29.

[7] Silberman, *Crisis*, p. 346.

293

active participation of large numbers of Woodlawn residents in pursuing, defending, planning, and administering projects that the organization had fought for and had some measure of control over: three hundred adults at a special meeting to defend the Youth Project, two to four hundred people at Model Cities meetings, one to two hundred parents and residents at monthly meetings of the Woodlawn Community Board. The observer would have noticed the community calm that was brought about through the Youth Project, the enthusiasm in the WCB meetings, and the optimism in Model Cities planning. A visitor to TWO in 1971 would be shown the Woodlawn Gardens housing, the shopping center, the TWO-Hillman supermarket, the TWO-Standard service station, and sites for the comprehensive health center and the proposed housing developments. He would visit the WESP office and the Woodlawn Service Program offices and the Child Health Center. He would be told about the environmental plan being reviewed by Model Cities and DUR. The observer would be impressed by all that was going on. But he would not write about "sense of dignity" or "community fights back." Nor would he find evidence of large community meetings to mobilize support around issues or to demand specific actions. Where Silberman could argue that "what makes the Woodlawn Organization significant is not so much what it is doing for its members as what it is doing to them,"[8] the recent observer would be more impressed by what TWO is doing *for* the community.

Clearly TWO was not, in 1971, the same kind of organization it had been in the early and middle sixties. Numerous changes had taken place both in the community and in the general strategy and style of the organization. Several of these developments warrant careful consideration.

By 1971, TWO had moved from conflict to coexistence. There was scant evidence of the innovative militancy that was the mark of the organization in the earlier years, no

[8] *Ibid.*

clear outside enemy, no inflammatory rhetoric, no mass protest demonstrations. Indeed on several occasions during the Youth Project, Schools Project, and Model Cities controversy, when the active constituency appeared eager to support vigorous protest action, the leaders of TWO managed to avoid precipitating direct confrontation with either City Hall or the agencies.

Why? Possibly TWO's experience supported several of Lewis Coser's propositions about the function of social conflict. "Conflict binds antagonists."[9] Sustained over a period of time, conflict provides the occasion for the development of mutually acceptable rules and relationships. TWO gradually developed working relationships with most of its former enemies, the University, DUR, school district 14, the Model Cities agency. The intricate web of relationships with foundations, federal agencies, and city departments also serves as a constraint. Militant action in one area might jeopardize programs and relationships in another. When TWO was in the final stages of negotiations for the Youth Project in the spring of 1967, it avoided protesting a DUR action which in earlier years would have triggered concerted community reaction. Social conflict, Coser also argues, stimulates the centralization of contending parties. The University, for example, soon valued TWO's capacity to speak for the community and sought to help the organization maintain its spokesman role. "A unified party prefers a unified opponent."[10] To facilitate communication and negotiation, contending parties tend to approximate each other's internal structure. TWO took on some of the characteristics of a formal agency. This made it possible for TWO more frequently to secure private settlements in potential conflict situations. Further, Coser points out that accommodation between antagonists is made possible, and

[9] Lewis Coser, *The Functions of Social Conflict* (paperback ed.; New York: Free Press, 1964), p. 121. The references to Coser in this paragraph are found in chap. viii of his book, pp. 121-137.
[10] *Ibid.*, p. 132.

likely, when each is aware of the relative strength of both. TWO's past conflict experiences had made the leaders sufficiently aware of the limits of TWO's power and the relative strength of other groups so that future conflict was less necessary. TWO is reluctant to engage in a confrontation over an issue which it knows it cannot win. And it can secure, without overt conflict, settlements which it can win.

The militant, direct, conflict tactics which built the organization were, by 1971, regarded as less necessary, desirable or permissible. The leaders of TWO saw that the organization had more to gain from coexistence with existing agencies than from militant conflict. And in many ways it did.[11]

The new situation was clearly revealed at a special meeting called by TWO in place of its regular steering committee meeting on November 16, 1970. Advertised as "Citizens' Information Night" the meeting was ostensibly to inform the 150 residents attending of the variety of programs operating in the community. However, a more significant message was conveyed. As TWO President McNeil cordially introduced representatives of DUR, the Urban Progress Center, the Model Cities office, the Police Department, and the YWCA and as these representatives responded with kind words about TWO, the common message was that the time of fighting each other was over. Herman Johnson, director of the Woodlawn Model Cities office observed, "A year ago I would never have met with TWO, especially at First Presbyterian Church." McNeil assured the gathering that "the government is not the enemy." There was an

---

[11] As TWO's need for financial resources paralleled its need for citizen support, the meaning of organizational survival and growth changed. Without IAF support after 1965, TWO had to secure its own funds. Dues, donations, and fund-raising efforts could not support the operation. TWO raised, by these means, $21,499 in 1967, $42,469 in 1968, and $32,512 in 1969, but this amounted to only between 4 and 7 percent of the total yearly receipts.

abundance of let-us-work-together rhetoric. It was no longer advantageous for TWO to fight DUR or Model Cities. TWO had developed a workable relationship with both agencies and was quietly but firmly pressing for the official endorsement of the Whitley and Whitley plan. The possibility of actual gains led to the transformation of TWO, though it is hard to see how it would have won the gains without the power and experience of almost a decade of conflict.

Secondly, by 1971 the focus of TWO activity had shifted from issues to projects. This gradual change had a significant impact on the organization. In early protest activity the issues were made clear. TWO's status and reputation depended upon its ability to identify and raise issues, politicize interests, mobilize citizen support, and negotiate settlements on clear issues of exploitation and outside control of Woodlawn. Success was measured in terms of the organization's ability to influence programs and policies administered by city agencies and to secure concessions from these agencies. Now TWO's reputation depends largely on its competence in administering its own programs, operating its own businesses, and managing its own housing projects. Success is measured in terms of its ability to make the TWO-Standard station a profitable venture, to avoid bankruptcy on Woodlawn Gardens, and to secure proper financing for Jackson Park Terrace. TWO's current stature rests, in short, more on its skill in managing its own projects than on its skill in identifying, pursuing, and negotiating issues.

This gradual change in focus from issues to projects created leadership needs as well as leadership problems. During the 1966-68 experience with the three major programs, more and more demands were placed on fewer and fewer leaders. Brazier, Finney, and two or three others carried out most of the negotiations with the mayor, agency leaders, federal officials, and the University. However, the active constituency was still knowledgeable about the projects and many participated fully in various stages of them. In the recent TWO transactions the intricacies of development corporations, special funds, health care systems, housing rehabilitation schemes, and business ventures have become so complex and sophisticated that knowledgeable participation is beyond the reach of all but a few residents and TWO is increasingly dependent upon the insights and advice of its staff, consultants, and specialists.

The technician replaced the organizer as the key to TWO's operation. Staff energies were devoted more to developing programs, writing proposals, seeking funds, consulting experts, and managing projects than to ringing doorbells and mobilizing the resident constituency. Bearing major responsibility in TWO's expanding programmatic agenda, the top staff members assumed leadership roles. With their own priorities and investments in TWO's future, members of the paid staff were frequently, and more openly, advocates of particular policies. Also, it is not insignificant that when Brazier resigned as president in 1970 he was replaced by a lawyer, E. Duke McNeil. As spokesman-negotiator Brazier was without peer. McNeil, however, brought to TWO a style and background that fit the techno-legal leadership needs of the organization.

The increase of community programs also brought new "leaders" to Woodlawn. Mrs. Sizemore, director of WESP, Herman Johnson of the Model Cities office, and Clinton McKay of the Woodlawn Services Program are three examples. Representing different perspectives and proposing different strategies, they appealed to constituencies that overlapped with TWO.

As a protest and spokesman organization TWO, with the aid of skilled organizers, was able to rally united support behind Brazier in combating insensitive professional bureaucrats and alien agencies. The development of projects gave rise to new leadership in the community. This was accompanied by increased competition and conflict between leaders both within TWO and in the community. That the entire TWO enterprise has become increasingly

298

complex and demands a new style of leadership may pose problems for the organization, but it is hardly a sign of weakness or failure.

Thirdly, it was readily apparent that by 1971 TWO faced new problems of internal tension and controversy. Having developed working relationships, or at least having clarified spheres of influence, with its former enemies, TWO could rely less and less on the glue of external conflict. In addition to having less to hold TWO together there was more to pull it apart. As Brazier told the steering committee, "TWO has problems it didn't have when we were carrying signs."[12] These were the problems of management, ownership, and administration.

As TWO moved from protest to program it began making policy and program decisions which did not please everyone. TWO experienced firsthand many of the same limitations for which it had previously criticized other agencies. For example, TWO had a long-standing policy in opposition to high rise housing until the organization itself became seriously involved in land use planning. Consultant Joyce Whitley confronted the ways and means committee with this dilemma. In a limited geographic area TWO had wanted low-cost housing, no high rises, more open space, more community facilities such as schools and hospitals, and a continuation of the present population density. This was obviously impossible. Hard choices had to be made.

TWO was a landlord. The problems in Woodlawn Gardens, from application policy to rectifying construction faults to tenant grievances, were brought to TWO. TWO had to evict people. As McNeil later expressed it, "It's hard to be a landlord and be a hero. It's hard to develop land without making deals. It's hard to manage housing without evicting people. TWO in some ways is the Establishment and should expect the heat."[13] TWO-Hillman and TWO-Standard both faced financial difficulties and there was

[12] Brazier to TWO steering committee, September 29, 1969.
[13] E. Duke McNeil, interview, May 24, 1972.

growing controversy within TWO about the priorities of the organization.

This increasing internal tension and frustration was unleashed on the floor of the annual conventions in 1971 and 1972. At the Tenth Annual Convention on April 25, 1971, McNeil, who had inherited the presidency at a time when the direction, leadership, and program of TWO were being questioned from within, was the most visible target. The dissidents, unable to persuade Brazier to reclaim his leadership position, ran a slate of officers headed by the Rev. Robert McGee, Brazier's assistant pastor and temporary president of TWO in 1961. McGee's candidacy tapped various undercurrents of dissatisfaction with McNeil and/or TWO's current strategy. The locals of the Social Welfare Union favored an alternative to McNeil's middle-class style, professional orientation, and lawyer image. McGee supporters argued that he was "a man of the people" who would restore popular democracy to TWO. Activists in the parent councils and WESP questioned McNeil's leadership on the Woodlawn Community Board. Several former TWO activists who had become disenchanted with the new programmatic efforts heeded McGee's call for a return to protest. "TWO and the Woodlawn community," McGee maintained in his platform, "have been victorious against our foes, winning many battles, UNTIL THIS PAST YEAR. . . ."[14] The statement went on to list TWO's recent failure to "speak out" and "take action against" city agencies. McGee's candidacy received behind-the-scenes support from some of the TWO staff whose own priorities were threatened by a strong president. An internal class cleavage, a top-level power struggle, and an ideological controversy were intermingled. Following the president's stirring State of the Community address it was evident that the McNeil forces would prevail. With the support from the Black P Stone Nation and the Disciples and most of the churches and

[14] From "Platform Statement" read by Robert McGee at TWO Annual Convention, April 25, 1971, on file at TWO.

block clubs, McNeil won handily by a three-to-one margin. To some of TWO detractors this heated internal controversy was a sign of the demise of the organization. Others, however, saw in the controversy itself the signs of new vitality.

The following year the convention was even more chaotic. The specific issues which triggered the breakdown of the meeting of over 130 delegate groups were not the characteristic issues signifying external domination. The volatile issues at the 1972 convention were internal housekeeping issues. One centered around constitutional changes which would strengthen the power of the staff and particularly the executive director, Leon Finney. The critical controversy was over the election of the treasurer of the organization. A woman who had previously worked at the mayor's Office of Inquiry and with the Model Cities Program waged a vigorous campaign for this office which had become a watchdog position through which the average participant was made aware of the organization's financial activities. Although she had a strained relationship with TWO in the past, the challenger was encouraged by Finney and supported by a large following. When, following a questionable voice vote, a roll call vote was refused by the chair, pandemonium broke out. Order could not be restored to continue the election of officers and other business of the meeting including the major address by guest speaker and gubernatorial candidate Daniel Walker. After several weeks and numerous negotiations between contesting groups a follow-up convention concluded the business, retained the incumbent treasurer, and healed the wounds.

The basic conflict was between TWO as a people's organization and TWO as a development corporation, between the power and authority of the nonpaid elected leadership and the paid staff, or, in personal terms, between president McNeil and Finney, who was executive director both of TWO and the Woodlawn Community Development Corporation. Finney's power in the organization had risen

301

with the expansion of community development programs. As director of WCDC Finney received a $26,000 salary designated by the Ford Foundation, the principal funding agent of the corporation. Neither the relationship between TWO and WCDC nor the role and accountability of Finney within TWO was clear. Although the efforts to strengthen his position further by favorable constitutional changes and by providing him with a more compatible treasurer failed, the veiled tension between Finney's leadership of the development corporation and McNeil's leadership of the organization remained. The steering committee and delegates meeting found itself repeatedly faced with various aspects of this tension between the dual aspects of TWO, grassroots organization and development corporation.

TWO had little experience in dealing with internal issues. The mechanisms of internal conflict resolution, delegation of authority, division of power, and formal representation—all the traditional governmental mechanisms—were less essential for a spokesman organization. A shared commitment against common enemies and a shared perception of the lack of representation in the larger society made the development of internal processes of representation less of an issue. TWO had been more concerned about speaking and acting with a strong united voice in its ongoing conflict with external forces and agencies than about adjudicating internal conflicts. As the organization moved from protest to program, it had to develop ways of resolving internal controversies, keeping its own house in order, and maintaining constituency support. That TWO faced increased internal tensions was not a sign of weakness but of growth. That it has thus far developed loyalty and support sufficient to offset and overcome the controversies that accompany its programmatic efforts is a mark of achievement rare in grassroots community organization.

Fourthly, by 1971 the mode, meaning, and value of citizen participation in the organization was changing. As a protest-spokesman-bargaining organization TWO's effectiveness was dependent upon an active participating constituency. There was a symbiotic relationship between TWO's capacity to influence external decision makers and the organization's ability to secure mass citizen support. The role and necessity of citizen participation were clear. Participants in the organization made a difference and it was a difference that they could see and about which they could share a sense of pride. When the Housing and Planning Committee of the City Council indefinitely deferred, in 1965, plans for a CHA high rise in Woodlawn, the eighty residents who attended the meeting had reason to feel that their participation in the protest made a desirable difference. When the local option referendum to dry up Baby Skid Row taverns won, the participants in TWO's effort could see the results of their action. The relationship between the 1966 community hearing attended by 1,100 residents and the subsequent designation of TWO-KMF as developers of Woodlawn Gardens was clear. This connection between active participation and visible results not only provided psychic rewards but also nurtured a political consciousness in the participants.

With the development of specialized programs, the decline of militant tactics, and the increased need for technical assistance, the significance of the participant role was diminished. The connection between participation and organized achievement became obscured and tenuous. There was no clear connection between active participation in TWO and the development of the TWO-Hillman supermarket, or the leasing of land from the University, or the securing of the National Institute of Mental Health grant. Since many of the plans, contracts, and transactions of TWO were the result of the work of experts and a few leaders, it was difficult for the average participant to sense personal gratification from these new accomplishments.

The TWO-Hillman store is one example. The anticipated success of this partnership venture was based largely on the presupposition that the residents would patronize a store

303

that they "owned." However, on the basis of initial response, this well-located and equipped supermarket appears to be regarded as just another store. There is no clear evidence of a sense of accomplishment or ownership on the part of the residents. The intricate arrangements, loans, and contracts had been worked out by TWO staff and consultants. There was no major controversy and no issue through which residents could gain a sense of having achieved a desired outcome. The significant struggle behind the TWO-Hillman venture was in the 1963 to 1966 protests, hearings, and negotiations during which several thousand Woodlawn residents participated in one way or another in having the land designated for development by TWO. But this activity, five years past, did not provide, except for a few TWO activists, the rewarding sense of accomplishment and ownership.

TWO's extensive program achievements do not generate the enthusiasm that was markedly apparent in the more modest outputs during the mid-sixties. The announcement of a $100,000 grant from the Ford Foundation or a $315,000 grant from the NIMH, or a $500,000 loan from the University was received at TWO meetings with perfunctory applause. In contrast, the announcement of a successful negotiation with a single landlord, especially if it followed prolonged controversy involving concerted citizen pressure, would trigger spontaneous cheers. TWO's capacity to develop, secure, and administer worthwhile programs is based more on staff skills, demonstrated competence, organizational stability and longevity, and general reputation than on active citizen participation. Of course, TWO has attained its prominent position largely as a result of concerted citizen involvement. But the present accomplishments, being less dependent upon direct and immediate citizen participation, are less rewarding psychologically. Alinsky argued that "to give people help without their having played a significant part in the action makes the help itself relatively valueless and constitutes nothing to the development of the individual that you are ostensibly 'helping.' "[15] If this premise upon which the spokesman style is built is right, it is questionable whether either past citizen efforts or present generalized support is "a significant part of the action."

While, with the proliferation of advisory boards, special committees, and corporations, there was more need for active participation, there was less gratifying activity for the ordinary resident. TWO had more going on, but the participants had less to do. This affected the make-up of the active TWO constituency. With the exception of a small number of loyalists, many of them older people for whom weekly participation in TWO had become a major part of their lives, the turnover in active TWO participation was noticeable. Of the fifty-five residents appointed to the six major working committees for 1970-71, only three had been on any of these committees three years earlier. Of the thirty-five officers and committee chairmen for 1970-71, eight had held leadership positions in 1967-68. Although the attendance at the weekly steering committee and the delegates meetings has remained about the same over the years, an increasing proportion of the active participants are employees or beneficiaries of one of the projects related to TWO, parent organizers, VISTA workers, etc. As it succeeds in securing and developing programs, TWO may be able to rely more on a form of patronage to maintain visible constituency support.

Peter Bachrach and Morton Baratz make a distinction between interest-oriented participation, the primary aim of which is "to provide a basis for the development of a widespread political awakening" and cooptative participation which is "to evoke the participant's interest, enthusiasm and sense of identity with the goals of the enterprise in question."[16] In the early and mid-sixties TWO, through un-

[15] Alinsky, "Citizen Apathy," p. 9.

[16] Peter Bachrach and Morton S. Baratz, *Power and Poverty* (New York: Oxford University Press, 1970), p. 206.

covering and channelling hostilities and politicizing neighborhood interests, was developing a "political awakening," a community consciousness. When the outcome of this awakening became a full agenda of projects and programs, TWO had greater need for cooptative participation, for active support of the ongoing enterprises.

This may be a sign of growth. TWO has sought to develop community institutions which would provide an ongoing and stable base for citizen involvement. Whether in the long run community development projects will be as effective as protest activities in sustaining the organization and in eliciting citizen participation remains to be seen.

Finally, by 1971, TWO's spokesman role was being fragmented. The central message of TWO had always been that the residents of Woodlawn were rendered powerless by the actions and policies of the agencies and institutions that operated in and on the neighborhood. The governmental and service agencies operate out of bureaucracies centralized downtown and related vertically to the various neighborhoods through "branch offices." Centralized internally, most of these agencies are decentralized from any formal public authority to which the Woodlawn residents might have access. The provision of services is fragmented, overlapping, and wasteful. The cycle of debilitating dependency would be maintained, TWO had argued, as long as the agencies were unresponsive to community interests, unconstrained by community groups, and unaccountable to an organized neighborhood constituency.

The heart of TWO's Model Cities plan was not in the new program ideas or the revision of delivery systems, but in the structure of control and responsibility. In essence, TWO proposed a first step toward a level of neighborhood government. Stymied in its move toward community control, TWO found itself with many of the pieces of its Model Cities plan, but not the center. Some of the innovative concepts in social welfare and education were being developed through the Woodlawn Service Program and WESP. With the National Institute of Mental Health grant the resident organizer-subprofessional training program was a possibility. A comprehensive health care system was being planned. Projects in housing rehabilitation, economic development, job training, and legal services were initiated. The pieces were there but there was little to hold them together. Rather than providing a center of accountability and control, TWO was itself being fragmented to fit the existing structure. In addition to the steering committee, the ways and means committee, ten standing committees, and the committees of the active constituency groups within TWO, there were at least sixteen special committees or bodies related to TWO concerns. Some were legal fictions; others demanded active participation.[17] Unable to develop or secure neighborhood centralization and local control, TWO duplicated the pattern it was resisting and developed *ad hoc* relationships and *ad hoc* programs. Like the agencies and city departments, many of these special boards and committees through which TWO is in touch with Woodlawn development, were semiautonomous bodies.

For TWO the special boards and committees had been a

[17] A partial list of boards and corporations in which TWO is involved would include the following:

TWO-KMF Development Association Board
Woodlawn Community Board for Urban Education Projects
Woodlawn Parent Council Advisory Board
Woodlawn Model Area Council
Mid-South Health Planning Council
Greater Woodlawn Assistance Corporation
Woodlawn Mental Health Center Board
Woodlawn Child Health Center Advisory Board
Woodlawn Drug Abuse Center Advisory Board
Mandel Legal Aid Clinic Advisory Board
Woodlawn Service Program Advisory Board
TWO-Hillman Corporation Board
Woodlawn Local Development Corporation
TWO Enterprises, Inc.
Woodlawn Redevelopment Corporation
Woodlawn Community Development Corporation

means of maintaining influence in programs it had negotiated (the Woodlawn Citizens' Committee in 1963, the Woodlawn Community Board), control over programs it developed (TWO-KMF Development Association Board, Woodlawn Community Development Corporation), continued attention to programs it had resisted (Woodlawn Model Area Council), "watchdog" surveillance of programs it welcomed (Woodlawn Mental Health Center Board, Woodlawn Service Program Advisory Board), or encouragement to programs whose usefulness might be developed (Legal Aid Clinic Advisory Board). It is entirely possible that for some agency leaders the reason for seeking advisory board participation from TWO was to achieve precisely the effects that were achieved, the dilution of TWO resources and the fragmenting of TWO efforts.

The irony of TWO's predicament is that it has been brought about largely because of the organization's strength. More things are happening in Woodlawn and there are more programs to which attention has to be directed. Some of these, like the economic development projects, are a direct result of TWO efforts. Some projects were stimulated by University professionals who wanted either to help or to experiment. Others, like several of the Model Cities projects, represented a competitive escalation of agency activity in response to TWO presence and pressure. Model Cities money was used to establish a competitive "experimental" school program within the geographic sphere of WESP influence. Shortly after approval of plans for TWO's health center, the Board of Health announced plans for a City Health Clinic two blocks away, again using Model Cities money.

Supervising a wide range of activities and maintaining vigilance over the escalation of agency activity poses a problem of fragmentation that many community organizations wish they could face, but few do. That TWO faces this problem is a sign of growth. That it has still maintained organization coherence is a major accomplishment.

During its first decade, TWO had evolved from a militant protest organization to a sophisticated administrator of community development programs. The table below summarizes some of the major characteristics on the growth of the organization. The organization problems TWO faced in 1971 were in many ways the problems of maturity, indeed, the problems of success. They were the problems of an established organization dealing with significant sums of money and developing major community renewal programs. If TWO appeared less interested in waging battle against City Hall, it also appeared more able to reap the rewards of past battles and more equipped to carry on the struggle for self-determination in Woodlawn in new terms.

TABLE 4. MAJOR CHARACTERISTICS IN DEVELOPMENT OF TWO

Year	Stance toward Outside Agencies	Major Task of Organization	Leadership Needs	Basis of Constituent Support
1962	Militant resistance	Build organization	Agitator-spokesman	Channeled hostilities
1965	Bargaining	Reallocation of resources	Spokesman	Politicized interests
1968	Community control	Redistribution of authority	Spokesman-manager	Community consciousness
1971	Coexistence	Community development programs	Manager-technician	Organized consent

A new dimension in this struggle became apparent by 1971. If TWO was different, it was even more clear that Woodlawn as a neighborhood was different. The casual observer in 1971 would wonder if there would be a neighborhood left to organize. Woodlawn, and particularly East Woodlawn, was being abandoned. This was not the result of direct action by the Department of Urban Renewal. In July 1971, the *Chicago Daily News* drew attention to what it called "the blitz of Woodlawn" in a five-article front page series;[18] that is, the article drew to the attention of the general public what was already painfully real to Woodlawn residents. The neighborhood was being burned down. The reporters counted 362 buildings that were either abandoned, burned out, or recently demolished. This epidemic of fires reached its peak in 1970 with 1,600 fires in the mile-square area of East and Central Woodlawn. Between 1967 and 1971, the population of this area dropped forty-six percent from 65,000 to 35,000. In what TWO and many residents regarded as a conspiracy to destroy Woodlawn, the people were being burned out. Evidence of arson in many of the fires was clear. But there was little effort to correct the situation. The Model Cities office, with a mandate to give priority to housing problems, did nothing. Owners of sound buildings found it impossible to secure loans for improvements or adequate insurance. Fire Department officials shrugged their shoulders. Among the beneficiaries of the fires, in addition to the few owners that were adequately insured, was the city of Chicago which was saved the demolition costs of many abandoned buildings. The greatest beneficiaries, TWO leaders argued, were the big land developers who had their eyes on Woodlawn. Stymied for years by the active presence of TWO, those who wanted to redevelop the prime land in Woodlawn for middle- and upper middle-income residents were waiting in the wings. TWO, so vigilant against agency proposals for massive clearance could do little to stop this gradual but relentless clearance by neglect, decay, and fire. It was clear that large portions of Woodlawn would have to be rebuilt. The questions, "By whom?" and "For whom?" remained. TWO saw the possibility of playing a major role in the survival and renewal of Woodlawn. But others had designs for this attractive piece of real estate bordered by two parks, a golf course, museums, Lake Michigan beaches, the University of Chi-

[18] Lois Wille, Betty Washington, and William Clement, "The Blitz of Woodlawn," *Chicago Daily News*, July 6-10, 1971.

cago, and a convenient transportation network. TWO was organized in 1961 around the issue of defending the neighborhood against the bulldozer. Ten years later, it faced the far greater task of defending the neighborhood against the outside developer. Although TWO could not prevent "the blitz of Woodlawn," it may have the resources, the contacts, and the expertise to play a determinative role in the rebuilding of Woodlawn. This, at any rate, is its task in the seventies.

The "blitz of Woodlawn," coupled with TWO's earlier inability to pursue successfully its major community controlled programs and the more recent turn toward less controversial development projects, posed serious questions about the general effectiveness of TWO as a community organization. If the neighborhood is slowly abandoned, TWO's continued organizational strength and programmatic accomplishments would seem to be pyrrhic victories. How can TWO be judged effective and successful if the physical and social conditions of the neighborhood it represents and serves continue to deteriorate?

Interpretations of success and failure depend on perceptions of what TWO has been about and anticipations of what it could become as well as on an analysis of the social forces within which the organization has operated. The condition of the organization and the Woodlawn community in the early seventies could yield several evaluations.

One line of evaluation would identify a causal connection between TWO's style and strategy on the one hand and continuing decay of the neighborhood on the other. Pierre de Vise, research sociologist, at least implied such a connection in a controversial address before the Hyde Park-Kenwood Community Conference in December 1971. After identifying TWO's position of influence in the community, de Vise made his point.

Largely because of the presence of these nationally eminent organizations, Woodlawn became the recipient of

311

about thirty five millions of federal, university and foundation support for experimental programs in housing, education, employment, youth, law enforcement, health and welfare. . . . Probably no other neighborhood in the nation had as much money and brainpower lavished upon it in the last ten years. . . . The result of a decade of these efforts is that Woodlawn lost 34 per cent of its people and 24 per cent of its housing. Only three of Chicago's ghetto communities lost more people and housing during the decade.[19]

It is implied that Woodlawn's decline is somehow the result of the concerted efforts secured and influenced by TWO's organizational prowess. Variants of this kind of argument are numerous. One is that the Black P Stone Nation, strengthened by a year of TWO support, went on to intimidate and frighten away segments of the community. Another is that TWO's early reluctance to cooperate with city agencies led to a decline of services, the final effect of which was not seen until the recent and rapid decay. A third is that TWO's militancy and potential strength made Woodlawn a target for selective neglect by agencies responsible for basic community services. Still another version maintains that TWO, by being able to prevent traditional programs of land clearance, invited "the blitz of Woodlawn" as a substitute. Whatever variant this argument takes, it results in blaming the victim.

A second type of evaluation of TWO, one which deserves more serious consideration, is that the organization abandoned its spokesman role and betrayed its vision of community control, leaving the community without a vigorous advocate and again at the mercy of exploiters. This assessment, most frequently leveled at the organization by critics from the Left, regards the emergence of TWO's paragovernmental strategy as the cause of TWO's decline as a spokes-

[19] Pierre de Vise, "Future Shock in Hyde Park and the Southeastside," *Hyde Park-Kenwood Voices*, December 1971, p. 9.

man organization and of the neighborhood's deterioration. This analysis assumes that there was a consistent pattern and clear direction in TWO's development from resistance to bargaining to control. This coherent pattern, identified as the spokesman style, was the bearer of TWO's basic message: that Woodlawn's problems are created and sustained by the domination and exploitation of outside agencies and operations that are neither responsive nor accountable to the residents of the neighborhood, and that the hope for Woodlawn lay in the nurturing of a people's organization which would fight unrelentingly against outside control and work diligently toward neighborhood self-determination. It was anticipated that once the cycle of powerlessness and dependency was reversed, the process of "decolonization" and the movement toward community control would be progressive.

The paragovernmental strategy of community development represented, from this perspective, a basic disjunction in the development of the organization, a fundamental shift in direction and style. Without the dynamic of external conflict the coherence of the spokesman style was lost. There were few clear targets. There was no clear vision of an alternative to the existing political process. There were no captivating issues. In place of issues were projects and advisory boards and development corporations. Without conflict, the rhetoric was less clear or compelling. Without conflict, citizen participation was robbed of much of its significance. In this development from conflict to coexistence, protest to program, and issues to projects, TWO lost some of the generative and therapeutic attributes of a spokesman organization. TWO was doing more but there was less enthusiasm. Once *the* organization *of* the community, TWO was becoming *an* organization *in* the community.

According to this interpretation TWO "bought in" to the Chicago political game. Having more to protect, the organization became less bold. Political expediency led TWO to trade a vigorous pursuit of community control for a stable

313

position in the existing process. Critics saw this as a failure of nerve, a collapse of vision, and an abandonment of TWO's charter. TWO, the argument goes, became so preoccupied with its own projects that it lost sight of Woodlawn. It was so concerned about Woodlawn Gardens that it failed to deal with the decay of other housing. TWO's programmatic achievements masked its inability to deal with community decay. From this perspective, informed by a particular vision of where TWO should be headed, the programmatic achievements of TWO in 1971 were little consolation. As a people's organization TWO was finished.

These negative assessments of the significance and impact of TWO draw attention to the community conditions which do not appear to have been improved by the organization's efforts. Externally, TWO's success had indeed been limited. Woodlawn, after a decade of TWO activity, continued to decline in many ways. Many social scientists, with quantitative measurements of success and failure, might simply write off TWO because the enduring external conditions of Woodlawn—unemployment, poor schools, decaying housing, police abuses—have not been solved. Even the casual observer might indeed wonder whether the decade of time, effort, and money expended were worth it. The visible and external signs of community renewal were not very impressive.

A third evaluation, one that is argued here, challenges these negative interpretations. TWO's inability in the sixties either to prevail over City Hall or to reverse the ghetto cycle is evident and uncontested. The fate of the organization's three major projects in the late sixties makes this clear. TWO faced the "limits of power." The systemic causes of urban decay and neighborhood decline were beyond TWO's reach. If one thing is learned from this experience it is that the ghetto cycle, being intimately related to powerful economic and political forces in the city and the nation, was basically unaffected by even the strongest neighborhood organization. That Woodlawn was not spared from these

314

forces is no reason to blame TWO. The established agencies, with far more resources and with the responsibility to deal with housing, education, crime, health care, and unemployment, not only have continued to fail in the central cities but also have jealously guarded their monopoly over planning and programs for these same areas in which they have so miserably failed. That the social and physical problems of Woodlawn have not been solved is, however unfortunate, not so clearly an indictment against TWO.

This evaluation of TWO, while recognizing fully the continuing plight of Woodlawn, would highlight aspects often unnoticed by both social scientist and casual observer, aspects of TWO's success which provide both a cause for admiration and a source of hope.

One, which is perhaps a negative tribute to the organization, is that TWO was able to retard the physical decay of Woodlawn and ward off real estate speculators and developers. Rather than being blamed for the decline of Woodlawn TWO should be credited for preventing the removal of Woodlawn. Unimpeded by the presence of TWO, the groups that were interested in clearing and/or redeveloping Woodlawn—the University, DUR, private developers—would probably have succeeded in the sixties. The traditional pattern of rapid neighborhood deterioration, massive relocation of residents, land clearance, and redevelopment for new and more affluent residents was checked. Furthermore, were it not for TWO's vigorous, even though belated, efforts, the epidemic of fires in Woodlawn would have continued and driven away even more of the population. Publicity, concerted and forceful action, and negotiations with the city Fire Commissioner led to a marked decrease of fires in Woodlawn by 1972. TWO's ability to impede the forces of decay is of no small significance. By slowing down this process, TWO has been able to maintain its power base, secure the resources, and develop the expertise to deal with the issues of conserving and rebuilding Woodlawn. TWO's stability and continuity amid the turmoil of the late sixties

315

and the fires of 1970 enabled the organization to direct its attention to organizing land as well as people. As the Reverend Jesse Jackson likes to tell his audiences on the South Side, the land is changing hands. Through gifts, options, and purchase TWO has been accumulating land in Woodlawn. In addition, smaller neighborhood development corporations, several of which were stimulated by TWO, were pursuing their own rehabilitation and building programs. Because of the presence of an experienced and stable community organization, Woodlawn residents and Woodlawn institutions have a real stake in the rebuilding of Woodlawn. TWO's ability to prevent, on the one hand, total deterioration of the neighborhood and to provide, on the other, resources and channels whereby the residents of the community might have a voice in the renewal of the neighborhood, is more than a modest accomplishment.

Another neglected aspect of TWO's impact on the community is revealed in the way it has functioned and continues to function in the lives of people in Woodlawn. It is a source of meaning and hope as well as a channel for action and communication. Leaders have been developed, ideas generated, competence gained. Although less tangible and less measurable than the external conditions in Woodlawn, these internal dimensions are no less significant as criteria by which to evaluate the organization. The presence of TWO has made, in the lives of thousands of Woodlawn residents, a difference which cannot be erased. The impressive expression of political independence in the March 1972 primary election where precinct after precinct in Woodlawn voted against the regular Democratic organization candidates is, among other things, evidence of this impact. The common struggles and the concerted efforts, the rallies, and the rhetoric, the confrontations with powerful forces that had controlled their lives, all these experiences that the participant in TWO has shared are etched in his consciousness. For some, fighting City Hall, standing up against injustice, participating in TWO, are habits they cannot give up. The

316

organization, with all its development programs, still maintains many of the characteristics of a spokesman organization. It still pays close attention to pursuing the grievances, the "bread-and-butter" issues which build a constituency. It still mobilizes pressure against city departments and agencies that neglect the neighborhood. TWO has also been able to develop new channels for citizen participation such as the parent councils, the social welfare union, and the local development corporations, and to refine its own internal processes of representation and decision making. Residents are demanding much of TWO partly because TWO in the past has educated the participants to expect much. The Woodlawn neighborhood will not disappear. Surprisingly, a community is being maintained during a process of external decay, mobility, and frustration. This, in no small part, is because of TWO. The movement toward neighborhood self-determination may be deferred but it will not be forgotten. People in Woodlawn are being prepared for self-government. As Woodlawn is rebuilt residents who received their awakening and gained their experience through TWO will be heard.

Finally, and perhaps of most significance, TWO's continuing health as a viable community organization in the face of numerous setbacks is itself a major achievement which is often misinterpreted or discounted. It is the contention of this analysis that TWO's move toward community development programming does not represent a new departure, a betrayal or an abberation, but is rather entirely consistent with TWO's abiding attention to institutional survival, continuity, and enhancement. The underlying consistency in TWO's development has been its pragmatic realism. TWO pursues what works, that is, what sustains and builds the organization. From TWO's perspective the reason is obvious: without a strong organization, opportunities for citizen action and the development of a voice for the community are impossible. Success for TWO is not so much in winning or losing particular issues, but in being around to pursue other issues and develop other programs. TWO's pragmatic flexibility, its keen sense for organizational survival, and its capacity to compromise skillfully have enabled it to seize the opportunities at hand.

TWO's approach has been more in line with Charles Lindblom's observation that "appropriate strategies always depend heavily on where we are now, what we see about us that we want to change, what our opportunities are— and only distantly and indirectly on our vision of the ideal community."[20] It is Alinsky's basic axiom that an effective community organization starts with and deals with the "world as it is." This "world as it is" is a volatile scene of struggle, bargaining, and compromise.

> In the world as it is, man moves primarily because of self interest.
> In the world as it is, the right things are usually done for the wrong reasons and vice versa.
> In the world as it is, a value judgment is rarely, if ever, made on the basis of what is best. . . .
> In the world as it is, "compromise" is not an ugly but a noble word. If the whole free way of life could be summed up in one word it would be "compromise."[21]

TWO's ability to bargain and compromise in this "world as it is," which from one perspective had led to the degradation of a protest style, has been TWO's basic strength and most consistent characteristic. TWO does what has to be done. There may be many reasons to fault TWO but not on the grounds that it failed in its purpose or betrayed its vision. The development of a strong stable organization is TWO's purpose. Continued existence is TWO's vision.

[20] Charles Lindblom, "Concepts of Community with Implications for Community Action" (unpublished paper prepared for Consultation on Community Organization, Center for Urban Studies, University of Chicago, April 12-13, 1968), p. 2.

[21] Alinsky, *Reveille for Radicals*, p. 225.

318

This interpretation identifies what has been most note-worthy about TWO, its capacity to survive under adverse conditions. In black neighborhoods in Chicago, where the life expectancy of neighborhood-based community organizations is short and where efforts to undercut and neutralize independent citizen activity is formidable, TWO's continued existence and programmatic growth is itself a rare accomplishment. Emphasis is placed on TWO's continued strength not out of any reverence for institutional maintenance as such, but out of a recognition that TWO's survival places it in contrast with numerous neighborhood organizations that have succumbed under the pressure of power politics in Chicago; and furthermore, that survival places TWO in a position to take advantage of opportunities as they emerge in the 1970s. This inclination and capacity to persist has been the key to TWO's success in the past and is its most hopeful characteristic for the future.

Because of its continued strength, TWO has established its reputation as a viable and credible organization that can handle major responsibilities over long duration. Governmental agencies can contract with TWO, business enterprises can enter into partnership, universities and foundations can make long-term agreements with the confidence that TWO will be around in the future. TWO found out the hard way that the governmental agencies are unable to solve—and sometimes even to recognize—the basic problems of the community. The private sector is increasingly wary of initiating programs in areas like Woodlawn where it does not have the support of the community. Through the Woodlawn Community Development Corporation, TWO can take the initiative in housing and economic development and invite the support of agencies—public and private—which have the resources and the concern. WCDC serves as a bridge between the outside agencies which have the resources but not the ability to make effective use of them in Woodlawn, and the various neighborhood groups

319

which have the capacity and credibility to sustain viable programs but not the resources. TWO's deep concern for the success of Woodlawn Gardens, TWO-Hillman, TWO-Standard, and Jackson Park Terrace lies in the fact that its credibility and indeed the future development of Woodlawn depends on the confidence which outside investors and benefactors have in the management capabilities of the organization. Only organizations that have demonstrated stability and competence can secure these kinds of commitments.

In addition, TWO is prepared for a long-haul struggle between centralized bureaucracies and neighborhood interests. In the long run community control, if it comes at all, may come less by intention than by default. This transfer of public authority will not be attained by forcible seizure of control or by federal stimulation or even by demonstrations of neighborhood competence. TWO found this out in the late sixties. The one factor compelling the transfer of authority will be, as Milton Kotler observes, "sheer utility."[22] Centralized bureaucracies are increasingly incapable of solving the basic problems of our cities. Many community organizations are quick to press demands and to offer advice on how to run the city, but among those organizations serious about neighborhood self-determination only the survivors will be fit. The task of a community organization from this perspective is to utilize federal resources when possible, make direct assaults on municipal sovereignty when possible, generate projects over which the community has direct control, but above all do what is necessary to survive and to build a government-in-exile capable of seizing opportunities and inheriting control from collapsing urban institutions.

If one looks at TWO not in terms of a success defined by its budget and level of programming or by its immediate impact on the neighborhood, but in terms of the ultimate goal of community control, then one can even argue that

[22] Kotler, *Neighborhood Government*, p. 8.

its present stance is calculated, over the long haul, to enhance the possibility of such control. How can TWO ever expect to win its fundamental conflict with the city? How can it sustain its sense of the issues? How can it work for participation? How, indeed, can it survive as a spokesman? One can argue that by compromise TWO has lost the conflict, fudged the issues, minimized participation, and lost credibility as spokesman. But the corollary to this is that some political configuration, of which we have no knowledge except for fleeting visions of revolutionary action, will rise to win by force what could not be won by TWO. If one rejects this corollary, one is pushed to answer the questions; and the answers offer a series of "rules for survival" and possibly the only route toward community control in Woodlawn.

How does TWO best keep alive the hope of victory in its conflict with the city? By moving from conflict to coexistence.

How does TWO keep the fundamental issues—external domination and self-determination—alive? By moving from the public raising of issues to the development of pragmatic programs which symbolize these issues.

How does TWO live out its initial assumption that it is unified by a common external oppressor? Today it does so by "maturing" beyond a simplistic oppressor schema and dealing with the subsequent internal tensions thus created.

How does TWO work for popular participation? Given the present impasse, it paves the way for future participation by concentrating on the development of specialized competence.

How, finally, does TWO ensure its spokesman role? Given today's reality, by turning from public spokesman to administration.

By moving from conflict to coexistence, from issues to projects, from external friction to the attempt to resolve internal tensions, from participation to technical competence,

321

from spokesman to administrator, TWO not only survives, but prepares for the day when it may be possible to carry on the battle for community control in a new key.

The story of TWO is a narrative of conflict and survival in black urban America. This narrative has taken on unforeseen significance in light of the travail of the late sixties. Of the many organizations that claimed the task of black self-determination, few have been able either to develop or maintain independence. When the trickle of federal money for citizen action programs dried up, when the political machines and urban bureaucracies saw the threat of black independence, many of the fragile vessels of self-determination and the halting efforts toward redistribution of public authority were torn between the two alternatives of retreat or revolutionary posturing, of accommodation to Edward Banfield's "unheavenly city," or indulgence in facile rhetoric of "power to the people." Attending to the unglamorous tasks of building organization, TWO has steered a precarious but steady course between the Scylla of radical rhetoric and the Charybdis of capitulation. The terms of TWO's success, obscured in the polarization of the late sixties, are now more apparent. TWO gained real power. It brought to Woodlawn resources, jobs, institutions, and services. It shifted relations with its strong neighbor, the University of Chicago, from enmity and paternalism to parity and mutuality. It has maintained citizen participation in a demonstrably more effective manner than other community organizations in Chicago. It has been able to bridge the chasm between the black middle class and the alienated poor. It has demostrated that for all the community-control rhetoric, the only vehicle is a power organization.

Ambivalence about TWO stems not from a lack of success but from the emptiness of success in these terms. Success within the limits and constraints of the existing system of power may be hollow. TWO simply cannot deal with the major forces that shape Woodlawn—unemployment, physical decay, official neglect. East Woodlawn is being abandoned. The black poor are being burned out, cleared out, and pushed further south. Neither can TWO override the policies of the established authoritative agencies. Complaints against TWO on these grounds should be directed at the system in which TWO operates. TWO's efforts to deal with the systemic causes of Woodlawn's problems were spurned by the authoritative institutions that have sustained the ghetto. However, if the present system breaks down for a multiplicity of reasons, empty success may be the basis for new hope, as the centralized agencies of control gradually yield to those neighborhood organizations who, while espousing community control, nevertheless have less interest in antiestablishment rhetoric than in getting on with the business of developing workable programs and moving toward a workable urban polity.

The Woodlawn Organization is a living organization. Evaluations of living organizations are hazardous. TWO's impact in the long run is not clear. What is clear is that a surviving and active TWO is Woodlawn's best hope. This assessment of TWO's experience and potential offers an implicit challenge to the thinking of several current urban theorists. This can be illustrated by considering the writings of three scholars of the urban scene: *The End of Liberalism* and *The Politics of Disorder* by Theodore Lowi, *Neighborhood Government* by Milton Kotler, and *The Unheavenly City* by Edward Banfield. Lowi, Kotler, and Banfield have provided provocative and insightful analyses of "the urban crisis" and have offered "solutions" to the basic problems facing our cities.

"Before our eyes," Lowi maintains, "politics and government have come unstuck and there is quite evidently a deep crisis in public authority."[23] The spectre is pluralism, or more accurately, official accommodation to pluralism. The basic reason for our plight is the general acceptance of a public ideology Lowi refers to as "interest-group liberalism" or

[23] Theodore J. Lowi, *The Politics of Disorder* (New York: Basic Books, Inc., 1971), p. xi.

323

government by bargaining. Dressed up in phrases like "creative federalism," "interest representation," "partnership," "maximum feasible participation," or "local option," government by bargaining is, according to Lowi, a self-defeating attempt to maintain consensus and order. The result, he claims, is the opposite. The parceling out of public authority to vocal and interested private and unregulated groups reduces the possibility of collective self-government and leads to the atrophy of public control and the loss of confidence in public institutions. Most important, interest-group liberalism cannot achieve justice. It can only, and temporarily, buy off discontent. And in doing so, government incurs cumulative damage to its capacity to govern equitably. Interest-group liberalism "transforms logrolling from necessary evil to greater good."[24]

In urban America the result is that "cities are well run but badly governed."[25] The pluralist approach to local government has led to fragmented authority and fractured government, the mushrooming of bureaucracies as "islands of functional power before which the modern mayor stands impoverished."[26] There is no polity, but only a multitude of publics with which to deal and bargain.

The solution is not decentralization. The cries for local influence and authority are part of the problem. Lowi's proposal? Juridical democracy. "Juridical democracy is a name for formal democracy, a majority rule democracy limited only by the requirement that government be run as closely as possible according to the way it says it is run."[27] Replace government by bargaining with government by rule of law. Replace interest-group liberalism with formal democracy. In urban America the first step of this "revolution through law" would be the elimination of the corporate city. "An easy and effective place to begin is with the complete destruction of the fiction of local citizenship and the sanctity

[24] Lowi, *End of Liberalism*, p. 76.
[25] *Ibid.*, p. 193.   [26] *Ibid.*, p. 201.
[27] Lowi, *Politics of Disorder*, pp. xvii-xviii.

of local corporate boundaries. . . . It is clear that the corporate city is contrary to public policy."[28] Local loyalties, interests, and attachments appear to Lowi as hindrances to justice and, like factions, mischievous to public order.

Like Lowi, Milton Kotler sees the fabric of city government coming unstuck. However, he casts this crisis of public authority in a much different light. The downtown financial and political oligarchy can no longer control the neighborhoods which are rising to claim local liberty after years of political subjugation. This renewed conflict is, for Kotler, a sign of hope. The struggle is between downtown and the neighborhoods. Kotler defines the neighborhood as "a political settlement of small territory and familiar association whose absolute property is its capacity for deliberative democracy."[29] Most neighborhoods are dominated by ruling oligarchies of "imperial city." Downtown areas have conquered (annexed) the outlying self-governing neighborhoods in order to enhance regional power, exploit regional resources, and to impose the burden of disproportionate taxation. Now both the conqueror and the conquered are paying the price. "Only," Kotler maintains, "by understanding the American city as it is today—a floundering empire, no longer in control of the neighborhoods it has annexed— can we see the force of neighborhood power in its claim for liberty."[30]

Kotler sees the possibility of increased national control but rejects this as inimical to the fundamental value of local liberty. The solution which Kotler sees emerging in a variety of forms is a radical decentralization of public power and wealth. Although the impulse toward decentralization is widespread, Kotler finds fault with various approaches, the New Left's preoccupation with national issues, Alinsky's willingness to settle for less than local liberty, the militant's insistence on separatism, and the pseudo-decentralization of

[28] Lowi, *End of Liberalism*, pp. 282-283.
[29] Kotler, *Neighborhood Government*, p. 2.
[30] *Ibid.*, p. 26.

liberal administrators. "The object of local power," Kotler insists, "can be nothing less than recreating neighborhood government which has political autonomy and representation in larger units."[31]

Banfield, of the three the most renowned as an urbanologist, does not share the alarm of Lowi and Kotler. In fact, as he surveys the urban scene he sees things getting objectively better in almost every area. Of course, there are problems but they are "important in the sense that a bad cold is important."[32] They will disappear not because of any governmental action but simply because time heals. Banfield points to economic growth, demographic changes, "middle-class-ification," and the decline of prejudice as the natural remedies of the hidden hand. If there is an urban crisis, it is not, in Banfield's view, located in the objective situation. It is found, rather, in the possibly self-fulfilling false definition of the urban situation. "In short," Banfield concludes, "wrong public definitions of urban problems may lead to behavior that will make matters worse despite the ameliorating influence of the accidental forces."[33] A convergence of rising expectations, false definitions, middle-class guilt, and professional alarm may create an "urban crisis" where none exists. "By treating a spurious crisis as if it were real, we may unwittingly make it so."[34]

If nothing else, the recent literature in urban politics confirms Robert Wood's observation that "students of urban politics constantly walk on eggshells, confront each other with apparently self-contradictory conclusions, and submit conflicting policy recommendations."[35] Lowi, alarmed by the spectre of pluralism buttressed by interest-group liberalism, advocates eliminating the corporate city as a political unit. Kotler, welcoming the collapse of "imperial city," calls for the restoration of neighborhood political units. For Banfield, the spectre is the incurable lower-class values combining

[31] *Ibid.*, p. 39. [32] Banfield, *Unheavenly City*, p. 6.
[33] *Ibid.*, p. 259. [34] *Ibid.*, p. 32.
[35] Wood, *Urban Form*, p. 100.

with insufferable middle-class activism to fabricate a spurious crisis.

Each of them, from different perspectives, would pass critical judgment on The Woodlawn Organization. For Lowi, the development of TWO illustrates what he, updating Weber and Michels, calls "iron law of decadence" or "rule of rigidification."[36] TWO, like other pressure groups, was sucked into the web of interest-group liberalism with the predictable outcome of becoming conservative, exclusive, and incapable of bringing about significant social change. Woodlawn has been used, energies have been wasted, a cause dissipated, and all that is left is an organization seeking to maintain its privileged position. Kotler maintained that TWO had the right idea but the wrong strategy. It has been mistakenly concerned more with "military" victory against central domination than with building local institutions of deliberative democracy. Kotler argued that "neighborhoods cannot presume to succeed in military action against central power since they are not defending any present liberty."[37] Because of TWO's inadequate strategy it suffered defeat and was left with the one alternative of settling for specialized programs. Banfield would argue that TWO has helped create and sustain a false public definition of the situation, thereby perpetuating a "reign of error."[38] This false definition, that the problems of Woodlawn are created by white racism, outside control, and insensitive bureaucracies, had led to the programs and "solutions" that are not only ill-founded and inadequate but also detrimental to the total well-being of the community. The "reign of error," according to Banfield, makes it impossible to get on with dealing realistically with the real social problems that do exist. These "real" problems are located primarily in the people who live in Woodlawn.

[36] Lowi, *Politics of Disorder*, p. xix; see also Ch. i: "Group Politics and the Iron Law of Decadence."

[37] Kotler, *Neighborhood Government*, p. 28.

[38] Banfield, *Unheavenly City*, p. 259.

According to these analysts, TWO is inadequate because it conformed to a false public ideology (Lowi), it employed a false strategy (Kotler), or it contributed to a false definition of the situation (Banfield). But what would they have suggested for Woodlawn? And what evidence would they marshal to justify their proposals and projections? Would Lowi have policy for Woodlawn determined by state officials or federal dictation? Given the state legislature's penchant for limited financial resources for areas like Woodlawn and the federal tendency to defer to Mayor Daley, would justice be served by such a policy? How would Kotler suggest that the transfer of authority be secured if not by the vigilant presence of a strong power organization? Not, certainly, by appealing to the good will of the mayor of Chicago. Until there is better evidence that Kotler's proposal has worked in the more open situation of Columbus, Ohio,[39] it is doubtful that it would be effective in Chicago. Would Banfield maintain that Mayor Daley and the agency leaders beholden to him provide a more adequate public definition of the situation in Woodlawn than the leaders of TWO and should, therefore, be allowed to operate unconstrained by local interests? And what evidence would he bring to show that the problems of the South Side of Chicago are being solved by the hidden hand? Would it be the decay, fires, and demolition of the buildings and the flight of nearly half the population?

The analyses by Lowi, Kotler, and Banfield are stimulating and certainly the judgments they level at TWO contain a modicum of truth. But when this "truth" is generalized and simplified and propounded as the solution to "the urban crisis," it becomes a distortion, offering, on the one hand, proposals like Lowi's and Kotler's that are "deceptively simple,"[40] and, on the other hand, scoldings like Banfield's that

[39] The East Central Citizens Organization in Columbus, Ohio is the best example Kotler used to illustrate his position. See *Neighborhood Government*, pp. 44-50, 82-87.

[40] Lowi's phrase (*End of Liberalism*, p. 297), to describe his own proposals, would also apply to Kotler.

are simply deceptive. Of course, it would be nice if government were run the way it says it is run and if local liberty were secured and, indeed, if expectations were not inordinate, but wishing it, contrary to Banfield's axiom,[41] will not make it so.

It may well be, as Kenneth Dolbeare argues, that "the discipline of political science itself is of marginal relevance to the problems and prospects of America's future."[42] This, of course, does not mean that there is no room for theoretical analysis, rational planning, and speculative projections. It does mean, however, that there is room both in our search for understanding and for social justice, for what political sage Reinhold Niebuhr called "the wisdom which resides in a hungry belly rather than a sophisticated mind."[43] This study commends the wisdom of TWO as a healthy corrective to the simplicities or impossibilities of the scholars. It suggests that democracy—even juridical democracy—is served by the kind of awakening and participation TWO has elicited, and that local liberty may be enhanced more by organized pressure than by political philosophy and that adequate definitions of the urban situation require a heavy dose of local wisdom.

The future of Woodlawn is not clear. The future of urban America is not clear. Our large cities are plagued with problems. Not least among them is that there is, especially among the residents of the inner city, a growing cynicism about either the inclination or the capacity of agencies of government to respect, represent, or serve the people. Similarly, there is a loss of confidence in the ability of research and scholarship to identify or address urban problems and in the ability of service organizations to recognize and meet human

[41] See Banfield, *Unheavenly City*, chap. iv, "Race: Thinking May Make It So."

[42] Kenneth Dolbeare, "Public Policy Analysis and the Coming Struggle for the Soul of the Postbehavioral Revolution," in Philip Green and Sanford Levinson (eds.), *Power and Community: Dissenting Essays in Political Science* (New York: Vintage Books, 1970), p. 109.

[43] Harry R. Davis and Robert C. Good (eds.), *Reinhold Niebuhr on Politics* (New York: Charles Scribner's Sons, 1960), p. 124.

needs. Woodlawn has been governed by what some regard as the most effective large city political organization in the country. Woodlawn has been "served" by numerous well-meaning agencies that have spent millions of dollars. Woodlawn is bordered by one of the country's outstanding universities with renowned specialists in all areas of urban research. The efforts and claims of these institutions in solving urban problems are no longer credible.

The source of hope for the people of Woodlawn lies not in the speculative offerings of urbanologists. Neither does it lie in the paternalistic efforts of bureaucratized city agencies, or in the escalation of federal programs, or in the designs of urban planners, or in the expanded patronage of a softening political machine. Hope for Woodlawn lies in the enduring efforts of citizens to shape their community and their future, in the continuing struggle of ordinary residents against those who exploit them, in a surviving and increasingly competent TWO. A slender thread? Perhaps. But the future of our deteriorating cities may depend less upon the brainwork of "experts" than upon the spirit of the citizenry, less upon the grand designers than upon incalculable contingencies. "Urban politics," Robert Wood reminds us, "is devoid of most of the properties of a manageable enterprise." Sensing the profound complexity of the urban scene, he adds:

> Dramatic breakthroughs, like a major reorganization or a renewal program, are more likely to be the result of accident, not design. They are not the creature of a conscious effort by a powerful coalition; they are incalculable occurrences of an improbable but possible convergence of forces in temporary agreement.[44]

Social and political forces in Chicago are shifting. The Democratic Machine, for example, so confident and resilient in the sixties, was, by 1972, shaken by primary election defeats, embarrassed by high level defections, plagued with program

[44] Wood, *Urban Form*, p. 113.

and administrative problems, and humiliated at the Democratic National Convention. There are even signs that city agencies, having failed in the past to deal effectively with the problems they supposedly address, may themselves become, out of their own survival interests, more open to neighborhood initiatives. TWO, because of its continuing vitality, stands ready to be a part of any new "convergence of forces," the outcome of which is unpredictable. But TWO will continue to press for increased community control which, if it comes at all, will come more, as Morton Grodzins indicated, by "mild chaos" than by design,[45] more by default than by intent. And it may not come at all: TWO has lost basic struggles with the city. It may not prevail in its extended effort to bring neighborhood self-determination. But its continued strength places TWO and the people of Woodlawn in a good position to continue the struggle. And continuing the struggle may be the best for which to hope.

[45] Morton Grodzins, "Why Decentralization by Order Won't Work," in Edward Banfield (ed.), *Urban Government* (New York: Free Press, 1961), p. 131.

331

BIBLIOGRAPHY

THE literature relevant to the study of community organization is voluminous. A thorough bibliography of 750 references is Richard H. P. Mendes, *Bibliography on Community Organization for Citizen Participation in Voluntary Democratic Associations* (Washington, D.C.: U.S. Government Printing Office, 1965). More current, although less extensive, bibliographies are found in some of the more recent literature. The following bibliography, selected from the items which have been most useful in preparing this study, is divided into three categories. The first includes general references which identify some of the issues and problems confronting inner-city neighborhoods as well as some of the social science and social ethical perspectives addressing those issues. The second section deals primarily with specific strategies of community organization, particularly with the approach identified with Saul Alinsky. The third section of the bibliography, and the one most essential to this study, includes references which deal specifically with The Woodlawn Organization and programs and projects with which it has been involved.

A record of TWO's priorities, programmatic efforts, and interpretation of events is found in its newspaper. In 1964, after TWO perceived that the *Woodlawn Booster*, one of a chain of South Side neighborhood newspapers published by Bruce Sagan, was not a sympathetic interpreter of the organization, TWO began its own paper. This paper has appeared under a variety of banners. The *TWO Newsletter* became the *TWO News* in September 1965, the *Woodlawn Observer* in January 1966, and simply the *Observer* in March 1968. Essentially there are two, not five, neighborhood newspapers in Woodlawn, the *Booster* and the TWO newspaper. The metropolitan press in Chicago is a resource for countless articles and news items on TWO and Woodlawn. This bibliography includes only some of the major bylined feature articles about Woodlawn.

GENERAL REFERENCES IN URBAN PROBLEMS AND ISSUES

Adrian, Charles R. (ed.). *Social Science and Community Action.* East Lansing: Michigan State University, 1960.

Altshuler, Alan A. *Community Control.* New York: Pegasus, 1970.

Bachrach, Peter, and Baratz, Morton S. *Power and Poverty.* New York: Oxford University Press, 1970.

Banfield, Edward C. *Political Influence.* New York: Free Press, 1961.

―――. *The Unheavenly City.* Boston and Toronto: Little, Brown and Company, 1968.

――― (ed.). *Urban Government.* New York: Free Press, 1961.

―――, and Wilson, James Q. *City Politics.* Cambridge, Mass.: Harvard University Press, 1963.

Beadle, Muriel. *The Hyde Park-Kenwood Urban Renewal Years, a History to Date.* Chicago: n.p., 1964.

Bellush, Jewel, and Hausknecht, Murray (eds.). *Urban Renewal: People, Politics, and Planning.* Garden City, N.Y.: Doubleday and Company, Inc., 1967.

Carmichael, Stokely, and Hamilton, Charles. *Black Power: The Politics of Liberation in America.* New York: Vintage Books, 1967.

Clark, Kenneth B. *Dark Ghetto.* New York: Harper and Row, 1965.

―――, and Hopkins, Jeannette. *A Relevant War Against Poverty.* New York and Evanston: Harper and Row, 1970.

Coleman, James S. *Community Conflict.* New York: Free Press, 1957.

Connery, Robert H. (ed.). *Urban Riots: Violence and Social Change.* New York: Vintage Books, 1969.

Coser, Lewis. *The Functions of Social Conflict.* Paperback ed. New York: Free Press, 1964.

Coulter, Philip B. (ed.). *The Politics of Metropolitan Areas.* New York: Thomas Y. Crowell Company, 1967.

Dahl, Robert A. *Modern Political Analysis.* 2d ed. Englewood Cliffs, N.J.: Prentice-Hall, Inc., 1970.

————. *Who Governs?* New Haven and London: Yale University Press, 1961.

Dodson, Dan. "Looking Ahead in Health and Welfare." Paper presented to the 55th Annual Conference of Health, Welfare and Recreation of the California Association for Health and Welfare, March 9, 1966. (Mimeographed.)

————. "To Work Effectively as Agents of Change." *Social Action,* XXXI (February, 1965), 26-36.

Donovan, John C. *The Politics of Poverty.* New York: Pegasus, 1967.

Easton, David. *The Political System.* New York: Alfred S. Knopf, 1964.

Elias, C. E., Jr.; Gillies, James; and Riemer, Svend (eds.). *Metropolis: Values in Conflict.* Belmont, Calif.: Wadsworth Publishing Co., Inc., 1964.

Fantini, Mario; Gittell, Marilyn; and Magat, Richard. *Community Control and the Urban School.* New York: Praeger Publishers, 1970.

Fortune, the editors of. *The Exploding Metropolis.* Garden City, N.Y.: Doubleday Anchor Books, 1958.

Gamson, William A. *Power and Discontent.* Homewood, Ill.: Dorsey Press, 1968.

Goodman, Paul. *People or Personnel and Like a Conquered Province.* First Vintage Book Edition. New York: Vintage Books, 1968.

Gosnell, Harold F. *Machine Politics: Chicago Style.* 2d ed. Chicago: University of Chicago Press, 1968.

Green, Philip, and Levinson, Sanford (eds.). *Power and Community: Dissenting Essays in Political Science.* New York: Vintage Books, 1970.

Greer, Scott. *The Emerging City: Myth and Reality.* New York: Free Press, 1962.

―――. *Urban Renewal and American Cities.* Indianapolis: Bobbs-Merrill Company, Inc., 1965.

Grodzins, Morton. *The Metropolitan Area as a Racial Problem.* Pittsburgh: University of Pittsburgh Press, 1958.

Gulick, Luther H. *The Metropolitan Problem and American Ideas.* New York: Alfred A. Knopf, 1966.

Havighurst, Robert J. *Education in Metropolitan Areas.* Boston: Allyn and Bacon, Inc., 1966.

Hawley, Willis D., and Wirt, Frederick M. (eds.). *The Search for Community Power.* Englewood Cliffs, N.J.: Prentice-Hall, Inc., 1968.

Hirsch, Werner Z. (ed.). *Urban Life and Form.* New York: Holt, Rinehart and Winston, Inc., 1963.

Hough, Joseph C., Jr. *Black Power and White Protestants.* London: Oxford University Press, 1968.

Hunter, David R. *The Slums.* New York: Free Press, 1964.

Hunter, Floyd. *Community Power Structure.* Anchor Books Edition. New York: Doubleday and Company, Inc., 1963.

Jacobs, Jane. *The Death and Life of Great American Cities.* New York: Vintage Books, 1961.

Kariel, Henry S. *The Search of Authority: Twentieth Century Political Thought.* New York: Free Press, 1964.

Kornhauser, William. *Politics of Mass Society.* New York: Free Press, 1959.

Kotler, Milton. *Neighborhood Government: The Local Foundations of Political Life.* Indianapolis and New York: Bobbs-Merrill Company, Inc., 1969.

Kraemer, Paul E. *The Societal State.* Mappel, The Netherlands: J. A. Boom en Zoon, 1966.

Krinsky, Fred (ed.). *Democracy and Complexity: Who Governs the Governors.* Beverly Hills, Calif.: Glencoe Press, 1968.

Lowi, Theodore J. *At the Pleasure of the Mayor.* New York: Free Press, 1964.

Lowi, Theodore J. *The End of Liberalism*. New York: W. W. Norton and Company, Inc., 1969.

——. *The Politics of Disorder*. New York: Basic Books, Inc., 1971.

—— (ed.). *Private Life and Public Order*. New York: W. W. Norton and Company, Inc., 1968.

Maass, Arthur (ed.). *Area and Power*. New York: Free Press, 1959.

Marris, Peter, and Rein, Martin. *Dilemmas of Social Reform*. New York: Atherton Press, 1967.

Martin, Roscoe C. *The Cities and the Federal System*. New York: Atherton Press, 1965.

Meltzer, Jack. "A New Look at the Urban Revolt." *Journal of the American Institute of Planners*, XXXIV (July, 1968), 255-259.

Memmi, Albert. *The Colonizer and the Colonized*. Boston: Beacon Press, 1967.

Merton, Robert K. *Social Theory and Social Structure*. Rev. ed. New York: Free Press, 1957.

Meyer, Martin. *The Teachers Strike: New York, 1968*. New York: Harper and Row, 1968.

Meyerson, Martin, and Banfield, Edward. *Politics, Planning, and the Public Interest*. New York: Free Press, 1955.

Michels, Robert. *Political Parties*. New York: Dover Publications, Inc., 1959.

Mills, C. Wright. *The Sociological Imagination*. New York: Grove Press, Inc., 1961.

Moynihan, Daniel. *Maximum Feasible Misunderstanding*. New York: Free Press, 1969.

Negro Self-Concept: Implications for School and Citizenship. Report of a conference sponsored by The Lincoln Filene Center for Citizenship and Public Affairs. New York: McGraw-Hill Book Company, 1965.

Nisbet, Robert A. *Community and Power*. New York: Oxford University Press, 1962.

Passow, A. Harry (ed.). *Education in Depressed Areas*. New York: Teachers College Press, 1963.

Pennock, J. Roland, and Chapman, John W. (eds.). *Voluntary Associations.* New York: Atherton Press, 1969.

Pettigrew, Thomas F. *A Profile of the Negro American.* Princeton, N.J.: D. Van Nostrand and Company, Inc., 1964.

Polsby, Nelson W. *Community Power and Political Theory.* New Haven and London: Yale University Press, 1963.

Pranger, Robert J. *The Eclipse of Citizenship.* New York: Holt, Rinehart and Winston, Inc., 1968.

Proceedings of the First Annual Conference on Social Issues at the University of Oregon. *Poverty: Four Approaches, Four Solutions.* Eugene: Associated Students of the University of Oregon, 1966.

Riessman, Frank; Cohen, Jerome; and Pearl, Arthur (eds.). *Mental Health of the Poor.* New York: Free Press, 1964.

Rossi, Peter H., and Dentler, Robert A. *The Politics of Urban Renewal.* New York: Free Press, 1961.

Royko, Mike. *Boss.* New York: E. P. Dutton and Co., Inc., 1971.

Schattschneider, E. E. *The Semisovereign People.* New York: Holt, Rinehart and Winston, Inc., 1960.

Schubert, Glendon. *The Public Interest.* New York: Free Press, 1960.

Sexton, Patricia Cayo. *Spanish Harlem.* New York: Harper and Row, 1965.

Simmel, Georg. *Conflict and the Web of Group Affiliations.* New York: Free Press, 1955.

Spear, Allan H. *Black Chicago: The Making of a Negro Ghetto, 1890-1920.* Chicago: University of Chicago Press, 1967.

Tax, Sol (ed.). *The People vs. the System.* Chicago: Acme Press, Inc., 1968.

Vise, Pierre de. *Chicago's Widening Color Gap.* Chicago: Interuniversity Social Research Committee, 1967.

Warren, Roland L. (ed.). *Perspectives on the American Community.* Chicago: Rand McNally and Company, 1966.

Warren, Roland L. (ed.). *Politics and the Ghettos.* New York: Atherton Press, 1969.

Waxman, Chaim I. (ed.). *Poverty: Power and Politics.* New York: Grosset and Dunlap, 1968.

Willbern, York. *The Withering Away of the City.* Bloomington: University of Indiana Press, 1964.

Williams, Oliver P., and Press, Charles (eds.). *Democracy in Urban America.* Chicago: Rand McNally and Company, 1961.

Wilmore, Gayraud S. *The Secular Relevance of the Church.* Philadelphia: Westminster Press, 1962.

Wilson, James Q. *Negro Politics: The Search for Leadership.* New York: Free Press, 1960.

Winter, Gibson. *Being Free.* New York: Macmillan Company, Inc., 1970.

————. *Elements for a Social Ethic.* New York: Macmillan Company, Inc., 1966.

Wright, Nathan, Jr. *Black Power and Urban Unrest.* New York: Hawthorn Books, Inc., 1967.

Young, Roland (ed.). *Approaches to the Study of Politics.* Evanston, Ill.: Northwestern University Press, 1958.

Younger, George D. *The Church and Urban Power Structure.* Philadelphia: Westminster Press, 1963.

Community Organization: Strategies and Perspectives

Alinsky, Saul. "Action to Equality of Opportunity." Chicago: Industrial Areas Foundation, n.d.

————. "Citizen Participation and Community Organization in Planning and Urban Renewal." Paper presented to the Chicago Chapter of the National Association of Housing and Redevelopment Officials, Chicago, January 29, 1962. Chicago: Industrial Areas Foundation, n.d.

————. "From Citizen Apathy to Participation." Paper presented at Sixth Annual Conference, Association of Community Councils of Chicago, October 19, 1957. Chicago: Industrial Areas Foundation, n.d.

————. "The I.A.F.—Why Is It Controversial." *Church in Metropolis*, VI (Summer, 1965), 13-15.

————. "Is There Life After Birth?" Paper presented before the Centennial Meeting, Episcopal Theological School, Cambridge, Mass., June 7, 1967. Chicago: Industrial Areas Foundation, 1968.

————. "Questions and Answers Regarding the Industrial Areas Foundation." On file at First Presbyterian Church, Chicago, 1959. (Mimeographed.)

————. *Reveille for Radicals.* Vintage Books Edition. New York: Random House, 1969.

————. *Rules for Radicals.* New York: Random House, 1971.

————. "The War on Poverty—Political Pornography." *Journal of Social Issues*, XXI (January, 1965), 41-47.

————. "You Can't See the Stars Through the Stripes." Paper presented to the Chamber of Commerce of the United States, Washington, D.C., March 26, 1968. Chicago: Industrial Areas Foundation, n.d.

Arnstein, Sherry. "A Ladder of Citizen Participation." *Journal of the American Institute of Planners*, XXXV (July, 1969), 216-224.

Bennett, John C. "The Church and Power Conflicts." *Christianity and Crisis*, XXV (March 22, 1965), 47-51.

Berliner, Robert W., Jr. "Alinskyism in Theory and Practice." Unpublished B.A. dissertation, Harvard University, 1967.

Christ, Robert. "The Local Church in a Community Organization." Presbytery of Chicago, 1961. (Mimeographed.)

The Christian Century. May 10, 31, June 6, 1961; July 18, 1962; February 12, June 30, 1965.

Cunningham, James V. *The Resurgent Neighborhood.* Notre Dame, Ind.: Fides Publishers, Inc., 1965.

Davidson, Robert. "If Justice Is the Goal—Organize." *Social Action*, XXXI (February, 1965), 5-14.

Fey, Harold. "Maintaining the Democratic Organization of Communities." *City Church*, XIX (September-October, 1963), 8-11.

Fish, John. "Community Organization and the Crisis of Public Authority." *Review of Religious Research,* IX (Winter, 1968), 72-79.

Fish, John, *et al. The Edge of the Ghetto.* New York: Seabury Press, 1968.

Fry, John R. (ed.). *The Church and Community Organization.* New York: Department of Publication Services of the National Council of Churches, 1965.

Lindblom, Charles. "Concepts of Community with Implications for Community Action." Paper presented at Consultation on Community Organization, Center for Urban Studies, University of Chicago, April 12-13, 1968. (Mimeographed.)

Renewal. "A Fleeting Talk with Saul Alinsky." March, 1968, 6-9.

Ridgway, James, "Saul Alinsky in Smugtown." *The New Republic,* June 26, 1965, 15-18.

Riessman, Frank. "Self-Help Among the Poor: New Styles of Social Action." *Trans-Action,* September-October, 1965, 32-37.

―――. *Strategies Against Poverty.* New York: Random House, 1969.

Rose, Stephen C. "A Layman's Guide to Community Organization." *Christian Advocate,* X (January 13, 1966), 7-8.

―――. "Power Play in the City." *Crossroads,* January-March, 1967, 8-12.

―――. "Saul Alinsky and His Critics." *Christianity and Crisis,* XXIV (July 20, 1964), 143-152.

Ross, Murray G. *Community Organization: Theory and Principles.* New York: Harper and Row, 1955.

Ruoss, Meryl. *Citizen Power and Social Change.* New York: Seabury Press, 1968.

Sanders, Marion K. *The Professional Radical: Conversations with Saul Alinsky.* New York: Harper and Row, 1970.

Schaller, Lyle E. *Community Organization: Conflict and Reconciliation.* Nashville: Abingdon Press, 1966.

Schroeder, W. W. "Protestant Involvement in Community Organization with Special Reference to The Woodlawn

Organization." *Cognitive Structure and Religious Research.* East Lansing, Michigan: Michigan State University Press, 1970.

Sherrard, Thomas D., and Murray, Richard C. "The Church and Neighborhood Community Organization." *Social Work*, X (July, 1965), 3-14.

Spiegel, Hans B. C. (ed.). *Citizen Participation in Urban Development.* Vol. I: *Concepts and Issues;* Vol. II: *Cases and Programs.* Washington, D.C.: NTL Institute for Applied Behavioral Sciences, 1968.

Still, Douglas. "The Churches and Community Organization." Church Federation of Greater Chicago, 1963. (Mimeographed.)

————. "Reviving the Democratic Organization of Communities." *City Church*, XIV (September-October, 1963), 9, 12-14.

Time. "Radical Saul Alinsky: Prophet of Power to the People." March 2, 1970, 56-57.

Von Hoffman, Nicholas. "Finding and Making Leaders." Distributed by Students for a Democratic Society, n.d. (Mimeographed.)

————. "Reorganization in the Casbah." *Social Progress*, LII (April 1962), 33-44.

Winter, Gibson. "The Churches and Community Organization." *Christianity and Crisis*, XXV (May 31, 1965), 119-122.

Witmer, Lawrence, (ed.). *Issues in Community Organization.* Chicago: Center for the Scientific Study of Religion, 1972.

WOODLAWN AND THE WOODLAWN ORGANIZATION

Black, Hillel. "This Is War." *Saturday Evening Post*, January 25, 1964, 60-63.

Blakeley, Ulysses B., and Leber, Charles T. Jr. "The Great Debate in Chicago." *Presbyterian Life*, June 15, 1961, 36-37.

————. "A Summary of Events Related to the Temporary

Woodlawn Organization for Community Planning and Rehabilitation: From February 7 to March 22, 1961." On file at First Presbyterian Church, Chicago, 1961. (Mimeographed.)

————. "Woodlawn Begins to Flex Its Muscles." *Presbyterian Life*, September 15, 1962, 12-15, 41-42.

Brazier, Arthur M. *Black Self-Determination: The Story of The Woodlawn Organization*. Edited by Roberta G. and Robert F. DeHaan. Grand Rapids, Mich.: William B. Eerdman Publishing Company, 1969.

————. "TWO Testimony at McClellan Hearing." *Hyde Park Herald* (Chicago), July 10, 1968.

Burrell, Curtis E. "KOCO Head Exposes Model Cities Program." *True People's Power* (Chicago), April 1969.

Cameron, William E., Jr. "Religious Leadership and The Woodlawn Organization." Unpublished B.D. dissertation. Chicago Theological Seminary, 1963.

Chicago Department of City Planning. *Proposal for a Program to Meet the Long-Term Needs of Woodlawn*. Chicago: Department of City Planning, 1962.

Chicago Journalism Review. "Mayor Daley's War on Gangs." June 1969.

Chicago Model Cities Office. "Response of the City of Chicago to April 21, 1969 Report of the Federal Regional Coordinating Committee on the Chicago Model Cities Application." Chicago: Model Cities Office, May 15, 1969. (Mimeographed.)

Chicago Sun Times. "Street Gangs and the GIU." Section 2. July 20, 1969.

Cofield, Ernestine. "The Battle of Woodlawn." *Chicago Defender*, November 19, 20, 21, 22, 26, 27, 28, 29, 30, and December 3, 1962.

Community Legal Council. "Citizen Participation in Chicago's Model Cities Program: A Critical Analysis." Chicago: Community Legal Council, May 15, 1968. (Mimeographed.)

Congreve, Willard. "Final Report: Institutional Collabora-
tion to Improve Urban Public Education with Special
Reference to the City of Chicago." Presented to U.S. De-
partment of Health, Education, and Welfare, Office of
Education, Bureau of Research, March 15, 1968. Chicago:
University of Chicago, 1968. (Mimeographed.)

Davidson, Robert M. "The Woodlawn Organization: A
Channel for Action." Church Federation of Greater Chicago, 1964. (Mimeographed.)

Davis, Richard H. "A Proposal for a Leadership Training
Program for the Blackstone Rangers." A proposal devel-
oped in consultation with the leadership of the Blackstone
Rangers and their adult contact, January, 1967, on file at
First Presbyterian Church, Chicago. (Mimeographed.)

Federal Regional Model Cities Coordinating Committee.
"Initial Response to the City of Chicago Model City Proposal." Chicago: Midwest Regional Office of U.S. Department of Housing and Urban Development, April 21, 1969.
(Mimeographed.)

First Presbyterian Church (Chicago). "A Statement Regard-
ing the Relationship of First Presbyterian Church and the
Blackstone Rangers." On file at First Presbyterian Church,
October, 1966. (Mimeographed.)

France, Erwin A. "Statement on Chicago's Model Cities Program." Presented to the Finance Committee, City Council
of Chicago, April 10, 1969. (Mimeographed.)

Fry, John R. *Fire and Blackstone*. Philadelphia and New
York: J. B. Lippincott Company, 1969.

———. Speech at Symposium on the McClellan Hearings.
Hyde Park Union Church, October 20, 1968. On file at
First Presbyterian Church, Chicago. (Mimeographed.)

———. Testimony before U.S. Senate Permanent Subcommittee on Investigations. Senator John McClellan Chairman. On file at First Presbyterian Church, Chicago, June,
1968. (Mimeographed.)

———. "The Word Is *Cool*." *Rebels with a Cause*. Chicago:
Urban Training Center for Christian Mission, 1967.

Geyer, Georgie Anne. "Woodlawn: A Community in Revolt." *Chicago Scene*, June 7, 1962, 12-17.

———. "Woodlawn Unit Has Big Goals." *Chicago Daily News*, April 7-13, 1962.

Grant, Brian W. A report by the Social Action Committee of University Church of Disciples of Christ, on file at University Church, Chicago, 1969. (Mimeographed.)

Gumpert, David E. "The Tragedy of Hyde Park High School." *The Chicago Maroon*, May 20, 1966.

Gunther, John. "Chicago Revisited." *Chicago Today*, II (April 1965), 2-36.

Hamilton, William. "The Cities vs. the People: Citizen Participation in Model Cities," *Everyman's Guide to Federal Programs Impact! Reports*, Vol. I, No. 2. Washington, D.C.: New Community Press, Inc., 1969.

Hamm, Kathleen M. "The Black P Stone Nation and the Book of Revelation: Conflict, Ministry, and Eschatology." Unpublished B.D. dissertation, Chicago Theological Seminary, 1969.

Hauser, Philip M. "Conflict vs. Consensus." *Chicago Sun Times*, December 13, 1964.

"History of Ranger Activity, Summer, 1966." On file at First Presbyterian Church, Chicago. (Mimeographed.)

Hyde Park-Kenwood Voices (Chicago). "Kids, Cops, and the Community." Special Supplement No. 1, February, 1969.

Jacobs, Jane. "Chicago's Woodlawn—Renewal by Whom?" *Architectural Forum*, May 1962, 122-124.

Johnson, Thomas A. "Blackstone Rangers, Street Gang Investigated by Senate Panel, Demanding Share of Power in Chicago." *New York Times*, August 3, 1968, 44.

Kellam, Sheppard G., and Schiff, Sheldon K. "Adaptation and Mental Illness in the First-Grade Classrooms of an Urban Community." *Psychiatric Research Report 21.* American Psychiatric Association, April 1967, 79-91.

———. "The Woodlawn Mental Health Center: A Community Mental Health Center Model." *Social Science Review*, XL (September 1966), 255-263.

Kuta, Jeffrey. "Political and Professional Responsibility in Woodlawn's Model Cities Plan: An Overview." Unpublished paper, University of Chicago Center for Urban Studies, February 28, 1969. (Mimeographed.)

LaPaglia, Charles. "On 'Gangs.'" An unpublished paper on file at First Presbyterian Church, Chicago, 1969. (Mimeographed.)

————. Testimony before Senate Permanent Subcommittee on Investigations, Senator John McClellan, Chairman. On file at First Presbyterian Church, Chicago, June 1968. (Mimeographed.)

Leber, Charles T. Jr. "Rev. Leber Tells History of 'Anti-South Campus' Group." *Chicago Maroon*, March 3, 1961.

Levi, Julian. "Levi Refutes Leber's Charges." *Chicago Maroon*, March 10, 1961.

————. "The Neighborhood Program of the University of Chicago." Office of Public Information, University of Chicago, 1961.

Lund, Neal G. "East Woodlawn Pilot Study." Unpublished paper, University of Chicago Divinity School, 1966.

Mid-South Model Area Planning Council. Minutes of meetings of the Council, February-June 1969.

Model Cities Target. Newspaper of the Chicago Model Cities Program. August 1968-August 1971.

Moore, Ruth. "Woodlawn—A Happy Future." *Chicago Sun Times*, July 5, 1965.

————. "Woodlawn: An Urban Battlefield." *Chicago Sun Times*, April 9, 1961.

The Observer (Chicago), March 1968-August 1971.

Pierce, Ken. "Church Supports 'Hate Group.'" *Chicago Maroon*, March 3, 1961.

"A Proposal Outlining the Woodlawn Cooperative Project." On file at First Presbyterian Church, Chicago, 1959. (Mimeographed.)

"Report to the Presbytery of Chicago from Its Committee Investigating Allegations of Wrongdoing Made Against the Reverend John Fry, Mr. Charles LaPaglia and Miss Ann Schwalbach of the Staff of the First Presbyterian Church, Chicago." Presented to the Presbytery of Chicago, September 16, 1969.

Richardson, Lincoln. "The Blackstone Rangers." *Presbyterian Life*, February 15, 1968.

Richey, Elinor. "The Slum That Saved Itself." *Progressive*, October 1963, 26-29.

Silberman, Charles. *Crisis in Black and White*. New York: Random House, 1964.

———. "Up from Apathy—The Woodlawn Experiment." *Commentary*, XXXVII (May, 1964), 51-58.

Sotnak, Otto A. "An Experience with Community Organization in Woodlawn: Description with Observations." Paper presented at Lutheran Consultation on Community Organization, Chicago, January 4, 1966. (Mimeographed.)

Spergel, Irving (Project Director). *Evaluation of the Youth Manpower Demonstration of The Woodlawn Organization*. Chicago: University of Chicago, School of Social Service Administration, 1969.

Spergel, Irving A., and Mundy, Richard A. "A Community Study, East Woodlawn: Problems, Programs, Proposals." Social Service Administration, University of Chicago, 1963. (Mimeographed.)

Spergel, Irving, *et al.* "Block Clubs in Three Neighborhoods." Unpublished paper on file at School of Social Service Administration, University of Chicago, 1966. (Mimeographed.)

Swenson, William. "The Continuing Colloquium on University of Chicago Demonstration Projects in Woodlawn." University of Chicago Center for Urban Studies, November 15, 1968. (Mimeographed.)

"The Temporary Woodlawn Organization for Community Planning and Rehabilitation." On file at First Presbyterian Church, Chicago, 1961. (Mimeographed.)

TWO News. September 1965-December 1965.

TWO Newsletter. January 1964-August 1965.

U.S. Commission on Civil Rights. *TWO's Model Cities Plan.* Washington, D.C.: Government Printing Office, December 1969.

U.S. Department of Housing and Urban Development, Model Cities Administration. *Program Guide: Model Neighborhoods in Demonstration Cities.* HUD PG-47, December 1967. Washington, D.C.: Government Printing Office, 1968.

———. *Technical Assistance Bulletin No. 3: Citizen Participation in Model Cities.* Washington, D.C.: Government Printing Office, December 1968.

Walker, Walter L. "The University of Chicago and Its Community." *The University of Chicago Magazine,* LXII (1970), 6-7.

Welfare Council of Metropolitan Chicago. *Chicago Community Area Profiles.* Chicago: Welfare Council of Metropolitan Chicago, 1964.

Wille, Lois. "Inside 'Ranger' Gangs." *Chicago Daily News,* August 1-5, 1966.

———. "Saul Alinsky Loves a Good Hassle." *Inland Architect,* February 1969, 26-27.

———. "The War Within Poverty War." *Chicago Daily News,* April 5-9, 1965.

Wille, Lois; Washington, Betty; and Clement, William. "The Blitz of Woodlawn." *Chicago Daily News,* July 6-10, 1971.

Williams, Charles J. "A Christian Approach to Community Organization—The Greater Woodlawn Pastors' Alliance." Unpublished B.D. dissertation, Chicago Theological Seminary, 1963.

Williams, Eddie N. (ed.). *Delivery System for Model Cities: New Concepts in Serving the Urban Community.* Chicago: University of Chicago Center for Policy Study, 1969.

Woodlawn Booster (Chicago). 1961-1969.

The Woodlawn Community Board for Urban Education Projects. Reports, proposals, and minutes of Board meetings, 1966-1968. (Mimeographed.)

Woodlawn Experimental Schools Project. Reports, proposals and minutes of the Woodlawn Community Board for the Woodlawn Experimental School Project, 1968-1970. (Mimeographed.)

The Woodlawn Observer (Chicago). January 1966-December 1967.

The Woodlawn Organization. "Total Manpower Demonstration Program for 700 Unemployed Young Adults." Application to Office of Economic Opportunity, November 1966, on file at TWO.

———. *Woodlawn's Model Cities Plan: A Demonstration of Citizen Responsibility*. Northbrook, Ill.: Whitehall Company, 1970.

Yondorf, Barbara. "Citizen Participation in the Planning of a Model Cities Proposal." Unpublished paper, University of Chicago Center for Urban Studies, March 3, 1969. (Mimeographed.)

351

STUDIES IN RELIGION AND SOCIETY

edited by

THOMAS C. CAMPBELL, W. ALVIN PITCHER,
W. WIDICK SCHROEDER, AND GIBSON WINTER
Center for the Scientific Study of Religion

OTHER MONOGRAPHS IN THE SERIES

Paul E. Kraemer, *Awakening From the American Dream:
The Human Rights Movement in the U.S. Assessed During a Crucial Decade, 1960-1970*, 1973
William C. Martin, *Christians in Conflict*, 1972
Victor Obenhaus, *And See the People*, 1968
Walter M. Stuhr, Jr., *The Public Style: A Study of the Community Participation of Protestant Ministers*, 1972
Lawrence Witmer, ed., *Issues in Community Organization*, 1972

*Order from the Center for the Scientific Study of Religion,
5757 University Avenue, Chicago, Illinois 60637*

OTHER BOOKS IN THE SERIES

Thomas C. Campbell and Yoshio Fukuyama, *The Fragmented Layman*, 1970.
John Fish et al., *The Edge of the Ghetto*, 1968
W. Widick Schroeder and Victor Obenhaus, *Religion in American Culture*, 1964
Gibson Winter, *Religious Identity*, 1968

Order from your bookstore

Library of Congress Cataloging in Publication Data

Fish, John.
  Black power/white control.

  (Studies in religion and society)
  Bibliography: p. 330
  1. Woodlawn Organization. 2. Black power—Chicago.
I. Title. II. Series: Studies in religion and society series.
HN80.C5F58   322.4'4'0977311   72-5379
ISBN 0-691-09358-X